Engaging Environments in Tonga

Pacific Perspectives:
Studies of the European Society for Oceanists

General Editors:
Edvard Hviding, University of Bergen
Toon van Meijl, Radboud University

Oceania is of enduring contemporary significance in global trajectories of history, politics, economy and ecology, and has remained influential for diverse approaches to studying and understanding human life worlds. The books published in this series explore Oceanic values and imaginations, documenting the unique position of the Pacific region – its cultural and linguistic diversity, its ecological and geographical distinctness, and always fascinating experiments with social formations. This series thus conveys the political, economic and moral alternatives that Oceania offers the contemporary world.

Volume 9
ENGAGING ENVIRONMENTS
IN TONGA
Cultivating Beauty and Nurturing Relations in a Changing World
Arne Aleksej Perminow

Volume 8
REVEALING THE INVISIBLE MINE
Social Complexities of an Undeveloped Mining Project
Emilia E. Skrzypek

Volume 7
IF EVERYONE RETURNED, THE ISLAND WOULD SINK
Urbanisation and Migration in Vanuatu
Kirstie Petrou

Volume 6
PACIFIC REALITIES
Changing Perspectives on Resilience and Resistance
Edited by Laurent Dousset and Mélissa Nayral

Volume 5
IN THE ABSENCE OF THE GIFT
New Forms of Value and Personhood in a Papua New Guinea Community
Anders Emil Rasmussen

Volume 4
LIVING KINSHIP IN THE PACIFIC
Edited by Christina Toren and Simonne Pauwels

Volume 3
BELONGING IN OCEANIA
Movement, Place-Making and Multiple Identifications
Edited by Elfriede Hermann, Wolfgang Kempf and Toon van Meijl

Volume 2
PACIFIC FUTURES
Projects, Politics and Interests
Edited by Will Rollason

Volume 1
THE ETHNOGRAPHIC EXPERIMENT
A.M. Hocart and W.H.R. Rivers in Island Melanesia, 1908
Edited by Edvard Hviding and Cato Berg

Engaging Environments in Tonga

Cultivating Beauty and Nurturing Relations
in a Changing World

━━━━━ ◆●◆ ━━━━━

Arne Aleksej Perminow

berghahn
NEW YORK • OXFORD
www.berghahnbooks.com

First published in 2022 by
Berghahn Books
www.berghahnbooks.com

© 2022, 2024 Arne Aleksej Perminow
First paperback edition published in 2024

All rights reserved. Except for the quotation of short passages
for the purposes of criticism and review, no part of this book
may be reproduced in any form or by any means, electronic or
mechanical, including photocopying, recording, or any information
storage and retrieval system now known or to be invented,
without written permission of the publisher.

Library of Congress Cataloging-in-Publication Data
Names: Perminow, Arne Aleksej, author.
Title: Engaging environments in Tonga : cultivating beauty and nurturing relations in a changing world / Arne Aleksej Perminow.
Description: 1st. | New York : Berghahn Books, 2022. | Series: Pacific perspectives : studies of the European society for oceanists ; Volume 9 | Includes bibliographical references and index.
Identifiers: LCCN 2021042538 (print) | LCCN 2021042539 (ebook) | ISBN 9781800734548 (hardback) | ISBN 9781805390657 (open access ebook)
Subjects: LCSH: Human ecology--Tonga--Kotu. | Kotu (Tonga)--Environmental conditions. | Sea level--Tonga--Kotu.
Classification: LCC GF852.T63 P47 2022 (print) | LCC GF852.T63 (ebook) | DDC 304.2/509612--dc23/eng/20211112
LC record available at https://lccn.loc.gov/2021042538
LC ebook record available at https://lccn.loc.gov/2021042539

British Library Cataloguing in Publication Data
A catalogue record for this book is available from the British Library

ISBN 978-1-80073-454-8 hardback
ISBN 978-1-80539-715-1 paperback
ISBN 978-1-80073-4-555 epub
ISBN 978-1-80539-065-7 web pdf

https://doi.org/10.3167/9781800734548

An electronic version of this book is freely available thanks to the support of libraries working with Knowledge Unlatched. KU is a collaborative initiative designed to make high-quality books Open Access for the public good. More information about the initiative and links to the Open Access version can be found at knowledgeunlatched.org.

This work is published subject to a Creative Commons Attribution Noncommercial No Derivatives 4.0 License. The terms of the license can be found at http://creativecommons.org/licenses/by-nc-nd/4.0/. For uses beyond those covered in the license contact Berghahn Books.

In grateful memory of the late Heamasi Koloa Pemoʻui
(1913–2000);

Hafukinamo, motuʻa tauhi fonua o Taufatōfua, ofisa kolo ki Kotu and *setuata* of the Kotu congregation of the Free Wesleyan Church of Tonga.

Contents

List of Figures — viii

Acknowledgements — ix

Introduction. An Environmental Puzzle — 1

Chapter 1. Moving to the Beat of a Marine Environment — 19

Chapter 2. Daily Motions of Merging and Separation — 35

Chapter 3. Lunar Motions of Growth and Regeneration — 54

Chapter 4. Creating Tableaus of Moving Beauty — 76

Chapter 5. Nurturing Flows between Hands That Let Go — 112

Conclusion. Calamity, Sacrifice and Blessing in a Changing World — 149

Appendix. Words of a World in Motion — 175

Glossary — 183

References — 210

Index — 219

Figures

─── ◆●◆ ───

0.1. The dying *vao* ('forest') between the village and the *liku* weather coast on Kotu Island in 2011. © Arne Aleksej Perminow.   6

0.2. *Vai tangata/Veifua* pool in the forest between the village and the *liku* weather coast on Kotu island in 1986. © Arne Aleksej Perminow.   7

0.3. *Vai fefine/Tōkilangi* pool in the forest between the village and the *liku* weather coast on Kotu Island in 2011. © Arne Aleksej Perminow.   7

2.1. Figure of diurnal dynamics. The illustration shows the main phases of day and night in Tonga. © Arne Aleksej Perminow and Kristine Lie Øverland.   47

2.2. Figure of tidal dynamics. The illustration shows the main phases of ebb tide and flow tide in *Namolahi* Lagoon. © Arne Aleksej Perminow and Kristine Lie Øverland.   48

2.3. Gunson's figure of Polynesian cosmology. Figure taken from Herda, Terrell and Gunson (eds), *Tongan Culture and History* (Target Oceania, 1990), courtesy of Neil Gunson.   49

5.1. Plan of *fale tonga* ('Tongan house'). The plan was sketched by the author under the directions of Heamasi Koloa, based on his memory of the Free Wesleyan Church of Tonga on Kotu Island, destroyed during tropical Cyclone Isaac in 1982. © Arne Aleksej Perminow and Kristine Lie Øverland.   123

Acknowledgements

◆●◆

In October 1986, Kotu Island in the Lulunga district of the Tongan group of Ha'apai appeared as a low silhouette on the Western horizon as the small boat we were in weaved its way through a channel in the fringing reef into the large lagoon surrounding the island for the first time. The tide was low, and the boat scraped the bottom and ground to a halt long before reaching the sandy beach in front of the entrance to the village. A tall and slender elderly man with short-cropped, silver hair greeted us with a smile as we waded ashore; he then escorted us through the village to the home of his family, next to the central village green. This was the late Heamasi Koloa Pemo'ui, town officer and steward of the Free Wesleyan Church of Tonga on Kotu; I am deeply grateful to him for opening his home and heart to us when we first arrived and forever indebted to him for his unfailing commitment to sharing his long experience and many insights about the ways of the world and how to cope with them. I remember with appreciation his gentle encouragements to have the patience and perseverance to 'grasp well' (*puke lelei*) our long conversations and discussions about how the world works before moving on to other topics. The subject matter of this book bears the mark of Koloa's support and his own patience and perseverance. Also, I am grateful to his wife, the late Meletoa Koloa; his daughter Melena'a; and his son Rev. Lea 'a e Peni Koloa and his wife, the late Alamani Koloa, and their family for generously accepting the added burden of caring for visitors from afar during the first two field visits to Kotu in 1986 and 1991. Over the three decades of field visits that this book is based on, too many people from Kotu to name individually have offered their friendship and contributed their knowledge and views to make this book possible. My thanks go to all of them for their interest, openness and acceptance of someone coming repeatedly from across the world to 'study the Tongan way' (*ako e 'ulungaanga fakatonga*). Special gratitude goes to families on Kotu and on Tongatapu, with whom I have enjoyed enduring relations of mutual support. This has been essential for the book's perspective on the characteristics and dynamics of local sociality; the family of the late Siale and 'Ofa Koloa; the family of

Rev. ʻIsikeli Hauʻofa Lātū and ʻAlai Fakapulia Lātū; the family of Manase and Ele Fakapulia; the family of the late Rev. Hateni and ʻOfa Pahulu; the family of the late ʻAtu and Meliame Hē; the family of the late Lisiate and Launoa ʻIlangana; the family of the late Sione Pelo and ʻAtalia Taʻufoʻou; the family of ʻAtolo and Sela Tuʼinukuafe; and the family of Feʻao and Lineti Fakapulia and in particular their son Paula Fakapulia for leaving his door open even at his new home overseas.

I am also very grateful to have benefited over the years from stimulating discussions about qualities and continuities in Tongan culture and society with the founder of the Atenisi Institute, the late Futa Helu; Hufanga scholar ʻOkusitino Mahina; *tufunga lalava* artist Sopolemalama Filipe Tohi; *tufunga tā tongitongi* woodcarver Sitiveni Feʻao Fehoko; and last but not least, the late ʻEpeli Hauʻofa for advising me to go to Kotu in the first place.

The making of this book spans three decades and has benefited from numerous contributions from many colleagues to whom I am grateful; any of the book's shortcomings are entirely my own responsibility. In particular, I acknowledge the encouragement of Edvard Hviding to reframe and rework the ethnography for a longitudinal analysis, and the generosity of Nick Thomas in offering a peaceful place at Cambridge to get the work started and of Rane Willerslev for granting a sabbatical to go there. I am also grateful for the contributions of good colleagues in the form of helpful feedback to develop the ethnography, which carries the chapters of the book. A special thanks goes to Bradd Shore, Ingjerd Hoem, Kjersti Larsen, Jan Simonsen, Øivind Fuglerud, Marina Prusac Lindhagen, Mike Poltorak, Svein Gullbekk and Peter Bjerregaard.

I also want to acknowledge the value of the steady support of the Museum of Cultural History, University of Oslo, which has allowed me to keep going back to Tonga and Kotu. The longitudinal approach of the current book has depended on such support. Finally, I thank my family and my wife Marte Lie Perminow for their unfailing faith that this book would come to be.

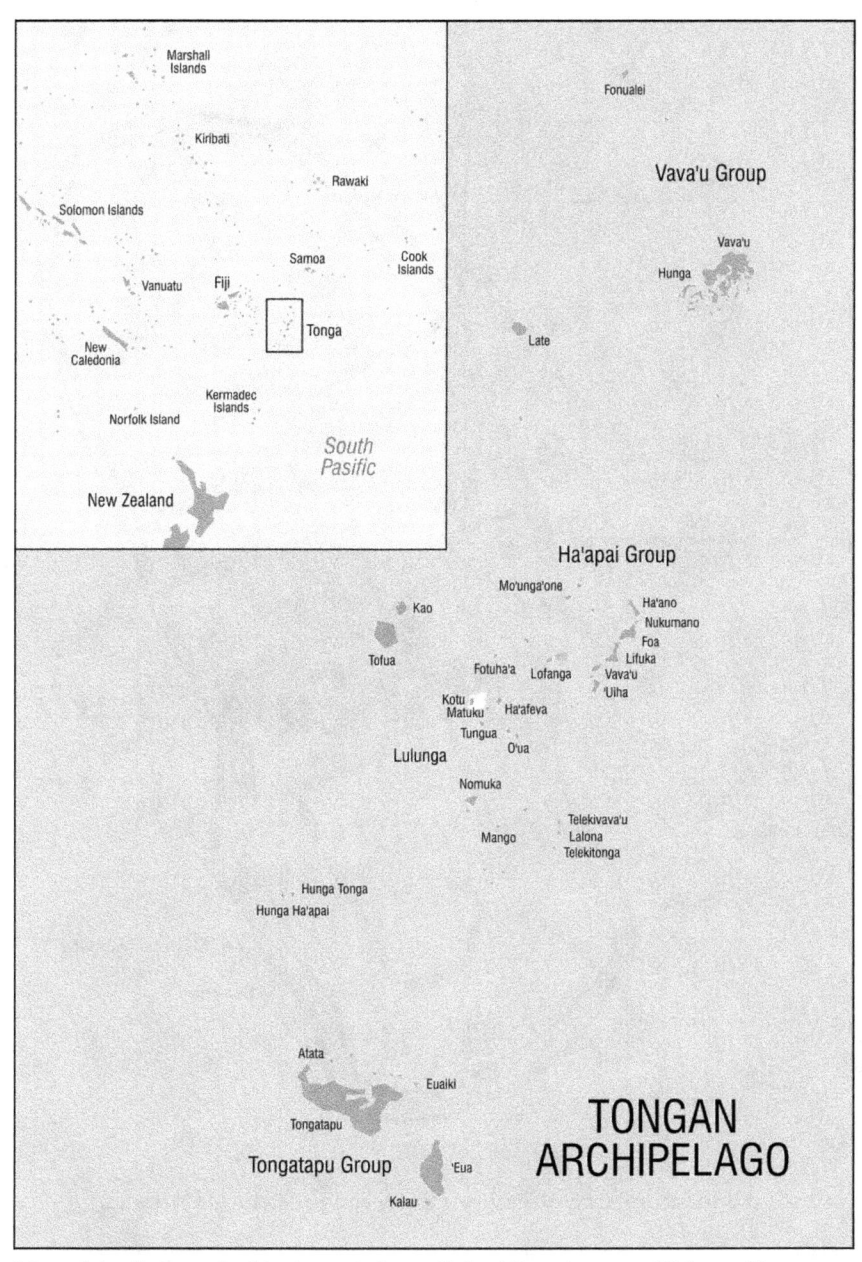

Map of the Tongan Archipelago. © Arne Aleksej Perminow and Johnny Kreutz.

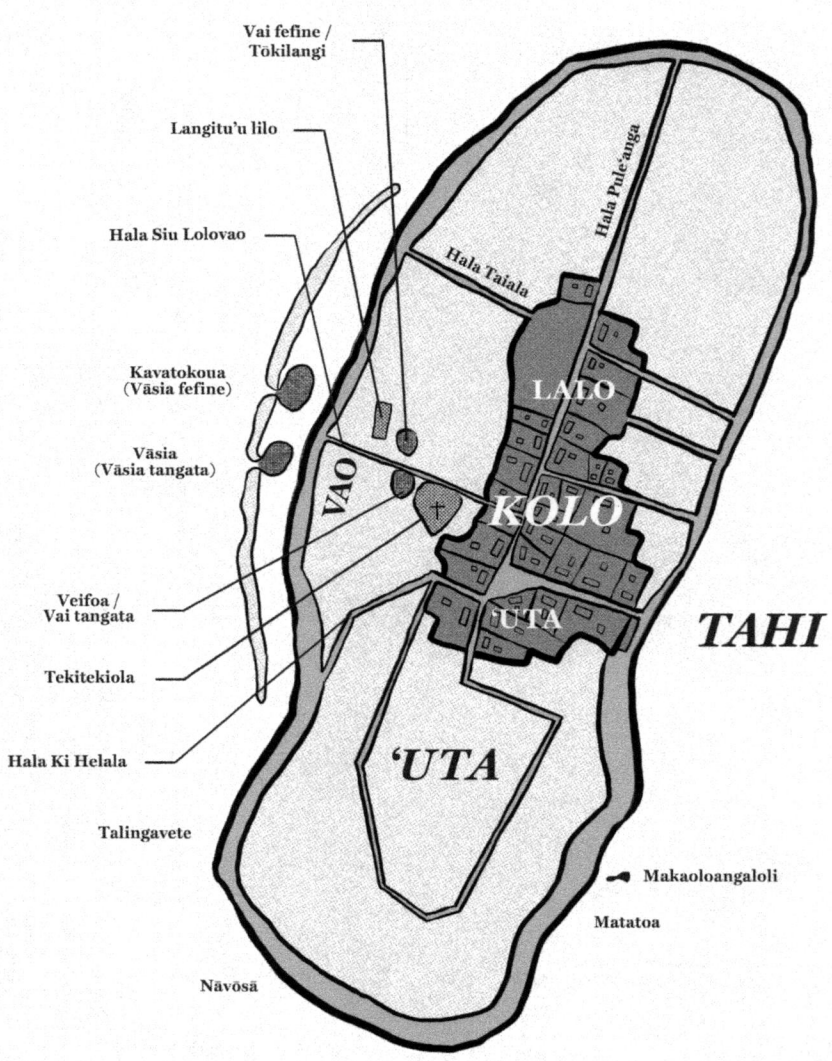

Map of Kotu Island. © Arne Aleksej Perminow and Kristine Lie Øverland.

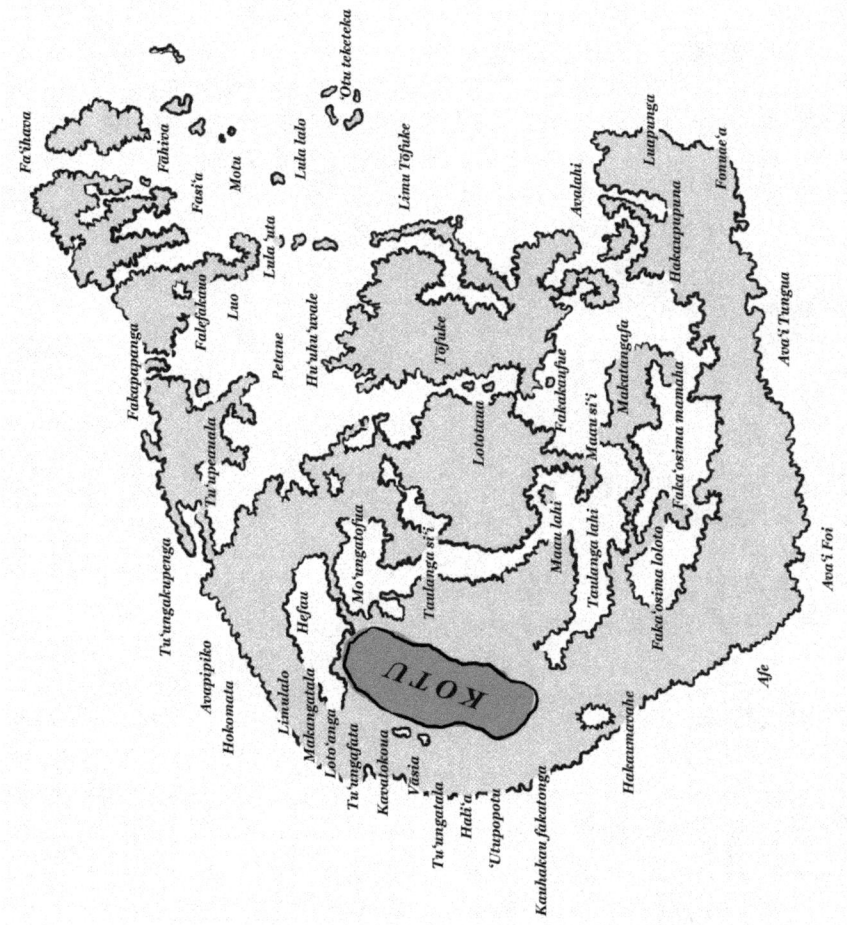

Map of *Namolahi* Lagoon. © Arne Aleksej Perminow and Kristine Lie Øverland.

Introduction

An Environmental Puzzle

'Red Wave' Moving In

On 11 March, 2011, catastrophe struck Japan in the form of a devastating tsunami caused by a great submarine earthquake off the coast of Tōhoku. A tsunami warning was issued for the Pacific: a giant wave may be on the move to threaten the low-lying islands in its path. Having heard the emergency radio announcement, the town officer of Kotu Island in the Ha'apai group of Tonga was now out on the main footpath running through the village to warn people. *Peau kula*; the unfamiliar word drifted out of the darkness.

I was sitting in front of the house I was staying at during a short revisit to Kotu. I had done several field visits to the island since the 1980s but had previously not been back since 2004. I had come to learn how ceremonial food presentations in a village setting in Tonga compare with food presentations among Tongan migrants in New Zealand (see Perminow 2015). At 11 PM, the new moon was leaving the village path in deep darkness. The path was unusually busy though, with people moving from the 'low' (*lalo*) to the 'high' (*'uta*) end of the island. *Peau kula*; 'Red wave? What sort of wave is that?' I wondered. A few women stopped for a moment at the low fence surrounding the *'api* ('home') I was staying in. One of them asked whether I had heard the radio announcement that a *peau kula* might be on its way towards us. She said that they were headed for the *'uta*, the garden lands occupying the slightly raised southern end of the island. Their rolled-up sleeping mats indicated that they meant to spend the night up there. As they were moving on, the loud voice of the town officer grew closer as he moved up the path from the 'lower end' (*lalo*) of the village. 'Attention all! A tsunami warning has been issued for Tonga. Bring food and water! Seek higher grounds and listen to the emergency updates of

Radio Tonga!' He stopped outside the low fence and called me over: 'They say on the news that there has been a great earthquake and a 'red wave' in Japan, killing many people. They say that a big wave is moving here and that it may come all the way to Tonga. It may get here in the early morning. So, leave for the garden lands before that time, eh …'

People were by no means panic-stricken. Yet many appeared to heed the warning and made their way towards the raised garden lands during the small hours. At about 3:30 AM, the women and children from the neighbouring home came to make sure I was awake and ready to come with them to a recently cleared bush allotment in *'uta*. By that time, the village was calm and quiet. The assembly hall of the Free Wesleyan Church of Tonga on the *mala'e* ('village green') where a handful of men earlier in the night had been drinking kava and watching a rugby match on satellite TV was now dark and silent. The 'higher grounds' of Kotu stand about 10 meters above sea level. As we made the short climb, someone mentioned that Kotu was lucky to have its garden lands on a hill in contrast to many other islands of Ha'apai, which are very low and quite flat. Kotu Island is small though; no more than about 1,800 meters long and about 600 meters wide. With its raised southern end, some of Kotu's people jokingly refer to it as the 'toothbrush' (*polosi fufulu nifo*). And indeed that is what it may look like when approached from the neighbouring Ha'afeva Island to the east.

The prospect of facing a tsunami from the raised end of a 'toothbrush' should not be expected to produce a great sense of security. Nevertheless, there was no sense of urgency or anxiety among those who had sought shelter there. On the contrary, muted conversations, humorous comments and the sharing of biscuits, fruits and tea created more of an atmosphere of a recreational outing than one of impending doom. Some dozed, and others listened for updated news bulletins on Radio Tonga. Some said that they found it hard to believe that an earthquake in Japan at the far end of the Pacific would create waves reaching all the way to Tonga. Others recalled that over the last few years several tsunami warnings had been issued and then cancelled when no 'red wave' appeared.

Tonga lies just west of the International Date Line along the so-called Pacific Ring of Fire. Here the Pacific plate subducts beneath the Indo-Australian plate in the Tonga Trench, which causes frequent earthquakes and volcanic eruptions. Tongans are quite familiar with volcanic activities and know well that very few earthquakes are followed by 'red waves' but will recall the 8.1 magnitude submarine earthquake close to Samoa and the 6-meter 'red wave' that 5 minutes later hit Niuatoputapu Island in September 2009, destroying 90% of the houses and killing nine people. It came suddenly, with no warning; many people on Kotu expressed that such events are not really 'predictable' (*me'a pau*; 'certain thing'); that forces of nature often strike suddenly and without warning.

Except for myself, all who were gathered in the particular bush allotment where we sought shelter from the *peau kula* in March 2011 were women and children. This made me wonder whether the menfolk might have less faith than the women in the tsunami prediction, or whether it might be considered unmanly to abandon their homes and the village in favour of the garden lands. When I asked my companions if the men remained in the village, the women around me said no. They said that I was the only man with no sister among the women present. 'The sister is taboo. They stay away because of "respect" (*faka'apa'apa*[1]) and seek shelter in other bush allotments,' one of the women said.

As night turned into day and the predicted time of the 'red wave' came and passed, people gradually returned to another normal day in the village. The only effect of the earthquake in Japan on Kotu's big lagoon was that the ebb tide turned midway down the beach and came in again a few feet further inland than the last high tide. Over the next couple of days, conversations with village men tended to touch upon the subject of who had chosen to make a stand, to *nofo 'i 'api* ('to remain in the homestead'), and who had chosen to seek safety, to *hola ki 'uta* ('to flee to the garden lands'). In a conversation with a steward in one of Kotu's churches, people's choice of where to spend the night of the tsunami warning turned into a moral question; a telling test of personal courage and faith. Replying to the question of where I had spent the previous night, I used the verbal *'alu*, signifying simply 'to go': 'I went with the people of the neighbouring homestead to the garden lands and stayed there until morning. What about you?' 'Oh, so you "fled to the garden lands" (*hola ki 'uta*) eh ...,' he stated with a deadpan look, and went on: 'Well me, I remained in my home doing my *lotu* ['praying'], trusting that God "shelters" [*le'ohi*] me.'

Many women, though, had claimed that most men actually spent the critical hours of the night on the elevated garden lands. The men encountered returning from the *'uta* the next morning were bringing back firewood or crops just as they would on any other Saturday in preparation for the following day of rest and worship, and therefore it was difficult to find out where men had actually spent the night and quite impossible to find men willing to admit to having 'fled to the gardens'.

Whether men actually remained in their homes or just said that they did so, their self-presentation as someone choosing to stand their ground rather than to flee in the face of potential disaster seemed to render the tsunami threat as a test of faith and moral fibre. More generally, I take their self-presentation to indicate that morality and calamity involving the elements and forces that surround people's lives may be mutually entangled in

Tonga. I do believe that a focus on such mutual entanglement is essential in order to understand how people perceive, explain and respond to dramatic events or changes in the environment of which they are part. Thus, I believe that a focus on people's perceptions of and engagements with the components, forces and dynamics they understand to surround their lives offers rich ground for discovering enduring ideas and practices underpinning sociality.

Many people on Kotu, then, appeared quite unperturbed by the tsunami warning in 2011. They were seemingly sceptical of the notion that such phenomena may be predicted and thus had limited faith in the human capacity to predict or control future destructive events. Just as Donner has argued to be the case regarding Fijian attitudes to weather as well as climate change, many Tongans appear to believe that destructive natural events lie within the 'Domain of the gods' (Donner 2007). This is clearly not because they are seldom affected by destructive consequences of forceful natural events. On the contrary, the effects of powerful and quite unpredictable natural events caused by Tonga's location at the Pacific Ring of Fire as well as within the cyclone belt are frequently demonstrated. Just six weeks prior to the tsunami warning of March 2011, Kotu was struck by a category 4 tropical cyclone. Cyclone Wilma had made an unexpected turn southward from Samoa to wreak havoc in Western Ha'apai before moving on towards New Zealand. The houses mostly withstood winds approaching 185 km/h, but many trees did not. According to those who were there, the waves had engulfed the lower part of the island. Indeed, the Tonga Islands, according to Patricia Fall, '… lie in the track of tropical cyclones, being struck by an average of two cyclones per year' (Fall 2010: 254). On 11 January, 2014, Kotu and the rest of the islands of Western Ha'apai remained on the outskirts of a category 5 tropical cyclone. Cyclone Ian did strike the islands of Eastern Ha'apai though, destroying 80% of the houses on Lifuka island. And in February 2016, the northern islands of Tonga narrowly escaped the tremendous destructive force of category 5 cyclone Winston. He brushed by Vava'u before veering westward to hit Fiji with wind gusts of more than 300 km/h, killing forty-four people.

Attitudes to predictions as well as the consequences of natural calamities are founded on experiential familiarity with forceful and dynamic realities that in Tim Ingold's terms may be said to make up a 'weather-world' (see Ingold 2011: 129–31). Experiences with 'weather-world' realities provide frequent instances of announced calamities being cancelled and destructive forces surprisingly and suddenly heading elsewhere after all.

Mole e fonua; 'Losing Land'

Not all events or changes affecting the surroundings with which Kotu people routinely engage are as sudden or dramatic as 'red waves' or tropical cyclones but may be a more serious threat in the long run. Thus, in 2011 it was mentioned by Kotu people who had moved to Tonga's capital, Nuku'alofa, that Kotu 'loses land' (*mole e fonua*) on the island's 'weather coast' (*liku*) to the west. 'I haven't been there to see it for myself,' said a church minister who had moved from Kotu to Tongatapu, 'but I have heard that land has disappeared on the weather coast' …

> They say that for some years now the sea 'enters land' (*hū ki he fonua*) when the tide is very high. I have heard that a lot of the 'forest' (*vao*) is already dead. There is a Tongan saying which fits the predicament of Kotu well: *Si'isi'i e kuma, toe vela hono hiku!* [Not only was the palm rat tiny, but it also burnt its tail!].

The saying speaks to the fact that as one of the smallest of Tonga's islands Kotu has little land to lose. 'Maybe when you go there, you could check it out for yourself,' he suggested.

Shortly after arriving in Kotu Island itself, I encountered a villager in his late seventies on the footpath between the waterfront and the lower part of the village and asked him about the rumours I had heard about the dying forest and the loss of land on the west coast of the island. 'Yes, so I've heard too,' he replied, 'but I haven't been there to examine it with my own eyes yet.' His answer was quite puzzling, since the area in question was just a few hundred meters from where we were standing. As it turned out, he was far from the only one on Kotu who claimed that they had not yet examined with their own eyes (*teeki ai fakasio*) what was going on in the *vao*, the forest between the village and the *liku* coast.

Moving on from the encounter with the old man, I went finally to see for myself what was happening inside the *vao* and at the *liku* coast. The standing stones surrounding two former freshwater pools at the entrance to the *vao* could barely be discerned at the edge of an extensive and very muddy swamp. In the 1980s and 90s, these two pools (*vaitupu*) had routinely been used by people to rinse off saltwater after swimming in the sea. Trees still grew on the *langi*, the 'chiefly burial mound' – known as *Langi tu'u lilo*, 'The hidden burial mound' – behind the two pools. Now, however, the mound was wholly surrounded by a swamp where dead and leafless trees and tree stumps were sticking out of a mudflat running to the sand barrier that separates the interior land from the beach.

Previously, the coast could be reached by walking under a canopy of dense forest along a path known by the elders as the *Hala siulolovao* – a very old name, which indicated that the walkway had been in existence for long enough to be considered a permanent feature of the landscape; it may be translated as 'Going under the forest to catch fish' (Churchward 1959: 433). Now, however, the path had disappeared altogether in the swamp. Jumping from tree stump to tree stump, it was barely possible to get across the mudflat to the weather coast. For a stretch of a few hundred meters up and down the sandy barrier between the beach and the interior land, littoral bushes were either dead or dying. Presumably, they were being nurtured by a saltier concoction than they could handle. Apparently, the natural sandy barrier had become an insufficient sea wall to protect the low-lying area within from the surrounding sea.

Compared to the conditions of the low-lying area in the 1980s and 1990s, the contrast was striking. The landscape had been transformed totally from a dense forest used by people to collect firewood, wild fruits and ingredients for 'waters of healing' (*vai tonga*) to a swamp covering a substantial part of the low-lying area between the weather coast and the village.

As mentioned, the standing stones that marked the place where the two secluded pools used to be were barely perceptible – submerged in the swamp. Some of the elders called the pools by their ancient names: *Veifua* and *Tōkilangi*.[2] They were mostly referred to, however, as *Vai tangata*

Figure 0.1. The dying *vao* ('forest') between the village and the *liku* weather coast on Kotu Island in 2011. © Arne Aleksej Perminow.

Figure 0.2. *Vai tangata/Veifua* pool in the forest between the village and the *liku* weather coast on Kotu island in 1986. © Arne Aleksej Perminow.

Figure 0.3. *Vai fefine/Tōkilangi* pool in the forest between the village and the *liku* weather coast on Kotu Island in 2011. © Arne Aleksej Perminow.

('Men's water') and *Vai fefine* ('Women's water') because of gendered use. The famous explorer Captain James Cook was shown the two pools when he disembarked on Kotu on his Second Voyage in 1777 (Beaglehole 1967: 120–21). So the pools were clearly a notable feature of the Kotu landscape two centuries ago. In 2011, however, the pools, like the path, had been claimed by the swamp.

Langi tuʻu lilo (the hidden burial mound), like the pools and the path, had according to oral tradition been around for centuries and was associated with the high ranking chief Tungī Mānaʻia, who lived in the seventeenth century. Some believed that what he had touched during a visit had become *tapu* ('taboo') because of Tungī Mānaʻia's high rank as the son of the daughter of Tuʻi Tonga's sister, the *tamahā*. Thus, the things he had touched were buried in the mound. Others believed that it was one of Tungī's concubines related to Taufatōfua, traditional chief of Kotu and Tōfua islands, who was buried there. Finally, some claimed that Tungī Mānaʻia himself had been buried there with his 'whale-tooth neck-rest' (*kali lei*) when he died on his way back from Tōfua island in the west to Tungua island east of Kotu.

Though still enigmatic, the mound was now definitely no longer hidden in the forest but stood out as a dry spot jutting out of a sea of mud. This transformation of the landscape did not, however, appear to preoccupy people greatly in 2011. Only a vague knowledge of environmental changes appeared to have reached beyond the island; no knowledge of it at all appeared to have reached beyond the Tongan Islands to overseas migrants. Thus, Tongans living overseas who originate from Kotu had not heard about the change in local sea level or its effects when I posted pictures on their Facebook group (*Kotu ʻiloa he lotu moe poto*) documenting the transformation in 2013. On Kotu itself, people appeared inclined to turn a blind eye to the changes. They were disinclined to dwell on them amongst themselves or broadcast the news about the changes beyond the confines of the island. As mentioned, many claimed not to have 'examined it with their own eyes' and few volunteered any theories about what might be causing the transformation.

A man in his early sixties whose homestead was located in the low-lying end of the village reported that not just storm surges but ordinary spring tides occasionally came right across the island to the very edge of his village allotment. But even he appeared quite unperturbed by this new development. The sea apparently first of all enters the interior across a natural sand barrier running along the weather coast, so stopping this overflow into the low-lying land seemed, in principle, conceivable. But in 2011 there had been no discussions or initiatives to construct some sort of wall or reinforce the sand barrier to keep the sea out. I wondered whether the town officer had reported the changes taking place to regional or central authorities, but no one knew of any initiatives taken to spread the news of the intruding sea.

This apparent lack of interest in the environmental changes that were taking place was all the more striking given that some changes were having a noticeable impact on everyday routines. A few days after the tsunami warning in 2011, I was sitting next to a woman in her late sixties one afternoon on the beach in front of the village. We were gazing out over the big lagoon waiting for the fishermen to return. 'Do you remember the time before, when you first came here, how the women used to collect shellfish and seaweed on the reef?' I arched my eyebrows as Tongans conventionally do to confirm something. She continued:

> Some say that it is because the women have become too lazy, but that is a lie! The sea is too deep now! Earlier we could walk all around the reef at low tide. We could walk out to places abounding in seaweed and shellfish and collect it in our baskets. But now the sea is too deep for us to get to those places even at low tide. The women do not dive, so now we cannot reach down to collect them. A thing happened a few years ago ... I think it was in 2006 ... There was a very big earthquake. And since that time the tide has not yet become really low again.

No one could volunteer any theories about what might be causing the transformation and seemed just as inclined to dwell on the benefits of the changes as its disadvantages. 'Do you remember how difficult it was to enter the lagoon at low tide in the past?' one man asked, and he continued: 'Nowadays the tide is never really low anymore so we may enter and leave the lagoon "whenever we please" (*noa 'ia pē*; lit. 'whimsically, indiscriminately').' Another man was sure that the recent environmental transformation had reduced Kotu's mosquito problem:

> The 'forest' (*vao*) and the two pools within it used to be breeding grounds for a lot of mosquitos before. Nowadays mosquitos are no longer a problem. Some of the young men went to Nomuka Island and brought back some *lapila* fish[3] from the big lake there. The *lapila* fish thrive in the muddy and brackish waters where the *vao* used to be. They are very useful, for they eat a lot of mosquitos. Now there are very few mosquitos on Kotu.

People seemed disinclined, then, to dwell on possible causes and the negative consequences of the quite radical transformation that had taken place over the first decennium of the twenty-first century. Also, they seemed markedly disinterested in spreading news beyond the island itself about what was going on in their immediate environment, even to people originating from Kotu. This may appear all the more puzzling in light of the establishment of a Pacific Adaptation Strategy Assistance Program (PASAP) in 2010 on nearby Lifuka, the main island of the administrative region to which Kotu belongs. Amongst other things, the project aims to assess precisely the vulnerability and adaptation to the rise in sea level that has occurred on Lifuka and which has caused significant erosion along the west coast. Apparently, the rise in sea level over the first decennium of the twenty-first century was significantly higher than expected based on global measurements or models and has most likely been caused by significant local subsidence of the land due to tectonic events within the Pacific Ring of Fire. According to the National Coordinator of the program, Lifuka was chosen as the site for the pilot project 'because it had already experienced sea level rise as a result of an earthquake in May 2006. The earthquake measured approximately 7.9 on the Richter scale resulting in a subsidence of 23 cm of the western side of the Lifuka Island' (Kitekei'aho 2012). It seems likely that the rising sea level on Kotu resulting in the end to low tide seaweed and shellfish collecting also prompted the establishment of the PASAP. However, news about the project had not reached Kotu in 2011 nor by my next visit in 2014. And likewise, news of Kotu's recent environmental changes had not reached Lifuka nor the Tongan Ministry of the Environment and Climate Change in the Tongan capital, Nuku'alofa on Tongatapu.

An Environmental Puzzle

With the global focus on climate change, as well as the interest within Tonga and within the Pacific region in general in the environmental consequences of rising sea levels, one might have thought people on Kotu would have found it in their interest to call attention to the ongoing environmental changes that are significantly affecting their lives. They, however, clearly thought otherwise. This book aims to produce an ethnography that may contribute to solving the puzzle of why they thought otherwise. Why the seemingly unshaken confidence in being safe in the face of dramatic and potentially catastrophic environmental events? Why the apparent calm acceptance, even complacency or secrecy, with regard to the drastic transformation of the forest? Why had so many people not yet gone 'to examine with their own eyes' the disappearance of historical landmarks contained in the forest, such as the two freshwater pools of *Veifua* and *Tōkilangi*, which attracted Cook's attention two and a half centuries ago? What about the loss of the path for 'Going under the forest to catch fish' (*Hala siulolovao*)? Or the threat that the 'Hidden mound' (*Langi tu'ulilo*), which links Kotu to the ancient and high-ranking lineage of Tungī Māna'ia, may soon disappear into the mud? Why the reluctance to see the consequences of the environmental changes as negative and the eagerness to look for the positive? Why the easy acceptance of the current state of affairs in their 'homeland', their *fonua*?

In order to solve the puzzle of why this was so, I suggest that it is useful to explore people's engagements with and understandings of the world that surrounds them. By exploring how people in the course of everyday life engage components, forces and dynamics in their surroundings, I aim to discover what Husserl once labelled 'a common horizon of expectations' (see Shore 1996: 282); a horizon of expectations contributing to make dramatic events and environmental changes in the surroundings meaningful to people and thus colour their attitudes toward them. By engaging environments in Tonga, I aim to produce insight into a particular cultural perspective on the relationship between people and the forces in their surroundings. By doing so, I hope also to contribute to an understanding of the relationship between people and environment in general and human responsiveness to environmental changes. The pieces for solving the puzzle have been collected through field visits over three decades. Although some of the data relate to quite recent events and ongoing environmental change, most of the pieces were collected long before and not with this particular puzzle in mind. The bulk of the ethnography of the book has been produced by having a sustained focus on routines of perceiving and engaging components and dynamics of the environment in order to explore the relationship between everyday experience, cultural aesthetics and sociality. In my view, such an exploration provides a promising point of departure for understanding people's puzzling attitudes to the environmental events and changes taking place on Kotu. I propose, then, to engage with the everyday life challenges and opportunities of people in Tonga. Thus, I also hope to show how knowledge embedded in people's everyday involvement with their surroundings may make it possible to discover as well as to deepen our understanding of cultural perspectives on what is true, what is beautiful, what is valuable and what is right. And as Mike Hulme has pointed out in *Why We Disagree about Climate Change* (Hulme 2009), precisely what people hold to be true, beautiful, valuable and right are key for understanding attitudes and responses to ongoing environmental changes. Most of the chapters of the book are devoted to producing insights into the interrelatedness of environmental and sociocultural dynamics. It is my belief that such insights are essential for an understanding of local attitudes and responses to ongoing environmental changes. Before moving on to an ethnographic exploration of environmental engagements and the aesthetics and sociality of everyday life, it is necessary to give a brief account of why people's everyday environmental engagement is somewhat underexposed in Tongan ethnography and what kinds of theoretical perspectives and methodology might be most helpful in exposing its significance.

Cultural Continuity in Engaging Environments

This book takes as its point of departure a mystery; the puzzling responses to the tsunami threat in March 2011 and to the environmental changes taking place on Kotu. But more than that, it is a book that explores the relationship between people and the environment in order to discover characteristic aspects of the make-up of the local world. One of the basic assumptions of the analysis is that the exploration of experience and knowledge related to everyday environmental dynamics makes it possible to discover widely shared notions about the makings of the world that are mostly taken for granted – what in Bloch's terms 'goes without saying' (Bloch 1992) as a largely mute background in people's conceptualization of society. In Eric Hirsch's terms from *The Anthropology of Landscape* (Hirsch 1995), I wish to develop a procedure of discovery to produce an ethnography that brings to the 'foreground' notions that tend to be taken for granted as part of 'background' realities (ibid.: 22–23) in people's lives. It is my view that knowledge and practices of coping with the everyday dynamics of the immediate environment remain an untapped resource for social analysis in Tonga and elsewhere in Polynesia. The idea is simple: people's responses to environmental events and changes do not happen in a cultural or historical vacuum. They must be informed by what people know about their world and how and why things happen in it. Through a focus on people's routines of referring to and engaging with components and dynamics that constitute their environment, the book aims to discover the characteristics of what people know and take for granted about the world that has been 'given' to them. Thus, the title, *Engaging Environments in Tonga*, is intended to imply that a focus on people's everyday engagements with their environment may produce a privileged point of departure for discovering fundamental notions that people share about the world around them. The subtitle, *Cultivating Beauty and Nurturing Relations in a Changing World*, is intended to imply that such shared notions may in turn illuminate the manner in which Kotu people aestheticized social events, talked about social and moral values and constituted social relationships.

Theoretically, the emphasis on the benefits of engaging environments for understanding cultural values and social dynamics is indebted to perspectives that understand humans as sentient beings intimately involved with environments that are made up of a lot of things other than people. Ingold emphasizes that man shares with other living organisms the capacity to engage with components of their environment, and like him I hold that in contrast to other living organisms people have the ability to disengage from the affordances of the environment and that this ability 'allows people to essentialise ranges of utilities, turning them into external objects that may be referred to' (Ingold 1992:

42–44). Thus, there are two modes of being in the world: 'It may be a feature of the human condition that we can switch back and forth between engagement and disengagement, between outward-directed action and inward-directed thought' (ibid.: 42–44). The current analysis has an ambition to explore the relationship between the two modes of being in the world. I hold that people's practical experiences with the qualities and components of their surroundings involve a kind of lived knowing from which their outlook on the world and what goes on in it can be understood along with what people hold to be true, beautiful and right. My emphasis on the potential for gaining insight into important notions that mostly go without saying by focusing on knowledge and experience in people's immediate environment is not, of course, an argument that this is the only environment people experience and have knowledge of. The Kingdom of Tonga as well as the island of Kotu had become part of global economic, political, religious and educational systems long before my first field visits there. George Marcus, who did fieldwork among Tongan chiefly elites in the 1970s, coined the term 'compromise culture' (Marcus 1980: 10) to describe the Tongan blend of traditions, values and social institutions two centuries after Captain James Cook first visited Tonga in the 1770s. Before that, Tongans, by their own navigational skills and those of other Pacific peoples, were interconnected within extensive regional economic, political and religious systems (Hau'ofa 1994; Besnier 2011: 37–38). As Nico Besnier demonstrates in *On the Edge of the Global* – a more recent analysis of modern Tongan anxieties – the steep growth in recent decades of flows of people, money, objects and ideas has intensified global entanglements, which are interwoven into the fabric of Tongan modernity. Tonga is culturally quite homogenous in the sense that people, whether they live in a small remote island of Ha'apai, the capital or even overseas, share quite fundamental ideas of what is valuable, what is beautiful and what is appropriate. In terms of the rhythms, practices and realities of everyday life, however, the differences between an urban and a village setting were certainly considerable when I did my first fieldwork in Tonga in 1986–87 and 1991–92. While people in the capital had cars and electricity – fridges, freezers, TVs and telephones – and acquired most of their food in shops or the Talamahu food market in the centre of Nuku'alofa, people on Kotu still got their food from fishing and farming and relied only on radio or post collected at the post office on neighbouring Ha'afeva island for news and announcements. Although everybody staying on Kotu in the late 1980s and early 1990s had close kin who had moved away to make a living elsewhere, very few of them had yet migrated out of Tonga to 'seek a life' (*kumi mo'ui*) abroad. Thus, the flow of money, things or news to Kotu from overseas migrants was still quite weak and slow. In the last decade of the twentieth century and the first decade of the twenty-first, a sharp increase in the number of overseas migrants originating from Kotu and a telecommunication revolution brought the rest of the world much closer. In 2011, solar technology made lighting affordable, significantly affecting people's everyday lives, with all homes on Kotu benefiting. Output from solar energy was still much too low, however, for cooking or keeping food cold, so it hardly affected patterns of production, distribution and consumption. Some homes acquired gas stoves and a few also washing machines powered by diesel aggregates, but people still mostly did the laundry manually and cooked on open fires and in earth ovens in order to save expenses on fuel. All in all, the rhythm and realities of local production, distribution and consumption were remarkably stable in the late twentieth and early twenty-first century. I do believe that the differences in the rhythms and realities of everyday living have an impact on the discovery of enduring ideas about what is valuable, beautiful and appropriate. A strong continuity with the past in daily routines made the village sociality of Kotu in the 1980s and 1990s a quite suitable point of departure for discovering the more enduring components of the cultural complexity that constitutes Tongan modernity. Thus, I feel that a methodology overdetermined by the facts of modernity and global integration could have the consequence of diminishing the potential for discovering enduring semantic structures – how the world is experienced and makes sense to people. Structures of the *longue durée* (Braudel, see Howard and Borofsky 1989: 249) – the 'essential dynamics' of 'streams of cultural traditions … exhibiting an empirical cluster of certain elements in syndromes that tend to persist over time' (Barth 1989: 131) – may easily be lost if following loops of global integration is not complemented by following threads of local signification.

In practical terms, my methodology is characterized by an interest in cultural perspectives produced by the fact that all places are connected to wider worlds by open-ended flows of persons, things and ideas as well as local conditions, routines of everyday life and ideas about reality. Thus, I see no reason why an awareness of the significance of global forces driving sociocultural change should reduce the ethnographic appetite for following the locally constituted conditions of cultural production of the present. From the outset, the production of an ethnography on Tonga seemed to rest on an idea of contemporary cultural inauthenticity. Five years before the publication of 'Tongan Society' (Gifford 1929), which was the first ethnographic account of Tonga made by a professional ethnographer, Gifford wrote 'a pioneer paper on acculturation' (Keesing 1947: 36) called 'Euro-American Acculturation in Tonga' (Gifford 1924a). By the time of the Second World War, the awareness among students of Polynesian culture of contemporary inauthenticity seems to have made urgency the predominant characteristic of cultural research: 'Changes under way will not wait for observers, and the need for pushing acculturation studies is urgent' (Keesing 1947: 39). Ernest and Pearl Beaglehole's book, based on eight weeks of fieldwork in the Pangai village of Vava'u just before the war (Beaglehole 1944), represented a rather isolated effort to collect material about everyday village living in Tonga. Others like Gifford (Gifford 1929), Collocott (Collocott 1919; 1921; 1928) and, later, Bott (Bott 1958; 1981; 1982) turned to those recognized to be most knowledgeable about authentic Tongan traditions of the past to salvage as much as possible before it was too late. However, the bias of Tongan ethnographic production in favour of the centre and elite traditions is probably first of all a result of what one of Marcus' Tongan informants called the 'aristocentrism' (Marcus 1980: 26) of Tongan society itself. Tongan conceptions of the distribution of knowledge about the 'Tongan way' (*anga fakatonga*) involve an ideological orientation around summits and centre. I think Biersack was right in pointing out that part of the reason 'the elite have continued to have a strong presence in scholarly writing about Tonga' is:

> the important role Queen Salote played as patron of anthropological and historical efforts, her interest in codifying elite practices and knowledge, and her sponsorship of particular scholars' efforts – ones such as Elizabeth Bott, Edward Winslow Gifford, Adrianne Kaeppler, and Sione Latukefu who have had a powerful impact on Tongan historiography and the anthropologist's perception of what there is to know about Tonga. (Biersack 1994: 3)

The aristocentrism of Tongan society combined with a sense of ethnographic urgency may seem to have synchronized scholarly efforts and the efforts of the Tongan elite to salvage the cultural heritage before it disappeared. I do not wish to suggest that the combination of scholarly and political urgencies in the history of Tongan ethnographic production has failed to produce useful ethnographies and interesting analyses of Tongan traditions. On the contrary, it has resulted in the collection and analyses of valuable material by Bott (Bott 1972a; 1972b), Leach (Leach 1972) Kaeppler (Kaeppler 1985; 1990; 1993), Gunson (Gunson 1990) Valeri (Valeri 1989), Herda (Herda 1990), Māhina (Māhina 1990) and others that would otherwise, no doubt, have been lost. Rather, the point is that Tongan 'aristocentrism' combined with scholarly and elitist urgencies may seem to have created a force field of Tongan ethnographic production that deflects cultural research away from the practices of contemporary everyday interaction, away from commoners and away from local community studies. Methodologically, this means that the archives, the centres and the knowledge of specialists have attracted more interest than village life, local knowledge of the present and a *contemporary* cosmology/world view. After seventy years of ethnographic production in Tonga, Paul van der Grijp's publishers were thus able to claim that his book *Islanders of the South* ' ... is the first book to examine the interplay of Polynesian and Western ideas within contemporary social and economic practices, not from the point of view of Tongan aristocracy, but from that of the common people' (Van der Grijp 1993a). Some village studies concerning aspects of commoners' strategies for coping with everyday realities have been undertaken, however, although only three seem to have resulted in books (Beaglehole 1944; Topouniua 1986; Perminow 1993a), with the rest comprising unpublished theses and numerous articles focusing on then contemporary ideas of kinship and village practices, written in the 1960s and 1970s by such scholars as Aoyagi (Aoyagi 1966), Decktor Korn (Decktor Korn 1974; 1975; 1976), Rogers (Rogers 1968; 1975; 1977) and K. Morton (Morton 1972; 1976; 1987). Since the late twentieth century, an interest in Tongan 'compromise culture' – defined as a '... complex of institutions, ideas, and practices, which integrates earlier Tongan culture with a version of *Papalangi* (European) culture' (Marcus 1980: 10; see also Howard and Borofsky 1989: 207) and characterized by changing gender relations and social changes relatable to the complex of migration, globalization and westernization (James 1983; 1990; 1991; Gailey 1987; 1990; Herda 1987; Cowling 1990a; Van der Grijp 1993b; Perminow 1993a; 1993b) – has dominated ethnographic production about contemporary Tonga. It is my belief that in the gap between the valuable works of cultural reconstruction of pre-contact Tonga and insights into the realities of contemporary cultural compromises sensitized to the significance of global impacts there is ample room to supplement the body of Tongan ethnography by delving deeply into the domain of local knowledge – that is, the conceptualizations of phenomena encountered by people experiencing and coping with local realities.

The first part of the book engages the immediate surroundings to produce insights about the make-up of the local world that has been 'given' to people and that is, thus, largely taken for granted. In the second part of the book, these insights will be used as a basis for approaching the enduring cultural significance of 'beauty' (*faka'ofo'ofa*) and 'orderliness' (*maau*) in ritual aesthetics and of 'compassion' (*'ofa*) and 'nurture' (*tauhi*) for sociality. The subtitle of this book, *Cultivating Beauty and Nurturing Relations in a Changing World*, is used to indicate that ritual aesthetics and sociality does not take place in a stable reality. Rather, they take place in a changing world that constantly transforms between different states or phases of being as tides move in and out, as day dawns and night falls, as the moon waxes and wanes, as the seasons change and as weather changes. Thus, the different phases or states of their surroundings afford people who routinely experience and cope with them very different opportunities to engage with and reflect upon the qualities of their environment and inform their understanding of the world and its workings.

This book, then, seeks to explore how engaging environments and their dynamics may improve our understanding of cultural aesthetics and sociality. It is my view that an effort to discover enduring and resilient ideas about what is real, what is effective, what is valuable, what is beautiful and what is appropriate is important for understanding people's responses and attitudes to things happening around them. Thus, this ethnography aims to discover the characteristics of how the realities of existence are seen to play out in everyday environmental dynamics. It aims to show how these dynamics are relevant for ideas of what must be done to achieve results in everyday production and what characterizes ceremonial aesthetics and notions of beauty and value, which in their turn constitute an important basis for relating to one another and to act appropriately. Finally, in the concluding chapter of the book, this ethnography of engagements with environmental dynamics in everyday routines, of cultivation of beauty in ceremonial events, and of nurturing relations in everyday sociality, will be crucial for a grounded understanding of local attitudes and responses to ongoing environmental changes.

Notes

1. The so-called brother-sister taboo involving constraints of conduct and avoidance related to eating and sleeping arrangements among cross-sex siblings and first, second and third cousins, who are all classified as *tuofefine-tuongaʻane* (sister-brother) vis-à-vis one another.
2. According to Churchward, *veifua* or *ʻumu veifua* signifies 'first cooked food presented to women after marriage or confinement or to shark-catchers on their return' (Churchward 1959: 537), while *Tōkilangi* might signify 'dedicated to chiefly burial mound' (ibid.: 482). Thus, the ancient names of the two pools seem to relate both to the path *Hala siulolovao* running between the pools and into the forest and the ancient chiefly burial mound *Langi tuʻu lilo* just behind them.
3. *Lapila* is the Tongan term for a kind of tilapia fish endemic to freshwater lakes in Africa and which is farmed extensively in Asia. It has been introduced to some areas in Africa as a measure to control malaria mosquitoes. *Lapila* were probably introduced to Tongan volcanic and brackish lakes in the twentieth century.

1

Moving to the Beat of a Marine Environment

Qualitative Nuances Read upon the Surface of Things

Going to the beach of the Great Landing (*Fanga lahi*) in the early morning to 'inspect the sea' (*fakasio e tahi*) was a common routine on Kotu. Finding out whether the tide was flowing or ebbing made it possible to form an opinion about what things would happen in the immediate future and was therefore important for planning the activities of the day. That marine realities should be important to people living on a small piece of low-lying land set in a large lagoon surrounded by the deep sea of the South Pacific should not be surprising. Still, I noticed during my fieldwork that marine realities blended easily into the mute background as something quickly taken for granted. I have suggested that the local response to environmental events and ongoing environmental changes may seem less puzzling if considering people's strong convictions about what is true and real in the world, what is desirable, what is beautiful and valuable and what is appropriate in dealings with one another. Thus, I suggest that a good point of departure is to start out by considering the significance of the tides as a timekeeper of everyday living.

The flow of time must be inferred by putting together memories of the past, images of the present and expectations about the future. According to Alfred Gell '… there are two logically quite distinct "basic experiences" of time. There are (1) that certain natural phenomena repeat themselves; and (2) that for the individual organism life changes are irreversible and death inevitable' (Gell 1992: 30). My purpose is not to discuss or decide whether different societies (or historical epochs) have different 'time conceptions'. I am not out to compare or explore local philosophies of time at all. Rather, I would agree with Gell, who, with reference to Kedang concepts of time (as described by Barnes), notes: 'The collective representations of "time" are not representations of the topology of the time-dimension, but are representations of what characteristically goes on in the temporal world ... The relevant distinction does not lie between different "concepts of time", but different conceptions of the world and its workings' (ibid.: 36).

I am interested in exploring the synchronization of people's daily activities with recurring natural phenomena, in order to gain insight about 'conceptions of the world and its workings'. Like Bourdieu, I think that this world does not make itself known to people as a stable reality but as 'qualitative nuances' (Bourdieu 1963: 59). What I hope to gain by exploring these nuances are insights into attitudes toward the world and its workings rather than attitudes towards time. To focus on the qualitative nuances of things on Kotu involves exploring the dynamics between several kinds of diametrically opposed states of being in which the routines of daily life are embedded. I shall use this exploration to identify and illuminate characteristic and enduring qualities of Tongan cultural aesthetics and sociality, which in their turn, I believe, are important for understanding how people responded to ongoing environmental changes.

What may be called the timescape of Kotu consists of numerous recurring phenomena that were important for timing people's everyday activities in the last decades of the twentieth century. Kotu was neither 'clock-less' nor 'calendar-less'. Still, its temporal topography may be described as one in which 'The effective points of reference in the continual flux of time's passage are qualitative nuances read upon the surface of things ...' (ibid.: 59). Terminologies of qualitative nuances existed to make it possible to map this timescape or topography: a terminology of the tides; a terminology of daily shifts and changes in the relationship between light and darkness; a terminology of moon nights; and the traditional Tongan calendar of yam cultivation. For my purpose, the significance of terminologies of qualitative nuances for the timing of everyday events is that they carry messages about the make-up of the world. The main difference between timing by reference to qualitative nuances and a terminology of quantitative differentiation, such as a clock or a date, is that the latter, *in itself*, provides fewer insights into the world in which it is embedded. Over the next two chapters, then, I shall explore everyday routines of coping with and referring to qualitative nuances related to tidal, diurnal and lunar changes on Kotu. The obvious significance of marine realities for everyday life on Kotu makes people's routine engagements with the dynamics of the *Namolahi* Lagoon an appropriate starting point for this exploration.

The Changing Faces of *Namolahi* Lagoon

Approximately every 6 1/4 hours a tidal transformation causes the marine environment to present a radically different face to Kotu people. The two tidal extremes of *tau 'a e tahi* (high tide) and *mamaha 'a e tahi* (low tide) are transitory moments in a continual process of transformation. The processes of *hu'a mai ke tau* (flood tide) and *mahu'i ke mamaha* (ebb tide) relate to the two diametrically opposed states. In addition, several intermediate states of the sea were recognized on Kotu. Twice a day, this process of transformation played itself out in the lagoon, used for its resources as well as to come and go from the island.

In his study of customary sea tenure, Edvard Hviding explored the sea as a cultural and relational focus for the people living around Marovo Lagoon in the Solomon Islands. He emphasized the terrestrial bias of the ethnographic documentation of coastal Melanesia: 'Even coastal populations have often been considered as overwhelmingly oriented towards agriculture, and their involvement with and dependence on the sea has tended to remain superficially documented at best' (Hviding 1992: 5). Navigational skills make up a topic in Polynesian ethnography, but the practical and experiential aspects of coping with the sea for everyday production is not well documented. Indeed, Hviding's conclusion about the sea-related ethnography of Melanesia appropriately describes also Polynesian ethnography: '… too little is known about the relationships … to the marine environment that forms such a significant context for their lives' (ibid.: 8). Thus, Bataille-Benguigui[1] in 1988 described the documentation of Tongan relations to the marine environment (Gifford 1929; Koch 1955: 244–90; Rogers 1975: 206–25; Halapua 1982; Dye 1983; see also Grijp 1993a: 51–59): 'Fishing techniques studied in the Tonga Islands have been described only by their operational methods and without investigating the possible symbolic aspects accompanying the acquisition of natural sea resources' (Benguigui 1988: 185).

On Kotu, the different parts of the lagoon were not associated with any social groups, nor did the people on Kotu hold common exclusive ownership, or usufruct, of it. Thus, people from the surrounding islands occasionally used the lagoon for commercial fishing.[2] There is no doubt, however, that *Namolahi* Lagoon has historically been particularly significant as a resource base for Kotu people. The references to Kotu island as *Namolahi* ('Large Lagoon') as well as *Tukulalo* ('Coastland' as opposed to 'interior'; *tuku'uta*) and subchief title *Hafukinamo* ('drifting before the wind to the lagoon') are all related to the fact that Kotu and its large lagoon historically has been considered as the marine part of Taufatōfua's territory. Kotu together with the high volcanic island of Tōfua, about forty kilometres west of Kotu, historically made up the estate of the non-noble chiefly title of Taufatōfua. Kotu people thus have a long history of commuting between the two islands in order to grow the kava pepper plant (*piper methysticum*) used to make the ceremonially important Pacific drug and also staple foods to supplement the limited production on Kotu, a practice locally referred to as *fakalahi kelekele* ('to enlarge the soil') (see Perminow 1993b). However, the significance of a focus on the lagoon is not a question of whether there has existed exclusive ownership, or usufruct, rather it lies in the importance of *Namolahi* Lagoon as a field of everyday experience.

The significance of a shift of focus from Kotu island to *Namolahi* Lagoon is to highlight the fact that the lagoon makes the area that people routinely use for purposes of production and transportation eighteen times larger. With its 685 persons per square kilometre, Kotu Island was the most densely populated island of Tonga in 1986 as well as in 1992.[3] The population density of Kotu Island, including the extensive *Namolahi* Lagoon which surrounds it, on the other hand, was only 38 persons per square kilometre. However, the main significance of this shift of focus is qualitative rather than quantitative; it is intended to draw attention to the significance of people's engagements and knowledge related to the marine parts of the environment, aspects of everyday experience that have suffered from more land-locked approaches. Thus, I would draw attention, as Hviding does in his study of life around the Marovo Lagoon, to the significance of the sea because it may contain: '... powerful connotations of fluidity, mobility, and other realms of life' that may serve to supplement insights gained from numerous terrestrially biased explorations in the Pacific (Hviding 1992: 10).

Moving in *Namolahi* Lagoon

Daily activities within *Namolahi* Lagoon involves coping with an environment in perpetual motion, with tidal dynamics bringing certain seascape features into temporary existence. The expression 'the lagoon is on the move/astir' (*loka 'a e namo*), for example, refers to occasional strong currents (*'au lahi*) creating 'water flows/rivers' (*vai tafe*). Other seascape features, such as fields of seaweed, deep spots, different kinds of coral formations and channels or passages in the fringing reef become more or less significant as tides change. From the perspective of those moving and working in the marine environment of *Namolahi* Lagoon, features brought to existence by the ebb tide constitute a complex seascape, creating specific facts of existence that have to be taken into account in order to act appropriately or effectively. Likewise, the flood tide creates a state where low-tide features lose their distinctiveness and constitute a different environment.

The routines of coming to or leaving Kotu Island may illuminate the practical significance of these natural marine dynamics, as demonstrated in the following account.

> The sea was calm and the full moon was high in the sky when the ferry from Nuku'alofa arrived at Ha'feva. 'Atu Hē had come from Kotu with his boat to pick up Kotu people who came on the ferry. 'What do you think?' 'Atu asked, 'Should we go ashore at Ha'afeva to wait for daylight, or should we go straight back to Kotu?' 'It's your decision,' I said, 'but as the sea is very calm, it would be well if we were to go straight to Kotu'. 'It is the truth,' he said, 'but look at the moon; it almost stands straight up (*meimei tu'u tonu 'a e mahina*). Very soon it shall be low tide.' He turned to discuss it with some of the other passengers, who all felt that it was worth a try. Because the moon provided ample illumination, he decided to 'attempt' (*'ahi'ahi*: 'probe', 'seek by trial and error') to enter *Namolahi* Lagoon by way of the 'Great passage' (*Ava lahi*). Approaching the *Namolahi* Lagoon, 'Atu sent a man up front as lookout for the passage between the submerged reef of *Tōfuke*, *Luapunga* ('permanently submerged head-coral') and *Fonuae'a*[4] ('sometimes visible land') leading through to *Ava lahi* ('Great passage') into the lagoon. After about half an hour of careful navigation involving exchanges of orders and information between 'Atu and the lookout about significant places of the fringing reefs surrounding the lagoon, we finally managed to enter the 'Great passage'. That 'Atu had found it was made evident by the boat making very little headway, even though he opened up the throttle of the 30 hp. outboard engine as far as it would go. Despite the fact that the boat had very little forward motion, the sea boiled whitely around the bow, and the boat shook and rocked violently. For some time, the power of the engine fought the force of the outgoing tide. But eventually 'Atu got us through and told the lookout to watch out for the submerged coral formation of *Fakakaufue* and *Maka tangafa* ('Humphead Wrasse Rock'), to direct us into the narrow channel between the partly exposed formations of *Maau si'i* ('Small Maau') and *Maau lahi* ('Big Maau') leading into the low tide anchorage of *Taulanga lahi* ('Large anchorage'). Tilting up the engine and zigzagging between massive 'coral boulders' (*punga/lua punga*), wide 'tabulate corals' (*hakau kahifi/makafale*), brittle and sharp coral mushrooms and fans and forests of entangled 'staghorn coral' (*maka feo*), as well as across deep sandy 'ponds' (*fo'i loto*) and shallow 'fields of seaweed' (*fo'i limu*), 'Atu brought the boat within 500 metres of the 'Large Landing' (*Fangalahi*), where we disembarked and proceeded to wade onto land.

The Places of *Namolahi*

The features of the marine environment make up a chartable seascape (see map of *Namolahi* Lagoon in the frontmatter). I emphasize, however, that the marine world of *Namolahi* Lagoon is inherently dynamic. A seascape map gives a sense of stability that is alien to the marine realities with which people deal. Like Weiner, I emphasize that the named places are part of an 'existential space' in contrast to '... Euclidean space of absolute, geometric dimensions'. This existential space, according to Weiner, is constituted as 'an intersubjective social one' through people's life activity (Weiner 1991: 32). The named places were of temporary and varying significance for the practical life activities that took place in the lagoon.

About fifty places in the lagoon had recognized names. These named places feature 'deep spots' (*fo'i loto*), 'coral formations' (*fo'i hakau*), 'coral boulders' (*fo'i maka*), 'passages' (*fo'i ava*) in the outer reefs and 'fields of seaweed' (*fo'i*[5] *limu*). Some of the terms describe characteristic qualities of the named place. Thus, as mentioned, the name *Ava lahi* means 'Great opening/passage', while the names of other passages include *Hakau fakapapanga* ('Smooth/Featureless reef'), *Ava pipiko* ('Crooked passage'), *Ava 'i Tungua* ('Passage toward Tungua') and *Hali'a* ('Grazing place'). Similarly there are the descriptive names *Hakau pupunu* ('Filled/stopped-up reef'), *Hakau mavahe* ('Divided reef'), *Kauhakau fakatonga* ('Southern reefs'),'*Utu popotu* ('Small crab rockface'; pitted with small holes among which small crabs scuttle) and *Luo* ('Hole/Depression'). The name *Mo'unga Tōfua* also seems to describe characteristics of the place in question, referring to a deep area in the lagoon becoming a 'lake' at low tide and mirroring the crater lake known as *Vai ko Lofia* in the interior of Tōfua Island.

Some of the names refer to activities associated with specific locations in the lagoon. *Tu'unga Kupenga* means 'Place of net-fishing', *Tu'u peau ala* may be interpreted to mean 'Standing in the waves collecting shellfish', while *Taulanga lahi* and *Taulanga si'i* signify 'Large anchorage' and 'Small anchorage'.

Some parts of the lagoon were associated with specific marine species; for example, Koloa, my host and Kotu's town officer, told me that *Maka he afe* ('Boulder of the bend'), *Hakau pupunu* ('Filled/Stopped up reef'), *Hakau fakapapanga* ('Smooth reef'), *Hefau* ('The Haul'; a sandy, shallow part of the lagoon) and *Kauhakau fakatonga* ('Southern reefs') were 'haunts' (*nofo'anga ika*; lit. 'dwelling place of fish') of the Yellowfin Goatfish or *Malili* (*fa'ahinga ika*[6]) (*Mullidae*; Randall et al. 1990). Similarly, Sweetlips or *Fotu'a* (*Haemulidae*; ibid.) were characterised as 'dependable' (*pau*) and were said to form 'schools' (*fakataha ika*) beneath the tabulate corals of the 'deep spot' (*fo'i loto*) close to the *Hakau fakapapanga* ('Smooth reef'). Most marine species were described as 'unpredictable' (*ta'epau*), in not having specific haunts or by 'scattering' (*mouvetevete*) when disturbed, and were associated with other kinds of marine terrain. The *Koango* (probably Thumbprint and Grass Emperor; *Lethrinidae*; ibid.) were associated with the lagoon 'fields of seaweed', while the *Tanutanu* (possibly Pink-eared or Orange-striped Emperor and/or Lancer; *Lethrinidae*; ibid) were associated both with the fields of seaweed and formations of staghorn coral, among which they habitually hide when alarmed.

The place known as *Tōfuke* was by some associated with 'octopus fishing' (*maka feke*). Similarly *Lula 'uta* (Higher *lula*) and *Lula lalo* (Lower *lula*) refer to two 'ends of a seaweed field' (*mui limu*) and identify a good 'place/bed for the turtle net' (*tu'unga/mohenga 'o e kafa fonu*). Similarly, a stone barrier named *Maka papa*, running along the west coast of the island, the 'pools' of *Vāsia* and *Kava tokoua*, the coral rock *Tu'ungatala* ('Perch of the *Tala* seagull') and the beach known as *Talingavete* ('Waiting for the goatfish') were associated with the Yellowstripe Goatfish (*vete*; *Mulloidichthys flavolineatus*; ibid.). These goatfish were referred to as 'fish belonging to the territory' (*ika fakafonua*), 'fish originating here on Kotu' (*ika tupu'a 'i Kotuni*) and 'fish from the days of old' (*ika fuoloa*) (see also Bataille-Benguigui 1988: 188).[7] According to Koloa, the *vete* is usually an 'unpredictable' (*ta'epau*) fish. In the warm season, however, they sometimes collect in great numbers. From his childhood and youth in the early twentieth century, he recalled that such occasions used to be referred to as 'fish days' (*'aho ika*). He mentioned that one should 'examine' (*fakasio*) the lagoon for signs of schools at 'low tide in the morning' (*pongipongi mamaha*) after the 'second quarter of the moon' (*tu'u efiafi e māhina*; lit. 'the moon stands in the afternoon'), at which time the fish were said to collect close to the 'Perch of the seagull' (*Tu'ungatala*) and sometimes along the barrier of the weather coast. If the fish were to collect along the barrier, they could be caught in great quantities by fishermen forming a line along the barrier and coordinating the throwing of their casting nets (*sīlī*). Some fishermen claimed that if the fish collected too far from the barrier one could attempt to get them closer by pounding kava and throwing it into the 'pools' of *Vāsia* or *Kava tokoua* or outside the barrier.

One man in his forties recalled vaguely that 'fish days' referred to an old technique of catching goatfish by throwing nets during December but claimed that the goatfish never came close enough to the coast nowadays. For a young man in his early twenties, the expression 'fish days' meant nothing, and he associated the places of the lagoon with quite different activities, like bathing, referring, like most youngsters, to the two lagoon pools as *Vāsia tangata* ('men's *Vāsia*') and *Vāsia fefine* ('women's *Vāsia*'), mirroring the references to the two 'pools/springs' (*vaitupu*) on the island itself, known as *Vai tangata* ('Men's Water') and *Vai fefine* ('Women's Water'). These pools were much used by young people in 1986, as well as in 1992. 'When the boys have been swimming in the *Vāsia tangata* [in the lagoon] they go to the *Vai tangata* [on the island] to rinse off the sea water'.

To sum up, then, particular features of the seascape serve as points of reference for particular activities and occurrences in the lagoon. Some of the place names of the lagoon have no doubt remained unchanged for centuries and are therefore stable. For instance *Fonuae'a*, marking the entrance of the 'Great Passage' into the *Namolahi* Lagoon, was an important point of reference when Cook visited Kotu in 1777.[8] On the other hand, other place names may be less stable and subject to change as routines and the marine environment changes.

Examining the Face of the Sea

As mentioned, in the morning, villagers routinely paid visits to the 'beach' (*matātahi*; lit. 'the face of the sea') of the 'Great Landing' (*Fanga lahi*), explicitly to 'examine, inspect' (*fakasio*) the sea. In the afternoon, people went to the sea to 'receive/welcome the fishermen' (*tali kau fangota*) or occasional visitors, to rest, cool down in the sea breeze, play or 'have a bath' (*kaukau tahi*). The term *fakasio* refers to reading the signs of a situation to make an informed judgement about it. Thus, an 'examination of the sea' first of all took into consideration the direction the tide was moving. The 'face of the sea' (*matātahi*) was examined for signs indicating either a 'flood tide' (*hu'a mai ke tau 'a e tahi*: 'the sea is flowing here to unite with land') or 'ebb tide' (*mahu'i ke mamaha 'a e tahi*: 'the sea is separating/detaching itself to become almost empty'). In practice, this was decided on by examining the sand to see whether it was 'wet' (*viku*) or 'dry' (*momoa*), 'clean' (*ma'a lelei*) or 'filled with litter' (*veve'ia/vevea*).

People's competence in identifying the 'turning point' of the sea (*ngata 'o e tahi*) varied depending on amount of marine experience, and there was quite often a lack of consensus about the direction of the tide. Joining a 17-year-old youth at the beach around high tide one morning, I asked him, 'What do you think; has the tide turned? Is it *tau hu'a* [attached but still flowing here] or is it *tau mahu'i* [attached but becoming separated/detached]?' Glancing at the beach, he said, '*Tau mahu'i pē* [It is detaching].' Five minutes later, a man in his early forties joined us, looked at the beach and said: '*Kei hu'a mai pē e tahi, eh?* [The sea is still flowing here, don't you think?].' Looking up, the boy exclaimed: '*Ueh! ... mo'oni pē 'ia* [I say! ... That is the truth!].' Later on, I discussed this instance of *fakasio* ('examination') with the boy's grandfather: '*Oku kei vale pē e tamaiki pea 'oku 'ikai te ne fu'u anga ki tahi* [The youth are still ignorant, and also this one has little affinity with the sea].'

After the 'turning point' (*ngata'anga*), it becomes easier to discern which way the tide is moving. And some 'dependable sign' (*me'a pau*; 'dependable thing') appears to make divergent interpretations quite impossible.

Between the extremes of 'high tide' and 'low tide', the tidal motion was terminologically arrested, so to speak, at several stages. Again, knowledge about these stages varied. Everyone knew the terms referring to the extreme ends of tidal motion, but only some were familiar with the numerous terms referring to intermediate states:

Tau 'a e tahi	'The sea is attached'. High tide.
Tau mahu'i	'The sea is attached but has started to detach'. High tide that has turned.
Takapau 'uluaki	'First reliable examining'. First stage of ebb tide. The term refers to the appearance of a band of debris left on the beach by the waves of the ebb tide. One of several meanings of the term *taka* is 'to examine with interest', while *pau* signifies 'certain/definite/reliable'.
Takapau ua	'Second reliable examining'. Second stage of ebb tide. The term refers to the second band of debris left by the receding sea.
Loto'one 'a e tahi	'The sea is in the middle of the sand'. Mid-ebb tide. The expression refers to the point when the ebb-tide state is such that 'the beach is divided into two equal parts' (*vaeua mālie 'a e matātahi*).
Toukilikili 'a e tahi	'The sea is at the pebbles'. More than half ebb tide. This refers to an ebb-tide state when pebbles (*toukilikili*) appear in the lagoon and 'make known that the sea shall soon be empty' (*mahino ai kuo vave 'a e tahi ke mamaha*).
Hā 'a e pala	'The appearance of the *pala*'. Late ebb tide. This refers to a tidal state when the soggy 'seaweed' (*limu*) appears to 'make known that sea of the lagoon shall very soon be empty' (*mahino ai kuo vave 'aupito ke mamaha 'a e tahi*). *Pala* means 'soggy' and 'rotting/rotten', and the expression *pala-tahi*, according to Churchward, signifies 'to be rotten by being wet for a long time in sea water' (1959: 400).
Mamaha mahu'i 'a e tahi	'The sea is almost empty but still separating/detaching'. Last stage of ebb tide.
Mamaha 'a e tahi	'The sea is almost empty'. Low tide.
Mamaha hu'a mai	'The sea is almost empty but is flowing here'. Low tide that has turned.
Puli 'a e pala	'The soggy seaweed has vanished'. First phase of flood tide.
Puli 'a e toukilikili	'The pebbles have vanished'. Second phase of flood tide.

Loto'one hu'a mai 'a e tahi	'The sea flowing here is in the midst of the sand'. Mid-flood tide.
Tau hu'a mai 'a e tahi	'Attached but still flowing here'. High tide that has not yet turned.
Tau 'a e tahi	'The sea is attached (to land)'. High tide.

Two observations about the practical significance of this terminology of tidal dynamics should be made. First of all, people more often referred to the phases close to the tidal turning points, such as *tau hu'a mai 'a e tahi* ('the sea is attached but still flowing here'), *tau* ('attached'), *tau mahu'i* ('attached but separating/detaching') as well as *mamaha mahu'i* ('almost empty but separating/detaching'), *mamaha* ('almost empty'), *mamaha hu'a* ('almost empty but attaching'). Secondly, people more often used terms describing the qualitative nuances of ebb tide than those describing the nuances of flood tide. The reason for this may be that the most important activities in the seascape of the lagoon occur during low tide. The finer distinctions of the flood tide, described by terms such as *puli 'a e pala, puli 'a e toukilikili, loto'one (hu'a)* were seldom used.

Everybody on Kotu knew the basics of tide movement: '*Kapau 'oku mamaha pongipongi 'a e tahi e toe mamaha pē he efiafi*' ('If it is low tide in the morning, it will also be low tide in the afternoon'). The same kind of statement was also made with reference to the occurrence of high tide. From my own observations, the interval between high tide and low tide did seem to be stable, remaining at about 6 hours 15 minutes. This means, however, that any tidal state is delayed by about one hour in one diurnal cycle. Also, because expectations were formulated in terms of the broad categories of *pongipongi* ('morning') and *efiafi* ('afternoon'), the sea quite often presented a quite different face from the one based on a previous 'examination' of the beach. Going by the beach early in the afternoon (around 3:00 PM) and seeing that the sea covers all of the beach, one would be quite right in deciding that it is 'high tide in the afternoon' (*tau efiafi*), especially if it is a 'spring tide' (*tahi lahi*), which means that even if the tide turned at 2:00 PM it may well still cover the beach an hour later. This might make it reasonable to assume that it would be 'high tide in the morning' (*tau pongipongi*). However, coming to the beach 17 hours later (at 8 AM) to examine the sea, the tide would not be high but very low (turning in at about a quarter to nine and well on its way to the uncommonly low tides following spring tide highs). This would, however, only represent an unpleasant surprise if one were to schedule specific activities in accordance with the faulty prediction. Thus, it would be frustrating if one had set one's mind on working on the plantation in the morning during the expected high tide and going fishing in the afternoon during the expected low tide. Such precise advance scheduling of specific everyday activities, however, appeared to be uncommon on Kotu. Also, predictions involved in timing specific future events were based on several considerations.

Acts of *fakasio* may be understood as routines of tuning into the marine environment for purposes of planning the more immediate future. Thus, utilizing what knowledge they had about the qualitative nuances of the sea would constitute an important part of people's planning of everyday activities. People's knowledge varied, but frequent acts of *fakasio* or 'examining' nevertheless contributed to establishing shared understandings about a tidal motion between very different states of the sea offering different opportunities.

Further Rules of Reading the Sea

In addition to acts of *fakasio*, some people took into consideration different types of tides. These are the most common expressions used to differentiate between them:

Spring high tide	*Tahi lahi*; 'Big sea' or *Ngata 'i 'uta 'aupito ('a e tahi)*: '(The sea) comes all the way up onto land (before turning).'
Spring low tide	*Maha 'aupito 'a e tahi*; 'The sea is altogether empty' or *Pakupaku ('a e namo)*: '(The lagoon is) absolutely dry.'
Neap high tide	*Tahi si'i*; 'Small sea' or *Ngata he loto'one ('a e tahi)*: '(The sea) ends/turns in the middle of the sand/beach).'
Neap low tide	*'Oku 'ikai ke fu'u mamaha a e tahi*; 'The sea is not very empty.'

Koloa claimed regarding neap tide conditions: 'If there is a small sea (at high tide) or if the sea ends/turns in the middle of the sand, the sea shall not become very empty.' And for spring tide conditions: 'If there is a big sea (at high tide), or if the sea comes altogether up onto land (during high tide before turning), the sea shall become altogether empty/the lagoon shall be altogether dry.'

But even these understandings were not absolutely dependable. Thus, for Koloa there was yet another set of considerations, bringing into the act of *fakasio* notions of the relative 'strength' (*malohi*) of the 'deep sea' (*moana*) 'outside the lagoon' (*tu'a namo*) and the sea 'inside the lagoon' (*lotonamo*): 'If the lagoon is "on the move/astir" (*loka'a e namo*), the sea shall not become very empty.' He also claimed that the strength of the *loka* overrides the effects of spring tide: 'Even if the sea is big (at high tide), with the lagoon on the move, the sea shall not become altogether empty (at low tide).'

It is not clear what oceanographic circumstances may produce the local phenomenon known as *loka* ('on the move/astir'). But it was people's observation that spring tides and neap tides are offset by other alterations caused by meteorological forces related to seasonal variations of air and sea temperature, which often made people hesitant about predicting states of the sea. Thus, according to Koloa, people's predictions tended to be quite tentative and 'unreliable' (*ta'epau*; 'non-dependable') and should be treated as *fakamahalo pē* ('conjectural statements/approximations') (see Decktor-Korn, 1983 for an interpretation of general attitudes to future events in Tonga).

To complicate the act of *fakasio* even further, the effects of the marine condition of *loka* on the lagoon varied depending on what kind of *loka* it was. Some people distinguished between *loka fakatokelau 'a e namo* ('Northern *loka*') *loka fakatonga 'a e namo* ('Southern *loka*') and *loka takai 'a e namo* ('*loka* all around'). The first kind of *loka*, although sometimes observable by the manner in which the waves break along the northern part of the outer reefs, was not believed to create a 'strong current' (*'au lahi*) in the lagoon. The two other kinds were known to create powerful 'flows' or 'rivers' (*tafe*) at ebb tide as well as at flood tide. Also they were known to create a powerful current in the passages between the lagoon and the deep sea, making it most convenient to leave and enter the lagoon at high tide. Ordinarily (even during spring tides), it would be possible with sufficient illumination and familiarity with the tides to enter the lagoon regardless of the tidal state. The marine condition of *loka* did, however, tend to bring temporary phenomena into existence, transforming passages into barriers. 'A lagoon on the move' appeared to bring about a general reorientation of people's mode of relating to the different states of the lagoon. Rather than representing potential for safe passage, 'the openings' of an ebb tide lagoon 'on the move' became a potential hazard, and the prospect of a bountiful catch was low. At the same time, a flood tide transforms the hazardous and difficult seascape of the ebb tide lagoon 'on the move' into a more tranquil seascape. Thus, a high tide has a practical significance during *loka* that it normally lacks; apart from making it possible to enter and leave Namolahi Lagoon, it was also of particular significance for Kotu fishermen because it transformed the difficult seascape of a lagoon 'on the move' into a state useful for purposes of production. 'Line fishing' (*taumata'u*) was said to be the only method of lagoon fishing undertaken during high tide and the only practicable method of fishing at times when the lagoon was 'on the move'.

Acts of *fakasio* must be very thorough in order to discover the signs that the lagoon is 'on the move'. Opinions about the state of the tide and expectations about the tidal near future were basically formed by examining the beach (*matātahi*), where *'uta* ('land') faces *tahi* ('sea'.) Signs that the lagoon is 'on the move', on the other hand, were basically read off the 'outer reefs/fringing reefs' (*'u'ulu hakau*), where the sea 'inside the lagoon' (*lotonamo*) meets the sea 'outside the lagoon' (*tu'a namo*). However, Koloa argued that this observation relies too heavily on appearances and that 'waves break very strongly on the reefs even when there is no *loka*'. According to one man in his late thirties, the condition of *loka* was easily observable because it coincides with a calm sea (*tofu*). Koloa argued that a calm sea alone was not in itself a sign; however: 'When the sea is calm and the waves still break strongly, then you know that the lagoon is *loka*.' The sea, however, keeps some of its secrets and would surprise people despite what acts of *fakasio* might have led them to expect. And with the condition of *loka* tending to last for four to seven days, it would always influence other information gained from examining the sea during this time.

Engaging an Environment in Motion

Habits of 'examining the sea' (*fakasio*) and practices of dealing with the sea mean engaging with an environment that constantly changes between states that are diametrically opposed. This, to my mind, is the greatest significance of the exploration of the marine environment on Kotu. The recognized qualitative nuances of this motion provide clues that may be followed in order to discover enduring qualities in Tongan cultural aesthetics and sociality that may contribute to solving the puzzle of local attitudes and responses to the environmental occurrences that I presented in the introduction. Thus, I shall, in the next two chapters, follow this motion between opposed states or phases into other fields of everyday experience and later on in the book use it as a central context in an ethnographic analysis of ritual aesthetics, cultural values and sociality. Before doing this, however, it is necessary to sum up central qualities of tidal dynamics by exploring marine realities as fields of everyday experience and local knowledge.

The two diametrically opposed states of the lagoon are not referred to as 'high tide' and 'low tide' but rather as 'the sea is attached (to land)' (*tau 'a e tahi*) and 'the sea/lagoon is empty/almost empty' (*maha/mamaha 'a e tahi*). References to the states of 'high' and 'low' and the movement of 'up' and 'down' are otherwise used very extensively in Tonga to elaborate on relationships of relative worth and significance. Thus, all relationships of rank may be described in the terms of *mā'olunga* ('high') and *mā'ulalo* ('low'). Occasions of ceremonial kava drinking, for example, involve procedures which may described in terms of distribution of kava moving 'up' and 'down' in the space between the position of the chief and the position of the 'kava maker/presenter' (*tou'a*) (Bott 1972b; Biersack 1991; Perminow 1993a; 1993b). Kotu Island was described as consisting of two 'places' (*feitu'u*) referred to as *lalo* ('down/low') and *'uta* ('land') on higher ground.

Still, as mentioned, tidal transformations of lagoon states on Kotu were not conceived in terms of vertical differentiation. The sea was seen to move between a state in which it is fully 'attached' (*tau*) to land and one in which it is separated. The Tongan term *tau* has an extraordinary number of meanings; Churchward lists seventeen (Churchward 1959: 461), including the inclusive plural pronoun 'we' ('all of us'); 'reach'; 'anchored'; 'fight' (locked in combat); 'hang'; 'to angle' (for fish); 'male animal mounting a female animal'; 'wring out'; 'leaves covering food in the earth oven'; and 'to be full' (of the tide). All these meanings signify a temporary and forceful joining together, a uniting or compressing of that which is otherwise apart. People, animals or objects become temporarily related by one strong line of attachment or as elements meld together to constitute a single whole. Thus, it is appropriate to describe the tidal motion of 'flood tide' (*hu'a mai ke tau*) creating a state of 'high tide' (*tau 'a e tahi*) as one that causes the multiple features of the lagoon seascape to meld together with the sea (*tahi*) as it becomes temporarily 'joined' to or 'united with' (*tau*) land ('*uta*).

A similar semantic exploration of the term for the tidal motion of 'ebb tide' (*mahu'i ke mamaha 'a e tahi*) reveals movement from a state of attachment, oneness and containment to a state of separation and multiple differentiation. The term *mahu'i* is thus interpreted by Churchward (ibid.: 318) to denote: 'to become wrenched off/detached by force'; 'to be weaned away'; 'to become separated by some influence'. These interpretations refer to the severance of a strong line of attachment or the forceful separation of that which has been joined together as one whole. This makes it appropriate to describe 'ebb tide' as a breaking apart of the completeness of the high tide seascape as the sea disengages from land and recedes outside the lagoon (*ki tu'a namo*) leaving a seascape of importance and multiple differentiation 'inside the lagoon' (*lotonamo*).

The general significance of conceptualizations in terms of high and low states and upward and downward motion may hardly be overemphasized in Tonga. Interestingly, then, it does not make very good sense to perceive the tides of Tonga in these terms. In a sense, the diametrically opposed states of unitedness and separateness and the dynamics that relate them are more fundamental in the sense that they involve the difference between an undifferentiated state and a state, making any differentiation, including that of high and low, possible. Seen in this perspective, the conceptualization of tidal dynamics also resonates with Tongan myths of the process whereby the world first came into being. Indeed, this resonance makes tidal dynamics look like an everyday version of the process of original diversification described in Tongan cosmogony. In the beginning, according to the Wesleyan missionary Collocott and the Tongan historian Māhina: ' … the sea's surface was diversified only by masses of floating weed (*limu*) and mud (*kele*), which at last came together … in Bulotu' (Collocott 1919: 234). From this union resulted the rock of *Touia 'o Futuna*, which later multiplied by giving birth to four pairs of brothers and sisters (Māhina 1990: 34), who became the ancestors of the Tongan Pantheon.

Kotu people were not very familiar with myths of pre-Christian cosmogony at the end of the twentieth century. It is quite intriguing, however, that the main themes of a cosmogony long gone should resonate so strongly with the mode of conceptualizing vital states, phases and processes characterizing the marine field of contemporary everyday activities. Although no longer used to answer questions of origin, central themes of cosmogony appeared to continue colouring understandings of the dynamics of the relationship between sea and land in the *Namolahi* Lagoon surrounding Kotu Island in the final decades of the twentieth century. This marine world still appeared to be caught up between 'united' and 'separated' states of being and 'uniting' and 'separating' phases of becoming. The indication of this kind of continuity in marine spaces offers an opportunity to discover fundamental shared understandings about the world and its workings that are highly relevant for the puzzle at hand. In the next two chapters, then, I shall look for similar kinds of continuity with regard to the phenomena and dynamics of the surrounding world and their significance in other fields of everyday experience.

Notes

1. This paper 'synthesises very briefly the main data' (Bataille-Benguigui 1988: 186) of an unpublished thesis (Bataille-Benguigui 1986) exploring 'Tongan relationships to the sea environment' (Bataille-Benguigui 1988: 186). As far as I know, the study has not been translated into English, but from the brief synopsis the focus seems to be on the significance of an association between some 'socialized fish species' such as the shark (*'anga*), goatfish (*vete*), octopus (*feke*) and 'milkfish' (*'ava*) standing apart from species of no ritual account. Thus, Bataille-Benguigui argues that rituals and taboos associated with these species serve to 'reinforce the traditional village hierarchy ... reduce social tensions since harmony, or even love in the sense of respect for others, is a necessary factor in fishing success' (Bataille-Benguigui 1988: 195).
2. In a context of resource management, this creates a situation not too different from that referred to as a tragedy of the commons. Even those fishermen of Kotu who held that the increasingly intense exploitation of lagoon fish species and shellfish for sale may be too taxing on the lagoon resources to be sustainable felt that there would be no point in reducing the intensity of exploitation only to have the resources exploited by fishermen from other islands of the district.
3. Clearly the population density would also decrease radically if figures were corrected for Kotu people's prolonged practice of ambilocal adaption 'between the volcano and the big lagoon'.

4. The first collection of island names of this part of Tonga made by Captain Cook's officers in 1777 seem to bear witness to the enduring significance of this coral formation. From Anderson's Journal from Cook's third voyage, it appears that *Foonooʻeia*, right next to the island of *Kotoo* (Beaglehole 1967: 869), was included as a place of sufficient significance to be perceived by the European explorers as one of the islands of the 'Kotu group'. In Anderson's list of Kotu- or Lulunga group islands, this was the only name for which Beaglehole was unable to find a referent. Both Anderson's conventions of transcription and the location next to Kotu make it quite likely that the place to which the Tongan informants of Anderson referred was the sometimes partly exposed coral formation of *Fonuaeʻa*, close to the main passage into *Namolahi* Lagoon.
5. The term *foʻi*, according to Churchward, signifies 'fruit of, egg of', as well as 'single, individual' (Churchward 1959: 196) and is used to describe any piece or unit for which the extent and boundary is clearly defined and easily perceived.
6. Four named kinds of goatfish were perceived to be related to one another as a 'family of fish'. The 'family' was not assigned a separate name, but the perceived relationship was expressed like this: '*oku nau kalasi kehekehe ka faʻahinga pē taha*' ('they are of different classes but of one kind'). This *faʻahinga* was perceived to consist of four 'classes', *vete* referring to Yellowstripe Goatfish, *malili* to Yellowfin Goatfish, *hikumanonu* to Freckled Goatfish and *Tukuleia* referring to about a dozen other kinds of goatfish marked by different kinds of bars, dots and colours. Finally, extraordinarily large specimens of this *faʻahinga* were called *Kalofiama*.
7. Bataille-Benguigui identifies the *vete* with the Yellowfin Goatfish (*Mulloidichthys vanicolensis*). Kotu people, however, referred to the Yellowfin Goatfish by the term *Malili* and used the term *vete* to refer to the Yellowstripe Goatfish (*Mulloidichthys flavolineatus*; Randall 1990: 208). Although both kinds of goatfish have a yellow stripe on the body running from the eye to the caudal-fin base and thus look rather similar, the Yellowstripe Goatfish does not have yellow fins. Kotu fishermen have no problem differentiating between them and clearly perceive the Yellowstripe Goatfish as the more significant of the two because they occasionally aggregate in very great numbers.
8. It may be doubtful, however, whether this named point of reference for entering the lagoon will survive another 200 years. In 1993, parts of the outer reefs close to the 'Great Passage' were blown up with dynamite to allow an easier and less tide-bound passage. Also, battery-powered signal lights have been placed on the outer reefs as points of reference for navigation.

2

Daily Motions of Merging and Separation

◆●◆

As we will see in Chapter 4 and 5, cultural continuity in perceptions of the surrounding world and how things happen in it can be helpful in understanding characteristic qualities of Tongan ritual aesthetics and sociality, including central ideas about how to cope with the realities of the world and one another. In the concluding Chapter 6, such ideas in their turn are explored as affecting attitudes and responses to what is happening in the world, including the kinds of events and changes that were taking place on Kotu and *Namolahi* Lagoon in the first decades of the twenty-first century. Thus, I believe that answers to the puzzle of people's attitudes and responses to ongoing changes can only be found by patiently following threads offered in the detailed ethnography of the world and its workings. In this chapter and the next, I follow clues that have been produced by the exploration of marine dynamics in the previous chapter onto dry land and into the sky above to explore conceptualizations and practices related to other everyday activities. Most importantly, the ethnography of these chapters will bring out the significance of knowledge embedded in everyday fields of experience and practice as a source of meaning and cultural continuity. An ethnography of the world and its workings produced through an exploration of shifts and changes related to the diurnal cycle is the subject matter of the current chapter, while shifts and changes related to the lunar cycle is the subject matter of Chapter 3.

In the 1980s and early 1990s, solar panels were not yet in use on Kotu, and apart from one generator run once in a while to cool a catch of fish waiting to be shipped on the weekly ferry to Nukuʻalofa or to illuminate ceremonial occasions, people relied on kerosene lamps. Since kerosene was considered quite expensive, its use in both public and private spaces was limited. This clearly made the practical significance of nightfall and dawn much more important than what has been the case since affordable solar energy became available and began to illuminate all private and public spaces on Kotu in the new millennium. This clearly also made it much easier to produce an ethnography based on knowledge related to shifts and changes of illumination over the diurnal cycle (as well as over the lunar cycle).

Such Is Night and Day

It may seem particularly appropriate to say that night falls fast in the tropics. At least in contrast to Scandinavia, where daylight wanes slowly. Still, night did not appear to be perceived to fall abruptly on Kotu in terms of how people referred to the many nuances between daylight and darkness. Rather, darkness was described as something gradual until finally 'overflowing' and 'engulfing' the world of daylight. I shall argue that like the tidal cycle, the terminology of the diurnal cycle is also modelled as a process of transformation between diametrically opposed states. Like 'high tide' (*tau 'a e tahi*) and 'low tide' (*mamaha 'a e tahi*), the states of *pō* ('night') and *'aho* ('day') were referred to in a way that made them phases in an ongoing process where numerous qualitative nuances relate opposite states to one another. Descriptive terms of the nuances of the diurnal cycle were characterized by being evocative, even quite poetic. In this chapter, I shall explore a body of temporal references related to diurnal dynamics. I believe that a focus on the descriptions of 'qualitative nuances' (Bourdieu 1963) with which people were familiar and routinely read 'upon the surface of things' (ibid.: 59) is helpful for the discovery of enduring aspects of Tongan 'conceptions about the world and its workings' (Gell 1992: 36).

Among the documents collected by the Tongan Tradition Committee, which was founded by Queen Sālote in 1950 'to conduct research into, and to maintain Tongan culture' (Campbell 1992: 168), are some typed manuscripts. In the typescript referred to as the 'Book of Havili Hafoka and Queen Sālote on Tongan Traditions' (Havili Hafoka n.d), the author describes and discusses Tongan ways of 'reckoning the passage of time' (*lau taimi*). The author refers to more than fifty terms describing occurrences and changes in the diurnal cycle. In late twentieth-century Kotu, references to phases of the diurnal cycle covered broad categories. But many people were also familiar with a terminology of finer qualitative distinctions and nuances. Despite the fact that most people of Kotu owned a wristwatch, and that some everyday occurrences involved the occasional practice of consulting it, a number of terms related to qualitative shifts and signal events in the surroundings were still routinely used in everyday life. Through semantic examination, I shall explore such terms as descriptions of moments in a perpetual process of becoming, analogous to the tidal motion explored in the preceding chapter.

Below are a few of the broad categories mentioned above that are most frequently referred to on Kotu:

Hengihengi	'Late night/Early morning' until the appearance on the eastern horizon of the golden red reflection of the sun immediately before sunrise.
Pongipongi	'Morning' from immediately before sunrise until the sun has ascended fairly high in the sky (around 10 AM). According to Havili Hafoka, 'The expression *pongipongi* refers to the "dazzling brightness" (*popongi*) of the sun' (Hafoka n.d).
Hoʻatā	'Noon' from around 10 AM till about 2 or 3 PM. Described as the phase when persons and things 'cast no shadow' (*'ikai 'iloa hoto 'ata*). The sun was perceived to remain at a position of maximum elevation, and 'noon' was also associated with silence.
Efiafi	'Afternoon/Early evening' described as commencing with 'the start of the decline of the sun' (*pale 'a e la'ā*). According to Hafoka, the expression *efiafi* refers to the 'lighting of the cooking fire' (*efi 'o e afi*) (Hafoka n.d).
Tūmaama	'Evening after dark'. The expression refers to the 'lighting of lamps'. It was described to last from some time after sunset, when it has become 'very dark' (*po'uli 'aupito*), until most people have 'put out the light' (*tamate maama*) to go to sleep.
Tu'uapō	'Deep night'. A prolonged phase of stable, changeless darkness and silence.
Longo'aho	'Late night'. A phase of night containing the first vague signs that the stable state of darkness is about to end. The term *longo* has several meanings, the most common of which is 'to be silent'/' to hold one's peace', but in some expressions *longolongo* and also *longo* (weaker) means rather 'to feel as if something were happening or about to happen'. Thus the expression *'oku longolongo'uha* means 'it feels like rain' while *longo'uha* means 'it feels like it may rain'. The expression *longo'aho* seems to refer to a parallel vague feeling that day is about to come.

These broad categories were in their turn subdivided into finer qualitative distinctions clustered around phases of rapid transformation or specific qualitative shifts or diurnal turning points. For instance, finer distinctions operated to constitute a specific sequence within the phase of transformation referred to as *hengihengi*[1] ('Early morning') by distinguishing between:

Ata 'a fa 'ahikehe	'Twilight of the other kind/spirits/devils'
Ata 'a puaka	'Twilight of the pigs'
Kuo mafoa 'a e ata	'Twilight has shattered'
Ata 'a tangata	'Twilight of man'
Kuo ma'a 'a e 'aho	'Day has become clean'

Describing the quality of the 'twilight of the other kind' (*ata 'a fa'ahikehe*) or the 'twilight of the devils/spirits' (*ata 'a tevolo*[2]), Havili Hafoka writes:

> First there is the twilight of the devils, the twilight of the other kind. This twilight was associated with the first springing up of light in the sky, but in a manner making it hard to know with certainty whether it was really the twilight of morning or just some peculiarity of the colour of night. People believed that only beings of 'the other kind' (*fa'ahikehe* i.e. spirits) truly knew the coming of the day, as this was the time when they should return to their holes in the burial ground. They believed that the spirits only roamed about during the night. (Hafoka n.d)

Koloa's description implied some of the same notions: 'This is a time when man is not yet up and about (*Koe e taimi ia teeki 'alu holo ai 'a e tangata*)'.

With regard to the two next phases of dawn, Koloa described 'twilight of the pigs' as 'the time of darkness immediately preceding "twilight has shattered"'. The latter phase he described as a time when 'night has divided off from/separated from the sky (*mavahe mei he langi*) so that the day sheds light.' Hafoka's manuscript sequenced them the other way round. Thus, after the 'twilight has shattered' (*kuo mafoa 'a e ata*), 'twilight of the pigs' was the time when the pigs woke up and started to stir. During this time, 'the Western parts of the sky are still dark' (ibid.).

Both stated, however, that men awake and start to stir in the 'twilight of man' (*ata 'a tangata*), 'when the sky is misty with the light of day' (ibid.), and that the expression 'day has become clean' (*kuo ma'a 'a e 'aho*) describes the final part of 'early morning' (*hengihengi*). Thus, Koloa described the 'clean day' (*ma'a 'a e 'aho*) as 'a time when the day illuminates well'. In Hafoka's manuscript, the same phase is described as 'The time when the "haze of day" (*nenefu 'o e 'aho*) has gone altogether' (ibid.).

The terms describing the transition from a night-time to a daytime state all involved some kind of sequencing of events of dawn. Shifts and changes in several different kinds of surrounding phenomena were sequenced in a parallel manner. Thus, a rich and nuanced vocabulary indeed was linked with every dawning day. Bird calls made up one other such sequence of signal events, progressively transforming the world from a night-time to a daytime state. Koloa and the author of the manuscript agree on the sequence of bird calls:

Tangi 'a Teiko	'Cry of the Teiko bird'
'U'ua 'a e moamu'a	'First cockcrow'
Kio 'a e manumu'a	'First bird call'
'U'ua tu'o ua 'a e moa	'Second cockcrow'
Kiokio tu'u ua 'a e manu	'Second bird call'
'U'ua fakaholo	'Crowing all around'
Kio 'a fuleheu	'Call of the Honeysucker bird'
Kio fakaholo/Kio fe'ilo	'Bird calls all around/Bird calls of mutual recognition'
Manu tala'aho	'Birds announcing day'

Finally, the rise of the stars known as *Fakaholofononga* and *Fetu'u 'aho* ('Daystar') was sequenced by Koloa as it is sequenced in Hafoka's manuscript. Thus, Koloa characterized the star *Fakaholofononga* as 'a star that rises shortly before the "Daystar" (*Fetu'u 'aho*)', with Hafoka writing: 'Immediately after the *Fakaholofononga* has risen, the "Daystar" rises' (ibid.).

A Feeling That Day Is Coming

In the transformation from night to day, there are moments that stand out as turning points or particularly significant qualitative shifts, including:

Longo'aho	'Feeling of day'
Mokomoko 'aho	'Coolness of day'
Ata 'a fa'ahikehe	'Twilight of the other kind'[3]
Lea fakamuimui 'a e manu tataki 'aho	'Last cry of the bird leading the day'
Kauata	'Belonging to twilight'
Fakalau 'a e ata	'Twilight begins to come on'

These expressions all seemed to refer to the same transition. Thus, multiple terms from different fields of experience appeared to cluster around a point when a stable reality of night may be said to be about to 'crack' or 'come apart'; when the world is on the verge of changing from a state of all engulfing darkness to one in which distinctions may just 'barely be grasped' (*ata*: 'to be slightly clear', 'to barely grasp'. All of these descriptions dwell on phenomena obliquely indicating a shift in the quality of the night; they are vague signs that give rise to expectations that night may be about to end but that precede certain or definite knowledge of its ending.

The term *longo'aho* ('late night/early morning'), interpreted as 'a feeling that day may be about to come', indicates the vagueness of the sign of such a shift in a linguistically straightforward manner. The expression *mokomoko 'aho* ('coolness of day') similarly indicates such a shift in terms of a drop in temperature said to sometimes occur late at night to bring news of the coming of day. As previously mentioned, *Ata 'a fa'ahikehe* ('twilight of the other kind') refers to a very fine change in the nuance of the darkness that may, according to Hafoka, either indicate 'the coming of day or be a peculiarity of the colour of night' (ibid.). This indefinable quality may only be interpreted dependably, however, by the spirit beings of 'the other kind' (*fa'ahikehe*) belonging to the night. Hence the description 'twilight of the other kind'.

Lea fakamuimui 'a e manu tataki 'aho ('last cry of the bird leading the day') seems related to a notion that a particular kind of seabird knows of the coming of day from sources still unavailable to man. Hafoka elaborated on this in his manuscript:

> There is a name for the Teiko-bird which is 'bird leading/guiding the day' (*manu tataki 'aho*), because of the manner in which these birds fish in the direction of the sunrise. Being birds that 'catch fish' (*siu*) very far away they are said to be the first to know about the coming of day, and thus they leave off their fishing to return to land. When people heard their cries they said that 'first the Teiko birds return to land' (*mu'a mai 'a e Teiko*), 'day following in their wake' (*muimui mai 'a e 'aho*). The Teiko-birds keep on crying out until immediately before 'the shattering of the twilight' (*mafoa 'a e ata*) ... There is an expression for this time going like this; 'the day has been lead/guided' (*Kuo tataki 'aho*) and that is the 'turning point/end of the night' (*ngata'anga 'o e pō*) when 'the light is on the verge of appearing in the sky' (*meimei 'asi 'a e maama 'i he langi*). (Hafoka n.d)

Similarly, the somewhat vague phenomenon referred to as *kauata* ('belonging to twilight') reflects a shift in the quality of the night, indicating that the turning point between a steady state of night and a phase of incipient day is at hand. Thus, the time of 'leading/guiding the day' (*tataki 'aho*) was said to coincide with that of the *kauata*:

> They believed that 'twilight' (*ata*) was preceded by some phenomena and thus 'examined' (*fakasio*) the phenomena of night in their search for signs indicating the coming of 'twilight' ... The reason it was called *kauata* was the belief that this 'small portion of night' (*ki'i po'uli ko ia*) 'belongs to/is a part of the twilight' (*kau mo e ata*) ... After mid-night, 'day and night are joined together' (*'oku tau 'a e aho mo e pō*), and then the *kauata* is the 'last moments' (*'aho faka'osi*) of darkness on the way to light. The '(phenomena) belonging to twilight' (*kauata*) were not dependable (*pau*) but looking for signs of 'twilight' (*ata*), one may some nights learn about its imminent arrival by the appearance of a 'small rainstorm' (*ha ki'i taufa*) or a cloud (*konga 'ao*) or some 'night-time rain' (*fakapo'uli pē 'uha*). (Ibid.)

Finally, Koloa felt that the term *fakalau 'a e ata* ('twilight begins to appear') pertains to the same point of transition: 'This is the "beginning of the preparation of the light of day to appear at the edge of the sky" (*kamata ia ke hā he tapalangi 'a e maama 'a e 'aho*).'[4]

United Phases, Separating Motions

The mode of referring to the transformation from night to day is characterized by descriptive terms clustering around particular points of transition. Furthermore, the manner of codifying diurnal dynamics strongly recalls the manner of codifying tidal dynamics. In fact, one of the expressions used by Hafoka to describe the steady state of night was a precise parallel of the standard expression used by everyone on Kotu to describe the state of 'high tide' (*'oku tau 'a e tahi*). Thus, Hafoka described the phase of 'deep night' (*tu'uapō*) as *'oku tau 'a e 'aho moe pō* ('day and night are joined together') (ibid.).

I have argued that many of the senses of the term *tau* have in common a forceful joining, merging or union of that which is otherwise apart. I interpreted the expression *tau 'a e tahi* ('high tide') as referring to the result of 'flood tide' (*hu'a mai ke tau*). Thus, flood tide may be described as a process that melds together the differentiated features of the lagoon seascape to establish a state in which 'sea and land are joined together' (*'oku tau 'a e tahi mo e 'uta*). This way of describing 'high tide' is clearly analogous to the description of 'deep night' (*tu'uapō*) as one in which 'day and night are joined together' (*'oku tau 'a e 'aho mo e pō*).

Exploring the codification of tidal dynamics, I also argued that the process of 'ebb tide' (*mahu'i ke mamaha*) was referred to in terms of detachment or separation. The term *mahu'i* refers to the severance of a strong line of attachment or the forceful separation of that which has been integrated as one whole. Ebb tide can be described as a coming apart of the unity of sea and land that brings into being a seascape of multiple differentiation within the lagoon. Again, a comparison of modes of referring to tidal and diurnal dynamics reveals an intriguing analogy. The precise turning point of the tide could not be established with certainty by people on Kotu until the appearance of the line of debris on the beach; the *taka pau 'uluaki* ('first reliable sign'). Likewise, the exploration of the terminology of the transformation from night to day indicated that the diurnal turning point could not be established with certainty until some 'dependable thing' (*me'a pau*) made it quite obvious that the point of transition had passed. As we have seen, quite a number of descriptions were clustered around the point of transition when it may be established *with certainty* that the union of night and day was at end from *Kuo mafoa 'a e ata* ('The twilight has shattered') to *Kio 'a fuleheu* ('The call of the Honeysucker bird').

Koloa stated, similarly to Hafoka in his manuscript, that the term 'twilight has shattered' (*kuo mafoa 'a e ata*) follows 'unreliable' (*ta'epau*) signs evoking a 'feeling that day is coming' (*longo'aho*). Hafoka elaborates on the expression 'twilight has shattered' (*kuo mafoa 'a e ata*) in terms of sequence: '"The twilight of the other kind" (*ata 'a fa'ahikehe*) precedes the time referred to as "twilight has shattered" (*kuo mafoa 'a e ata*)' (ibid.). Koloa focuses on this transition in terms of separation: 'This is the time when "darkness has been separated/divided off from the sky" (*kuo mavahe ai 'a e po'uli mei he langi*) and the "day sheds light" (*maama 'a e 'aho*).'

Koloa's description in terms of 'separation' (*mavahe*), as well as the use of the term *mafoa* ('to shatter', like a broken bottle, or 'divided', like a split coconut), makes clear that the ebb tide 'separation/detachment' (*mahu'i*) and the transformation to a daytime state are codified in the same manner. The prefix *ma-* implies (among other things) 'a state or condition that has come about … spontaneously … or by some unknown agency' (Churchward 1953: 259).

'Twilight of man' (*ata 'a tangata*) may be described both in terms of human activity and the quality of illumination. Koloa described it as the 'time when man awakes', while in Hafoka's manuscript it was described as the 'time when the sky is misty with the light of day' (*kakapu 'a e langi 'i he maama 'o e 'aho*). 'Twilight of man' was described to coincide with the last moments of 'dawn' (*hengihengi*), referred to as 'day has become clean' (*kuo ma'a 'a e 'aho*). Thus, this phase of final separation was by Koloa described as 'a time when "day lights well"' (*maama lelei 'a e 'aho*) and in the manuscript as a time 'when "the haze of day has gone altogether"' (*'osi 'aupito 'a e nenefu 'o e 'aho*).

The expression 'day has become clean' (*ma'a 'a e 'aho*), descriptions of the disappearance of 'thick mist' (*kakapu*) and the ending of a 'blurred/hazy' (*nenefu*) state of appearances describe the final phase of transformation from night to day as one completing a process of separation. Indeed, the use of the term *ma'a*, denoting 'clean, free from dirt or impurity' (Churchward 1959: 348), makes the blurring fog appear as a remnant of night-time briefly lingering in a world of increasingly clear distinctions. Finally, the signal event of the 'twittering of the Honeysucker' (*kio 'a fuleheu*) was described as coinciding with 'twilight of man' (*ata 'a tangata*), when 'night-time has come to an end' (*'osi ia 'a e taimi po'uli*) and when people should 'rise from their beds' (*'ā mei honau mohenga*).

Motions of Merging

The period of 'morning' (*pongipongi*) may be subdivided into six phases coordinated to the positional relationship between the sun and the 'land' (*fonua*). The relatively prolonged phase of 'midday' (*hoʻatā*) may similarly be subdivided into three phases. Also, there are several terms clustered around a particular point of transition between 'midday' (*hoʻatā*) and 'afternoon' (*efiafi*), when it may first be established with certainty that the sun has started to move west, or decline, or lose some of its potency. All in all, however, qualitative nuances were far fewer during prolonged and silent periods of the day (from around 10 AM until about 3 PM, and from around 10–11 PM until about 3–4 AM). The vocabulary describing environmental conditions and events became much richer, however, with reference to the transition from day to night. A short period sometime after sunset stood out both in terms of the sequencing of several rapidly passing phases and in terms of several terms clustering around a particular point of transition.

I have emphasized that the transformation from night to day (as well as from 'high tide' to 'low tide') is codified as a motion of detachment or separation. If such an interpretation is sensible, it can be no surprise that the inverse transformation from day to night is codified in terms of the merging of that which has been separate. The qualitative descriptions made by Koloa and by Hafoka's manuscript are illuminating. Five terms refer to dusk, from some time after 'sunset' (*tō ʻa e laʻā/tapalika*) until night has become an undeniable, stable reality. Descriptions of the qualities of dusk all describe 'light' (*maama*) and 'darkness' (*fakapoʻuli*) as intermingling properties creating different degrees of mixedness and blurredness. In Hafoka's manuscript, the phase known as 'evening of dim light' (*ataata efiafi poʻuli*) was described:

> This is the time when 'the colours of the night appear in the lingering light of the evening' (*ʻasi mai ʻa e lanu ʻo e poʻuli ʻi he kei maama ʻo e efiafi*). When the sun sets the light is still strong, and then comes the dim evening when 'this strength has perished' (*mole ʻa e malohi ko ia*) but the light is not altogether spent. (Hafoka n.d)

Likewise, the time referred to as 'the blackness of the dirt/soil/ground' (*ʻuʻuli kelekele*) was described as ' ... the time when "the night is known in the ground while the light still appears in the free/open space" (*ʻoku mahino ʻa e poʻuli ʻi he kelekele ai, kae kei ʻasi ʻa e maama ʻi he ʻatā*)'(ibid.).

Koloa elaborated on this expression in slightly different terms, but this too involved the merging of elements that had been apart during the day: 'This is the time when "the sun falls into the soil/ground" (*tō kelekele ai ʻa e laʻā*).' One should note that this expression refers to qualities of illumination far past sunset. It does not, then, refer to the sun descending or falling below the horizon, which is referred to as *taitai tō 'a e la'ā* (probably 'gradually descending towards the sea') and *tō 'a e la'ā* ('the sun sets'). What may 'fall into the ground', then, would not seem to be the sun itself but the light lingering on after sunset. Whether described in terms of 'light falling into the ground' or 'darkness growing out of the ground', the notion of merging appears to remain central to the conceptualization of the process of transformation from day to night.

Connotations of the term *'u'uli kelekele* ('blackness of the ground') suggest that it mirrors the transition between 'early morning' (*hengihengi*) and 'bright morning' (*pongipongi*). I described the final phase of separation (morning) as a transition between a state in which a 'thick mist, fog/haze' (*kakapu/nenefu*) lingers on and where remnants of night-time have been swept away to leave a 'clean day', 'free from dirt/impurity' (*kuo ma'a 'a e 'aho*). The terms *'u'uli* and *kelekele* connote a similar mixed state as day turns into night. As mentioned, the term *'uli* means primarily 'dirt' and 'dirtiness'. In the form of complete reduplication, *'uli'uli* means 'black'. According to Churchward, such reduplication indicates intensification (Churchward 1953: 264; Naylor 1986). In the form *'u'uli*, the partial reduplication probably operates to moderate *'uli* in the same way as *māmāfana* ('lukewarm') moderates the meaning of *māfana* ('warm'). The verbal form *'uli'i* means 'to make dirty' and also 'to work with the soil'. The term *kelekele* means 'land, soil, earth, ground' but also 'dirt' as 'matter out of place' (James, see Douglas 1966: 165), as, for instance, on the hands at a meal, on the feet at a kava party or in the water that you want to drink. It is possible, then, to interpret the expression *'u'uli kelekele* as referring to an incipient 'soiling' of the daylight world by properties of the ground below starting to blend with the properties of the sky above to constitute a phase that is both day and night and neither of them at the same time. This phase, then, has a truly liminal quality. For Mary Douglas, the 'blackness of the ground' as a liminal phase in the process of merging may be described as 'Dirt ... created by the differentiating activity of mind' (Douglas 1966: 162). In her terms, this would be a different kind of 'blackness/darkness' than that of true night: 'In ... [the] final stage of total disintegration, dirt is utterly undifferentiated' (ibid.: 163).

Another term of reference in use on Kotu related the phase of merging, or blurring, directly to human perception. It was known as 'the time of mutual recognition', or *fē'ilo'ilongaki*. Koloa described it as '... a time when people can still recognize each other, so that if two men meet they are each able to recognize one another in the "deep shade of the night" (*he mamalu 'a e po'uli*)'. The 'time of mutual recognition' was the temporal site of a great number of Kotu people's encounters with 'devils' (*tevolo*) or those of 'the other kind' (fa'ahikehe); the kind of beings that were believed to emerge from the ground to which they were said to return in the 'twilight of the other kind' (ata 'a fa'ahikehe) in the 'early morning' (hengihengi). From the point of view of Kotu people, a part of the liminality and magic of dusk may have been the mingled presence of people still going about their business and potentially 'naughty' spirits (pau'u) of the night. Routines of exchanging greetings on Kotu indicated this. As 'mutual recognition' (fē'ilo'ilongaki) becomes increasingly more difficult, routines of exchanging greetings tend to turn into a practice of identifying that which is rapidly blurring. The identity of any shape moving through the village at dusk is thus routinely ascertained by people tentatively calling out the name of the person they resembled (e.g *Sione ē?*, 'John isn't'?) and the person calling out in return. This made the routines of greeting someone quite different at dusk than during the day. In the daytime, the conventional way of greeting someone was consistently *'alu ki fē?* (lit. 'Where are you going?'). That the question of identity should take precedence over the question of direction of movement as it becomes harder to decide who people are is not surprising. Given the fuzzy border between the realm of people and the realm of 'the other kind' (fa'ahikehe) in the liminal phase of late evening, the effort to identify someone makes sense, not only in terms of distinguishing one person from another but also in terms of distinguishing people from 'beings of the other kind'.

Finally, the conceptualization of the transition from day to night implies an expansion of darkness, an overpowering of daylight by the growing strength of night. Koloa described the phase of *mamalu efiafi* ('evening of deep shades') as '… the time when "darkness comes to cover the surface of the land" (*'oku 'ūfia ai 'e he po'uli 'a e funga fonua*).' In the manuscript, the term *efiafi fakapo'uli* is said to refer to '… the time when "darkness has become stronger than the light of day" (*mālohi ange 'a e po'uli he maama 'o e 'aho*)' and represents 'the "ultimate stage of the reckoning of day" (*ngata'anga ia 'o e lau 'aho*)' (ibid.).

Images of Constitutive Motions

This brings us full circuit from one state of stable darkness to another. As a whole, the vocabulary of the diurnal cycle described ongoing dynamics that I have chosen to refer to as a motion of merging and separation. Intriguingly, such a process or motion is quite clearly paralleled in characteristic narratives of pre-Christian Polynesian cosmology. Before elaborating further on this parallel, however, I shall briefly re-present the image of the diurnal motion, emphasizing what appears to be the most significant features of the way in which it was conceptualized.

Taking as a point of departure a 'united state' of stable night (*tau 'a e 'aho mo e pō*), the sky and the ground are seamlessly joined together to constitute one dark whole. As such, it is wholly undifferentiated. An appropriate graphic image of such an undifferentiated whole would be the shape of a seamless sphere. In the 'Deep night' (*Tuʻuapō*) nothing much happens; then numerous nuances of the night in the form of 'unreliable' (*taʻepau*) signs give rise to a 'vague feeling' (*longoʻaho*) that some shift is about to occur. Keeping within the image of the sphere, it is 'cracking' or 'shattering' (*māfoa*), so to speak. Coming apart, the crack grows into a widening gap, and elements of the two parts of the sphere cling to one another in decreasing degrees of intermingling, captured by terms of qualitative nuances read upon the surface of the components of the surrounding world. When man rises at the 'Twilight of Man' (*Ata 'a tangata*), the two halves of the sphere have come apart (*mavahe ua*), although a few remnants of the night-time linger in the form of 'haze/fog' (*nenefu/kakapu*) in the growing gap before disappearing altogether. The gap between the half below and the half above keeps on growing steadily in the 'dazzling morning' (*pongipongi*) as the sun rapidly moves through stages to arrive at its station of maximum elevation (*tuʻu tonu 'a e laʻā*), brilliantly illuminating the space between the half below and the half above. Then, for a while, nothing much happens (*hoʻatā*) until the 'small step of the sun' (*maleʻei 'a e laʻā*) indicates that the daylight world has reached a turning point and the gap starts to decrease again. As the gap shrinks, the world passes through phases of increasing degrees of intermingling. Thus, fine qualitative nuances describe how properties of the half sphere below emerge to mingle with the properties of the half sphere above, challenging the human capacity to discriminate in the shrinking gap in between. Finally, the gap narrows down to a thin line, which disappears as the two halves merge to reconstitute the all-encompassing shape of a seamless sphere. Expressed graphically, such a diurnal motion might look like Figure 2.1.

The conceptualization of the tidal motion explored in the previous chapter may be graphically expressed in an identical model (Figure 2.2).

Steady State of Cosmic Order

Intriguingly, a very similar dynamic may seem intrinsic to many Tongan and other Polynesian mythological narratives. First of all, it appears to resonate strongly with pre-Christian myths of creation. In an attempt to reconstruct the 'spiritual geography of the shaman's world in Western Polynesia' (Gunson 1990: 15), Gunson describes Tongan cosmological beliefs in the following manner:

Daily Motions 47

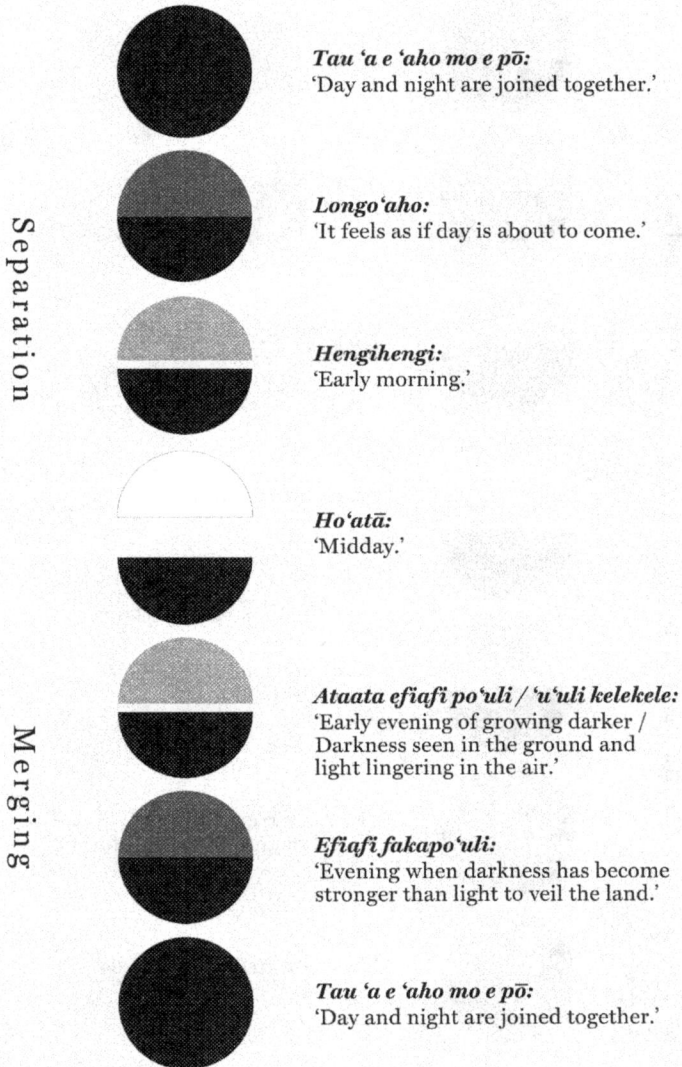

Figure 2.1. Figure of diurnal dynamics. The illustration shows the main phases of day and night in Tonga. © Arne Aleksej Perminow and Kristine Lie Øverland.

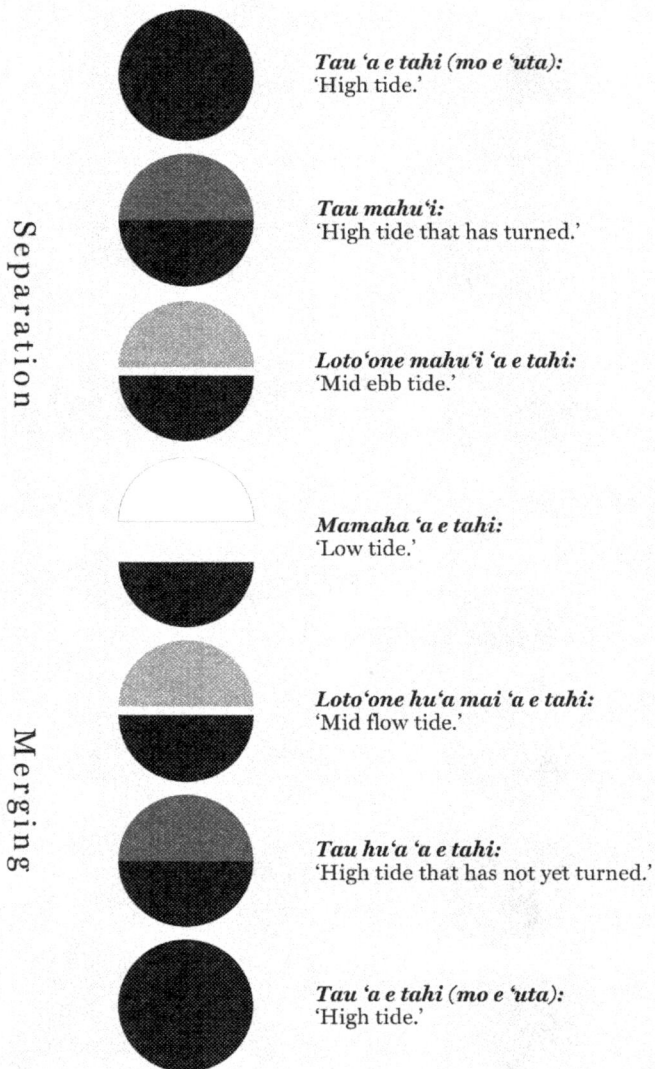

Figure 2.2. Figure of tidal dynamics. The illustration shows the main phases of ebb tide and flow tide in *Namolahi* Lagoon. © Arne Aleksej Perminow and Kristine Lie Øverland.

By way of illustration take a coconut and cleave it in two. Imagine the ocean floating in the lower half. The rock of creation rises in the centre. The world in the shape of one's particular islands rises to one side. On the other, out of sight because it is far away, is Pulotu, a mirror image of the world … Under the Ocean is the Underworld, known in Tonga as Lolofonua, the realm of Maui. At the base of the coconut shell is a cavern of volcanic fire … Under the top half of the coconut are seven layers of heaven which appear to rest on the tops of gigantic trees. The tree on the home island is a huge toa tree used by one of the gods or 'otua to come to earth. The tree on Pulotu is known as either 'Akaulea or Pukolea … At its roots is a lake or spring called Vaiola … The seven heavens constitute the Sky ruled by the gods or ancestors known as Tangaloa. The Underworld constitutes the realm of the gods or ancestors known as Maui. The Ocean is the realm of the 'otua Hea Moana 'Uli'Uli … Pulotu constitutes the realm of Hikule'o represented by a kind of lizard whose tail is tied by a sennit cord secured in the Sky above and the Underworld below. (ibid.: 16)

Graphically, Gunson has described these cosmological beliefs in Figure 2.3.

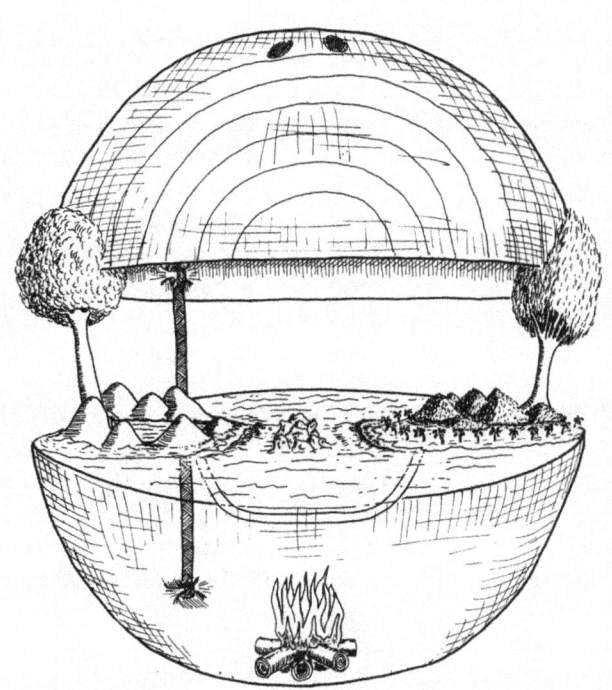

Figure 2.3. Gunson's figure of Polynesian cosmology. Figure taken from Herda, Terrell and Gunson (eds), *Tongan Culture and History* (Target Oceania, 1990), courtesy of Neil Gunson.

Comparing Figure 2.3 with the figures used to illustrate the referential wholes of the diurnal and tidal motions, it clearly represents the middle figure in the series; the one depicting a prolonged steady state of optimally differentiated 'day' (*'aho*) and 'low tide' (*mamaha 'a e tahi*). What seems to be elaborated, then, is a steady state of separateness rather than the dynamics of separation and merging. To my mind, the significance of exploring the referential wholes of tidal and diurnal dynamics is that they invite us to look beyond the steady state of differentiated order. This is a point of fundamental importance because later on it will enable us to fathom local attitudes and responses to environmental change, which this book aspires to do.

Separation, differentiation and orderliness are themes that have received much attention from Polynesianists as well as from Polynesians themselves. The discovery of a dynamic of separation and merging in the referential wholes of transformations that keep recurring in the world that people experience and work with on a daily basis implies a regenerative dynamic in which separation and orderliness is but a passing phase. The discovery of how the fundamental rhythms of the surrounds with which people engage appeared to be caught up in a motion between separation and orderliness, on the one hand, and unitedness and indistinguishability on the other is a very important finding for the ethnographic analysis to follow. It will be important for the ethnographic analysis of ceremonial aesthetics and sociality undertaken in later chapters in this book, which in its turn will constitute an important ethnographic basis for understanding local perspectives on why things happen and what to do about it and thus for understanding people's somewhat puzzling responses to ongoing environmental changes. Furthermore, the discovery of a strong resonance between Polynesian pre-Christian cosmological dynamics and perceptions of fundamental dynamics in the environment of everyday experience is quite important in identifying a source of cultural continuity in a society where Christianity has become a cultural cornerstone. Before undertaking the ethnographic analysis of ceremonial aesthetics and sociality, then, it is necessary to delve somewhat deeper into this resonance between what went on in Pre-Christian cosmology and myths and in the world which still surrounded people in the last decades of the twentieth century. As we saw in the introduction, Tongan Christianity appears to have played a significant role in informing people's attitudes and responses to environmental events and therefore it is quite important to understand what kind of Christianity this was.

We can also see continuity between myths of the past and practices of the present in the lunar cycle. Thus, I shall first sum up the exploration of the conceptualization of diurnal dynamics on Kotu and then in the next chapter go on to explore the conceptualization of lunar dynamics, which constantly transform the surroundings by producing varying conditions of illumination, varying conditions for growth and varying conditions for socializing.

Let There Be Light

The phases that transform night to day and day to night were paid intense attention in the codification of diurnal dynamics. In quantitative terms, there was a certain difference between expressions describing the nuances of the night to day transition and those describing the transition from day to night. Almost half the collected terms described qualitative nuances of daybreak, while about a third described those of nightfall. In qualitative terms, there was also a difference. A sense of inevitability and liminality comes through more strongly in the nuances describing the 'late evening' (*ataata efiafi po'uli*). The qualitative nuances of 'early morning' (*hengihengi*), on the other hand, evoke a very strong sense of uncertainty and impatience. This may seem consistent with what Gell refers to as a Polynesian preoccupation with elaborating separation and differentiation (Gell 1995), and what I would refer to as a continuous struggle to separate and differentiate that which inevitably and productively merges. However, the sense of impatience and uncertainty may also reflect the significance of these qualitative nuances for practical purposes of timing specific activities. In a discussion about the practical utility of wristwatches for people on Kotu, Koloa claimed that a watch was very handy if you wanted to go octopus fishing (*maka feke*):

> If you want to go octopus fishing in your canoe at Putuputua [about 3 km north-east of Kotu Island] and wake up during the night, it is hard to know when you must leave in order to arrive at Putuputua before sunrise. The fishing should start around sunrise, but when you look at the dark sky it is very hard to find a dependable thing telling you when you must get going. If you have no watch you very often end up arriving at Putuputua too late or much too early and get cold sitting in your canoe and fed up with waiting for the sunrise.

Additionally, however, the sense of impatience and uncertainty appears also to be linked to a general cultural emphasis that life is fragile and the future uncertain. Thus, the coming of a new day should not be taken for granted but is something to be looked upon eagerly and ascertained by the occurrence of some dependable signs to be received with joy and gratitude. Numerous conventions of greeting in Tonga seem to emphasize that individual survival through the night should not be taken for granted. What must be translated as 'good morning' means literally 'congratulations on things being well until this morning' (*malo e lelei ki he pongipongini*) or 'congratulations on having reached all the way to this day' (*Malo e tau mai ki he 'ahoni*) or *Malo e tau lava* ('Congratulations that we have all made it'). In contexts of more extraordinary circumstances or some crisis, the feat of surviving the night to see another day may be expressed by saying: 'We may all of us be thankful for having lived through the night' (*Malo pe 'etau 'ahoia*[5]). It may be argued that these are mere conventions of greeting and, as such, no more likely to evoke specific ideas about the human condition than the conventional greeting of 'good morning' among English speakers. I would argue, however, that the semantic implication that surviving the time of darkness to reach another day is an achievement is not merely a conventional greeting. Thus, it was paralleled by a general attitude to human existence as inherently fragile and the future as inherently unpredictable. People were very much aware that life comes with no guarantee of duration and were unwilling to speak about individual futures without expressing this awareness. For instance, all Kotu people with whom I discussed the grief and bereavement characterizing farewells among close kin as well as the intense joy characterizing reunions emphasized the bitter possibility that a farewell may very well be the last farewell, while the happy (*fiefia*) occasion of welcome (*tali*) called for a celebration that life had been granted to make a reunion possible. The intensity of expressions of bereavement that characterized the farewells among close kin on Kotu was rivalled only by the stylized expressions of *tangi* ('crying') and total bereavement as close relatives bid the deceased their final farewells at certain points during funerary ceremonies (See also Kaeppler 1993: 476): 'Oiaue, 'Oiaue. 'Alu a 'alu a, or 'Alas! Alas! Farewell, farewell.'[6] It is fair to say, then, that there existed a quite general emphasis on the inherent fragility of life and a marked consciousness of the inherent unpredictability of the future. Intriguingly, this emphasis is paralleled in the very mode in which diurnal transformations were codified. On the grounds of widely shared understandings of the world and its workings, then, an awareness of an inherent unpredictability of the future and the fragility of life figured prominently. In order to appreciate responses and attitudes to when things appear to go awry, I shall over the next chapters show how coping with such realities and achieving a good life, good relations and a good community on enduring grounds was not seen as something that may be taken for granted but as a challenge demanding knowledge, effort and discipline for it to be achieved.

Notes

1. Often the term *Uhu* was used when referring not to the phase of 'early dawn' itself but to some action undertaken in this phase. Thus, it was perhaps more common to speak about the timing of events in this phase by using the expressions *'auhu*

('next early dawn') and *'aneuhu* ('last early dawn') than by using the expressions *'ahengihengi* and *'anehengihengi*.

2. The term *tevolo* is the Tongan word for 'devil'. *Kautevolo* is used together with *fa'ahikehe* ('the other side/half') to refer to ghosts or spirits of the dead that are associated with the *fonua* ('land/homeland'), in general, and with the *vao* ('uncultivated bush') and *fa'itoka* ('cemetery') in particular. These beings are basically supposed to keep to their *luo fonua* ('pit, earth grave') or *fonualoto* ('vault, chiefly stone grave') during the day, but they may sometimes roam about in the bush. During the night, however, their movements are less restricted, and they may be encountered even 'within the village' (*lotokolo*).
3. Although the English term *twilight* is strongly associated with the evening, I use it also to refer to 'the light between' or the 'twilight of dawn' '(see Webster's dictionary, 1979).
4. In Churchward's dictionary, the term *'oku fakalau mai ke 'aho* is translated as 'Daylight is just beginning to appear' (Churchward 1959: 59).
5. The term *'ahoia* is also used to describe the quality of nights during which the moon stays in the sky until after sunrise. This occurs a little beyond full moon, when the sun and moon alternate to provide illumination throughout the diurnal cycle.
6. *'Oiaue* is an interjection expressing grief, pity, regret and annoyance, while *'alu a* is the conventional expression for 'goodbye'. From the point of view of the one who stays, it means literally 'you go, leave'; for the one who leaves, 'goodbye' is expressed as *nofo a*, meaning literally 'you stay'.

3

Lunar Motions of Growth and Regeneration

◆●◆

So far, then, this ethnographic exploration has revealed that a dynamic of a never-ending motion of separation and merging characterizes people's conceptualization of tidal and diurnal transformations. This kind of knowing, embedded in routines of experiencing and referring to environmental qualities and events, is important in revealing a layer of considerable cultural continuity with regard to fundamental perspectives on the world and its workings. Such perspectives in their turn are important for deciding how to cope with the world, what is desirable, beautiful and valuable (see Chapter 4), how to interact appropriately with one another (see Chapter 5) and how to respond when things go wrong (see Chapter 6).

In this chapter, I turn to perceptions of qualitative nuances related to a kind of environmental dynamic understood to directly affect the conditions for achieving well-being – that is, the cycle of lunation, understood to affect profoundly conditions of growth and regeneration. Before moving on, then, to an analysis in the next two chapters of what people appreciated and deemed appropriate in their dealings with one another, I shall use an exploration of the relationship between lunation and cultivation as a stepping-stone. Thus, I turn to an exploration of lunar dynamics, conceived in terms that imply they bring about the growth and regeneration of all 'living kinds' (Bloch 1993) by a motion of mutual attraction and repulsion between entities that both compete with and complement one another.

Such Is the Moon

'Why are the dead on Kotu buried with their heads towards the West?', I asked. 'The life of men is like the sun,' said Kafa'ongo, a man from Tongatapu who visited Kotu in 1992. Kafaʻongo worked in one of the Ministries in Nukuʻalofa. He held several talking-chief titles and enjoyed a reputation of being knowledgeable in matters of the 'Tongan way' (*anga fakatonga*):

> The early morning corresponds with childhood, when people are 'still small' (*kei siʻi*). At noon, man is still 'good looking' (*kei talavou*), while in the evening he becomes 'old' (*motuʻa*) and 'weak' (*vaivai*). The 'place of the sunset' (*tōʻanga laʻā*) and the 'place where man sets' (*tōʻanga tangata*) are the same. The 'manner of the body of the dead' (*anga ʻa e sino ʻo e mate*) should be the same as the 'manner of the sun' (*anga ʻa e laʻā*).

When I discussed the same topic with a Kotu woman in her late sixties, she said: 'It is said that on the Last Day Jesus shall come from the "place of the sunrise" (*hopoʻanga laʻā*). The dead are buried on their backs with their heads towards the 'place of the sunset' so that they may rise to face Jesus when they wake on the Last Day.' ʻAmanaki Havea, the president of the Free Wesleyan Church of Tonga, offered the following:

> In the 'times of darkness' (*taimi fakapoʻuli*) people were not buried in an orderly manner in cemeteries as they are today but 'disorderly all over the place'[1] (*noaʻia pē*). But I have heard that people used to be buried on their backs with their heads towards the east, so that they could rise to face the place where the sun sets and find their way to Pulotu, which was believed to be in the west. Because Christ is said to come from the opposite direction on the Final Day, people were turned around to face him, instead.

Although versions varied the reasons had in common that bodily burial posture should correspond with phenomena profoundly affecting people's existence. Finally, in a discussion of Kafaʻongo's analogy between the motion of the sun across the sky and the process of ageing, Koloa provided his own interpretation:

> It is a nice 'comparison' (*fakatatau*). But this is my thinking; the fisherman, if he looks to the sun to learn something, he will get nothing. If he would learn something about his fishing he must look to the moon. It is the same with the farmer; he gets nothing from the sun but everything from the moon. If you want to know about weeding or clearing new land, planting and harvesting, these are all matters that should be done 'according to the moon' (*fakamāhina*). It is the same with the 'sickness of women' (*mahaki fakafefine/fakamāhina*, i.e. menstruation), matters of pregnancy and birth; much can be gained from the moon.

I asked Koloa what may be learnt about the sickness of women and birth from the moon. He answered:

These are things that I have only heard and do not grasp very well. You must ask the women about these things. The thing is, many useful things may be known from looking to the moon, but the sun is almost the same from day-to-day and gives us nothing. This is perhaps why, according to my way of thinking, it is fitting for the posture of the body in the grave to be towards the place where the 'new moon' (*māhina foʻou*) 'rises' (*hopo*) in the West after having been 'dead' (*mate ʻa e māhina*). I have heard that people believed that Pulotu was in the West. If so, then maybe this would help people to come to life in Pulotu after death, just like after the 'old moon' (*māhina motuʻa*) has died 'the new moon' (*māhina foʻou*) comes to life in the West.

I was somewhat confused by all this. Particularly, I was puzzled by his claim that the new moon rises in the west, so I was not able to be of much help when Koloa asked me how this can be, but intrigued I decided to investigate further the extent to which this perception of lunar dynamics was shared and what other notions it could be related to.

Growth and the Motions of the Moon

The changing states of the moon create conditions that strongly influenced productive activities and other routines of everyday living on Kotu. Particularly, the states of the moon were perceived to influence garden fertility and growth. The correlations between the state of the moon and local knowledge about conditions of natural vitality may be approached in two somewhat different manners. Firstly, lunar dynamics may be explored as an autonomous flow of sequenced phenomena. Just as tidal and diurnal dynamics could be explored by examining the referential wholes that their descriptive terminology constitutes, the conceptualization of lunar dynamics may be explored in a similar manner – that is, as sequenced, natural phenomena related to one another by a dialectical process between extreme states; those of 'dead moon' (*mate ʻa e māhina*) and 'full moon' (*māhina katoa*). Secondly, the emphasis may be put on how lunar dynamics modify other sequences of natural phenomena. The changing states of the moon create conditions of illumination that modify the conditions produced by the diurnal oscillation between night and day. Nights are not equally dark but vary between extremes of no lunar illumination at all, around 'dead moon' (*mate ʻa e māhina*), and a full moon alternating with the sun to provide illumination throughout the diurnal cycle, conditions of illumination that were referred to as *fēʻahoʻaki* ('reciprocal/mutual day').

On Kotu, variations in lunar conditions influenced levels of night-time activity and night-time use of space. Around full moon, groups of laughing children played far into the night. Outdoor kava parties with no other illumination than that of the full moon were common. Pairs or groups of unmarried women could be encountered strolling along the beach, and small groups of young men would quite often decide to sleep on the beach. During the other phases of the moon, the night-time spaces temporarily made larger by the full moon would again shrink, leaving the arena to men engaged in night-time activities of fishing and others willing to risk close encounters with persons up to no good or spirit beings of 'the other kind' (*fa'ahikehe*).

In another conversation, Koloa went on to describe lunar changes and to elaborate on the significance of the qualitative nuances of the moon for different sorts of activities.

> There is a night when the rise of the 'old moon sickle' (*lausi'i motu'a*) in the east coincides with the time of dawn known as 'twilight has shattered' (*kuo mafoa 'a e ata*). This time of the 'weak moon' (*māhina vai*), in the reckoning of the nights of the moon (*lau pō*), is called *fungaata* ('the upper part of twilight') and also *māhina lekeleka* ('tiny moon'). For a short time, the weak moon may be seen, but when the sun rises the moon disappears in the dazzling light of morning. The next morning, the narrow, old moon sickle sometimes 'appears weakly' ('*asi vaivai*) very close to the sunrise. Then it disappears altogether in the growing light of the sun.[2] About the following night it is said, 'the moon is dead' (*mate 'a e māhina*). That is the last night of the moon. The 'new moon' starts from this first night, which is named *faka'uluaki* ('the first one') and also *fua tu'u 'a e māhina* ('the moon prepares to stand'). But this night is also known as *pō fa'ahikehe* ('night of the other kind/spirits') because during this night the moon 'is known by those of the other kind' ('*iloa 'e he fa'ahikehe*). Next comes the night named *fakaua* ('the second one') or *pō toutai*, because on this night the moon may sometimes be 'known by the sailors/fishermen' ('*iloa 'e he kautoutai*) who are at the beach of the weather coast or at sea in the evening. On 'the third one' (*fakatolu*), the narrow 'new moon sickle' (*lausi'i fo'ou*) may be seen by all people to stand low on the western horizon in the 'dimness of the darkening evening' (*ataata efiafi po'uli*). It is called *pō 'o e tu'u 'a e māhina* ('night of the standing moon') or *pō 'a e maama* ('night of the world') because this night the moon 'is known by man' ('*iloa 'e he tangata*). It is said about the 'third one' (*fakatolu*) that it is a good day for 'trolling' (*fakatele*).
>
> In the 'planting season' (*tō ta'u*; from May/June to November), the farmer may start planting from this time. The following nights of the moon are counted by numbers. The 'fifth one' (*fakanima*) is said to be good for trolling and also for planting the 'early yam' (*tokamu'a*) in the beginning of the planting season. On the 'eighth one' (*fakavalu*), the moon is 'divided in two' (*vaeua mālie*), and it is called *tu'u efiafi* ('standing in the early evening') because this is when 'the moon stands straight up in the early evening'[3] ('*oku tu'u tonu efiafi 'a e māhina*). The 'ninth one' (*fakahiva*) is also 'suitable for' (*aonga*) trolling and planting, but in my thinking the best time

for planting the yam is when 'four or three days remain' (*toe 'aho e fā pē ko e tolu*) until full moon. When two days remain until full moon, the moon sets a short time before the beginning of (the morning) twilight, and this night of the moon is named *fakatauata* ('leading to twilight'). It is still time to plant, but the time before this is better suited. There should be no planting after the 'full moon', or at 'reciprocal/mutual day' (*fē'aho'aki*) when the moon sets in the early morning, or after this when there is a 'first moonrise' (*'uluaki hopo*) on the eastern horizon. Before this, all plants 'live well' (*mo'ui lelei*) and are 'hard to kill' (*matengata'a 'a e 'akau*), but afterwards all plants 'die easily' (*matengofua 'a e 'akau*). This may be known if you try to clear a garden or weed before the moon has become full. If you want to put fire to a tree it will not burn. Afterwards, trees burn much more easily. Clearing and weeding become easier. The time after 'full moon' is better suited for that kind of work.

There are some nights 'in this part of the moon' (*vahe ko ia 'o e māhina*) that are well suited for 'fishing with hook and bait' (*taumata'u*) for *koango* [ertain Emperors, Lethrinidae, such as Thumbprint- Grass- and Pink-eared Emperor; Randall, Allen and Steene 1990: 200] in the lagoon. From the third to the sixth night after 'full moon', the moon rises soon after the sun has set. These nights may be referred to as *fakamāhina hopo* ('corresponding with moonrise') because one should look for the *koango* in the 'fields of seaweed' (*'i he limu*) just as the moon rises. After this come the nights that are 'partly dark' (*konga po'uli*), referred to as the *kaupo'uli* ('the dark ones') because the night becomes truly dark before the moon rises. These nights are better suited for 'night diving' (*ama uku*) because the fish stay put in easy places. Before this, in the nights when 'the moon lights very much' (*fu'u maaama lahi 'a e māhina*), the fish move about or stay in the shade of difficult places. It is said that the period when the 'moon stands in the evening' (*tu'u efiafi*) is better suited for trolling than after full moon, but there is one day towards 'dead moon' that is suited for trolling. But the day is 'not dependable' (*ta'epau*) and must be sought by 'trial and error' (*'ahi'ahi*). Finally, the 'old moon sickle' (*lausi'i motu'a*) appears in the 'shattering of the twilight' (*mafoa 'a e ata*) in the eastern sky 'to die' (*mate*) on the final day of the month.

In truth, a lot of useful things may be taken from the moon and nothing from the sun. The only way that the sun changes is that it rises and sets in different places when 'days are long' (*'aho loloa*) in the 'warm season' (*taimi mafana*) and when 'days are short' (*'aho nonou*) in the 'cool season' (*taimi momoko*). The moon is much more useful because it is different when days are long and short and also changes from night to night.

Koloa's mode of contrasting the practical significance of solar and lunar differences is all but identical with Eliade's in his cross-cultural examination of the moon and its mystique:

The sun is always the same, always itself, never in any sense 'becoming'. The moon, on the other hand, is a body which waxes, wanes and disappears, a body whose existence is subject to the universal law of becoming, of birth and death. For three nights the starry sky is without a moon, but this 'death' is followed by a rebirth: the 'new moon' ... This perpetual return to its beginnings, and this ever recurring cycle make the moon *the* heavenly body above all concerned with the rhythms of life. It is not surprising, then, that it governs all those spheres of nature that fall under the law of recurring cycles. Water, rain, plant life, fertility ... (Eliade 1958: 154)

Two points of transition stand out in Koloa's description of lunation: firstly, the shift from a 'weak and dying moon', engulfed in the east by the morning sun, to a rejuvenated moon reappearing in the west in the evening dusk some days later. Secondly, the shift from a waxing moon that made growing things easy ('hard to kill' (*matengata'a*)) to a full and waning moon that made things hard to grow ('easy to kill' (*matengofua*)). Koloa had also hinted that there may be a similar correspondence between lunar states and the 'sickness of women' (*mahaki fakafefine*), pregnancy and birth, but he told me to ask his wife Meletoa about these matters. According to her, variations of lunar states were first and foremost a useful timekeeper of menstruation, pregnancy and birth:

If a woman gets the moon sickness (*mahaki fakamāhina*[4]) at dead moon, she may know that she will get sick again at next dead moon. It is the same with the moon standing in the evening, full moon and 'waning half moon' (*kalipa*). It is the same thing with birth. If a woman gets the moon sickness at full moon and then she does not become sick again on the next full moon, she may know that she is pregnant. She then goes to the 'midwife' (*mā'uli*) to learn when she will give birth. The midwife will ask her: 'When was your last moon sickness?' If she answers that it was at full moon in February, the midwife will count nine moons ahead and say, 'Te ke fā'ele koe he kātoa 'a e māhina he novema'. ('You shall give birth at full moon in November'.) But if she answers that it was at *matofi 'a e māhina* (a named moon-night a night or two before the fourth quarter), the midwife will say, 'You shall give birth at *matofi 'a e māhina* in November.'

Meletoa agreed that it was indeed helpful to look to the moon to keep tracks of events within these female fields of experience. She stated that she did not believe that there were lunar states that were more suitable than others with regard to human fertility.

You ask me if it is more easy to become pregnant during the first part of the month, but it is not the same with people and plants. Becoming with child is different from woman to woman. For some it is very hard, and others become pregnant very easily.

> Sometimes a woman may live with a man for many years and never become pregnant, and then she lives with another and becomes pregnant very quickly. It is the same with the time of death. The life of man is not like that of plants that are 'hard to kill' (*matengata'a*) before full moon. Men die according to the manner of their illness, or death may come suddenly whether it is before or after the full moon.

For women coping with menstruation, pregnancy and birth, the significance of lunar dynamics was not that they were perceived to correspond with varying conditions of human fertility and growth. Rather, they were used to order and predict routine events in women's daily life and important events in their lives. Koloa, on the other hand, clearly approached this from the point of view of one coping with planting, weeding, cultivating and cropping in his garden, and evidently felt that also female fertility and the 'planting' and growth of the child may be expected to correspond with lunar dynamics.

The Moon also Rises

The claims that the new moon 'rises' (*hopo*) in the west and that a qualitative shift occurred when the full moon suddenly started to rise in the east were striking, if somewhat puzzling, features of elicited moon-lore. In order to understand these claims, it is necessary to approach the moon and its motions as components in the everyday environment. What circumstantial knowledge and routines of observation existed to make such claims and notions of lunar motions possible? Certainly no one on Kotu had witnessed a new moon rising in the west, in the sense of observing its ascent from beyond the western horizon.

Most city dwellers of an electrified era are unfamiliar with lunar dynamics. Also the moon changes in somewhat different ways at different latitudes. Thus, it is necessary to present a description of how the moon actually changes over the lunar cycle at the latitude of Tonga in order to make sense of local knowledge about the moon. On the first day when the moon starts to reflect the sun's light to earth, the only thing that may be observed is the narrow crescent moon. The new moon crescent appears low in the western sky in the aftermath of sunset before it drops below the western horizon. Over the next days, the moon's magnitude increases. The apparent distance between the sun and the moon in the sky increases, and the time lag between sunset and moonset increases. As the distance between the sun and moon increases, it first becomes possible, and then quite easy, to catch sight of the moon in the daytime sky. At some point, the magnitude of the moon, distance between sun and moon, and time lag between sunset and moonset make it hard *not* to see how the waxing moon (like all heavenly bodies) moves from east to west (as the earth rotates) across the sky during the day.

The notion that the moonrise suddenly shifted from west to east indicates that other knowledge and, I would argue, specific routines of observation existed to make the daytime appearance of the moon insignificant or irrelevant. Discussions with other informants on Kotu illustrated characteristic notions about lunar motions that may indicate a correlation between conceptions of the moon and general agricultural competence.

Sitting on the steps of the communal water tank one evening as a waxing half moon (*māhina tuʻu efiafi*) grew brighter in the failing light, I asked my companions, mostly men in their late thirties and forties, where this moon had risen. After some hesitation, one man offered his opinion that it had risen out of the west. He went on to explain that it would continue to do so until 'full moon'. Then it would start rising from the east. Another wanted to moderate this understanding of lunar motion. He claimed that, initially rising out of the west, it actually starts to rise out of the east a few days before full moon. He believed that it travels a great part of its westward journey across the sky before it becomes dark enough for the moon to attract attention to itself. Yet another held that the moon rises in the west until it 'stands in the evening' (i.e. waxing half moon). Then it shifts over to rise in the east and completes half the passage across the sky before evening. A couple of days later, one of Koloa's sons, a man in his forties who had been present in the moon discussion but had offered no opinion himself, asked me if I agreed with any of the men. He himself was uncertain but questioned the notion that a waxing moon rises in the west and then suddenly shifts to rise in the east. He felt that this was a belief of old people and thought that it was perhaps the common belief in the old days. He suspected that a close inspection of the actual motion would reveal that the moon always rises in the east. His belief was that the moon lags increasingly behind the sun and crosses a decreasing portion of the sky before sunset. Finally, Koloa's 18-year-old grandson, who had just dropped out of secondary school and had not been present in any of the moon discussions, quite simply stated: 'The moon always rises in the east, but the new moon is about to set in the west when it becomes dark enough to notice it.'

Data indicate a quite strong correlation between age and notions of lunar motions; older people tended to disregard observable daytime states of the waxing moon altogether. Middle-aged people included such daytime states earlier in the lunar cycle, while some of the younger ones seemed to include the hardly observable daytime states of the moon throughout the entire lunar cycle. I would suggest that this makes good sense in terms of correlations between age and competence/knowledge about the cultivation of garden crops. Typically, young boys start out as universal assistants, perceived as capable of undertaking chores under close supervision and detailed monitoring. Young men are understood to be 'still incompetent' (*kei vale*) for a long time but are expected to turn to the sea as fisherman to become 'competent/knowledgeable' (*poto*) before turning to farming. Looking back on his life, Koloa described his own career as one in which he was 'disposed towards the sea' (*anga ki tahi*) when he was young (*kei talavou*). When he was in his late forties, he began to feel the cold of the sea and gradually became disenchanted with staying in the water; then he became 'disposed towards land' (*anga ki 'uta*) and turned to gardening. Other people on Kotu confirmed that this was indeed the typical turn of affairs.

Since the early 1970s, many young and middle-aged men cultivate kava on Tōfua island, 40 kilometres west of Kotu, where Kotu farmers have access to land. Growing kava on Tōfua is considered strenuous work; older farmers prefer to stay on Kotu throughout the year. The increased significance of kava as a cash crop has changed the strategy of cultivation, with older farmers feeling that the kava – as well as the high status variety of yams known as 'chiefly yams' or 'chief's yams' (*kahokaho/'ufi 'eiki*) and other tubers, such as 'giant taro' (*kape; Alocasia macrorrhiza*; Churchward 1959: 252) and 'Tongan taro' (*talotonga*) – grown by young and middle-aged farmers on Tōfua had come to be planted *noa 'ia pē* ('without order'), or haphazardly. Koloa described the changes like this:

> Towards the end of the 'harvesting season' (*utu ta'u*) in March is a suitable time to go to the garden and cut off the leaves of the *kahokaho* yams that are to be used as seed yams. When the leaves have been cut off, the yam must be left in the ground for two or three weeks and then dug up and brought home to become nice and dry. It is good to 'cut it up to be planted' (*tofi ke tō*) close to the 'moon standing in the evening' (*tu'u efiafi e māhina*) at the beginning of the 'planting season' (*tō ta'u*; commencing with the 'new moon' in May/June). This is seldom done nowadays, but the yam cuttings should be planted in accordance with the part of the yam they come from. This makes the growth of the yams in the garden more beautiful and more orderly. When planted *noa'ia pē* ('aimlessly/non-orderly'), the yams grow *noa'ia pē*, some shoots appearing here and some over there, but the garden is not so beautiful. It is the same with the time of the planting. It has changed. Nowadays many plant the *kape* ('giant taro') on Tōfua not with the 'planting of the late/large crop' (*tō tokamui/ta'u lahi*) in August/September to the 'end/turning of the year' (*ngata'anga 'o e ta'u*) in November. Instead, they often do it before the 'planting season' in February and March. This makes the leaves of the crop big and strong, but the 'tubers' (*foha*; lit. child/son) become long and narrow. If it is planted later 'with the planting season' (*he ta'u*), the tubers taste the same but look much better. They become 'rounder' (*fōpotopoto ange*) and 'more full-bodied' (*sino ange*). It is the same with kava. It is planted *noa'ia pē* today because the farmer looks only for the speed of growth and thinks little of the

beauty and strength of a full-bodied 'limb of kava root' (*kataʻi kava*). Kava planted before the 'planting season' in March, in the 'time of rain' (*taimi uha*), will grow fast, but it will be weak, and the limbs of the kava will be 'long and slim' (*hako loa*). Such a kava may be cut down and sold in two or three years. Kava planted 'with the crop' (*he taʻu*), when there is little rain, will grow more slowly but will be 'stronger' (*mālohi ange*), more full-bodied and more beautiful.

It may seem, then, that the increasing significance of kava as a cash crop is involved in committing younger and middle-aged farmers to planting 'aimlessly, haphazardly and disorderly' (*noa*) from the perspective of the most experienced subsistence farmers. The main point, however, is that horticultural expertise involved knowledge about key events in the lunar cycle. Thus, commitment to the experiential field of subsistence farming involves paying attention to changes in the moon perceived to be of relevance for growing things rather than observing how it actually moves across the sky.

Hawaiian Nights of the Moon

As far as I am aware, apart from the manuscript held by the Tongan Tradition Committee (Hafoka n.d) there has been no material produced in Tonga (nor elsewhere in Western Polynesia) that may contribute insights into the relationship between conceptions of growth, gardening practices and codification of lunar dynamics. Such material has, however, been produced for Eastern Polynesia in *Kepelino's Traditions of Hawaii* (Beckwick 1932), by Kepelino Keauokalani, 'a descendant of the priestly race of Paao, a man well acquainted with priestly lore' (ibid.: 4), born on the island of Hawaii in about 1830. Some of Kepelino's descriptions of Hawaiian moon nights may seem to indicate a similar notion of a new moon 'rising' in the west: 'On the evening when *the new moon rose* until the next day was a good time for planting ... On *Ku-kahi*, the third night of the moon, the moon is to be seen in the western sky ... *Ku lua rises* on the fourth day of the month ...' (ibid.: 98, my emphases). Furthermore, in the Tongan reckoning of the nights of the moon, the time of optimal growth referred to as *Fuaʻaho* and *Punifanga*, when four nights remain until full moon, was also described as the most suitable time for planting in Hawaii: '*Ole-pau* is the tenth night of the moon. On this night farmers who are on the lookout for good crops plant their fields. It is a productive day, say the cultivators ... No other days of the group are like this one. Cultivators do not think anything of the other days, but this is important to them.' (ibid.: 106).

On closer examination, however, these similarities may seem somewhat facile. It is not clear whether the notion that the new moon *rose* in Hawaii has been produced by the translation of the original Hawaiian text into

English. Both the translations 'rises on ... night of the moon' and 'is the ... of the moon' refer to the Hawaiian formulation: '*ka mahina i kau ai*' (ibid.: 103), which appears to be a statement that the moon 'has come' rather than one implying from whence it has come. Also, the description of the days that correspond to suitable nights of the Hawaiian moon for planting imply that there is no shift into a time when the moon has stopped waxing when planting should no longer be undertaken. On the contrary, seven of the days of the waxing moon are described as days *avoided* by cultivators, while only one of the days of the waning moon should be avoided. Thus, apart from the two first days of the new moon, only the four last days of the waxing moon are described by Kepelino as suitable for planting. What Koloa's and Kepelino's conceptualizations of a relationship between growth and lunar dynamics had in common, then, seems to be that plant fertility turns and peaks at certain points in the lunar cycle. Apart from both referring to a peak of garden fertility four days before full moon, their conceptualizations of the relationship between gardening and lunar dynamics seem to be inversions of one another: Kepelino's most suitable days for planting seemed to be Koloa's least suitable days for planting, and vice versa.

The main point, however, is that the moon 'rising' in the west was given relevance specifically within the context of subsistence farming. The moon was paid particular attention at dusk and in the twilight of dawn to gain some knowledge about the state of the world in order to know how to act rather than to gain exact knowledge about astronomy.

Motions of Merging and Separation in the Sky

Individuals voiced different opinions in our discussions about where the waxing moon rises. Routines of taking note of the qualitative nuances of the state of the moon, however, seemed to consist of paying particular attention to events of the western evening sky in the early part of the lunar cycle, where the sun and moon may be described as moving away from one another. Thus, the sun and moon may be said to move apart spatially in terms of the apparent distance between them in the sky and temporally in terms of the time lag between the events of sunset and moonset. In the late part of the lunar cycle, on the other hand, the most dramatic events occur in the eastern morning sky, where the sun and moon may be described as having come together. The sun and moon may be seen as drawing closer to one another day by day in terms of the apparent distance between them in the sky and in terms of time lag between the event of moonrise and sunrise. For three or four nights around full moon, significant events occur in both the east and the west as the moonrise in the east coincides with sunset in the west. The sun and the moon are as far apart as they can get in terms of apparent distance in the sky and in terms of time lag between moonrise and sunrise.[5] This state of extreme separateness at the same time brings the diurnal shifting between a daytime state of brilliant light and a night-time state of utter darkness to a halt. Instead, the full moon alternates with the sun to create the condition of *fē'aho'aki* ('reciprocal/mutual day') and provide illumination throughout the diurnal cycle. Finally, for the three or four nights around 'dead moon' (*mate 'a e māhina*), between the last observation of the 'old moon sickle' (*lausi'i motu'a*) in the east and the first observation of the 'new moon sickle' (*lausi'i fo'ou*) in the west, no significant observable event occurs, neither in the east nor in the west. On the basis of the trends of the last days of the old moon and the first days that the new moon can be seen, however, people would be quite justified in assuming that the sun and moon have 'come together'. This state of merging at the same time makes the diurnal oscillation between darkness and light reassert itself fully. No lunar intervention offsets the motion by which all things merge in the evening and become separated in the morning.

I have argued above that the manner of referring to a shift between a merged state (of 'high tide' and 'stable night'; *tau*) and the beginning of separation (towards states of low tide through *mahu'i* or 'detachment' and day through *mafoa* or 'shattering') implies that the beginning of this transition was perceived to occur in a place or manner inaccessible to man. That some shift has taken place may only be grasped vaguely by the interpretation of uncertain indicators. Likewise, the manner of referring to the transition between 'dead moon', when the sun and moon appear to be in the same place, and 'new moon' (*māhina fo'ou*), when the sun and moon appear to have moved apart, involved references to events 'known by beings of the other side' (*'iloa 'e he fa'ahikehe*) but not yet known with certainty by man (*'iloa 'e he tangata*). As may be clear by now, I am arguing that the dynamics of the lunar cycle were conceptualized in terms of a perpetual motion of coming together and coming apart paralleling the conceptualization of tidal and diurnal dynamics explored in the two previous chapters. In the monthly motion separating and merging the sun and the moon, conditions of growth or garden fertility were perceived to become favourable when the new moon could be seen to have separated from the sun (*Fakatolu*; *'iloa 'e he tangata*). The conditions of growth were described as becoming increasingly favourable for as long as the moon and sun kept moving apart. At full moon, the sun and moon are as far apart as they can get. And immediately the capacity for growth and multiplication known to expresses itself in plants becoming 'hard to kill' (*matengata'a*) was believed to stop short and become inverted, making plants 'easy to kill' (*matengofua*). Growth, vitality and multiplication, then, correspond with the motion separating that which has become merged and that shall re-merge. Thus, the state of maximum separateness around full moon was not perceived to produce conditions of maximum garden fertility but conditions particularly ill-suited for putting seed yams into the ground.

Hina and Sinilau: Tales of Attraction and Repulsion

Exploring people's fields of experience constituted by their daily engagements with their environment, I have chosen to take seriously and focus strongly on the subtle qualitative nuances that characterize significant processes within these fields. I have argued that descriptions of the qualitative nuances of the tidal, diurnal and lunar cycles imply that these basic rhythms of everyday living were conceptualized in parallel manners. As descriptions of shifts and changes in the surrounding world, they all appeared to take the form of a dialectical process moving between the diametrically opposed states of separateness and oneness. Rather than depicting the world as a single and stable reality, they envisioned the surrounding world as a multiple and dynamic reality caught up in a perpetual motion of merging and separation. In exploring notions about changing conditions over the lunar cycle, we have seen how the motion of merging and separation between the two principal natural sources of illumination were strongly related to notions about garden fertility and growth.

The dialectics of merging and separation, then, appear to run through several fields of routine experience. As an ongoing story experienced by people engaging their surroundings, the flow of events and the ways of conceptualizing tidal, diurnal and lunar dynamics appear to make up a tale of attraction between complementary elements constituting one whole by coming together or by one engulfing the other. But it is also constitutes a tale of repulsion or struggle as two united elements coming apart or by one tearing away from the encompassment of the other. In the conceptualization of nightfall, merging seemed to occur by night seeping out of the ground, so to speak, to encompass the daytime world. In the morning, on the other hand, separation occurred by daylight forcing darkness and the beings belonging to it back into the ground. Likewise, in the conceptualization of lunar dynamics, the sun and the moon appeared to come together at the end of the cycle, the dazzling sun overtaking the waning moon on the eastern horizon. And they appeared to separate again as the new moon 'rose' in the west, tearing itself away to stand apart from the sun. In such a tale, the sun and moon are both like lovers, drawn to each other and complementing one another, and like adversaries, fighting for the upper hand and engaging one another in pursuit and flight. To my knowledge, the dynamic relationship between high tide and low tide or night and day has not been explicitly elaborated in collected Tongan myths or tales. Neither has the relationship between the lunar states of 'dead moon' (*mate 'a e māhina*), 'new moon/known by man' (*fakatolu/'iloa 'e he tangata*), 'moon standing in the evening' (*tu'u 'efiafi*) and 'reciprocal/mutual day' (*fē'aho'aki*) as sun and moon come together in the east, as the new moon tears away in the west, as they move apart in the western sky and as they become separated by all the sky to stand on opposed horizons. On the other hand, the dynamic relationship between adversaries and lovers, repulsion and attraction, increase and decrease of beauty and strength are very common themes in numerous mythical narratives collected from Tonga and elsewhere in Polynesia. In some cases, the resonance between the structure of mythical narration and the dynamics of lunation are quite striking. The mythical cycle of Hina and Sinilau, who in contemporary popular culture and numerous T-shirt decorations figure as 'Lovers of Ancient Tonga', consists precisely of tales elaborating on attraction and repulsion, with growth and loss of love or compassion, beauty and strength as the main characters move together and come apart. Many of these tales of attraction start out with a young man and woman of extraordinary status, beauty and fame learning about one another and admiring one another from a distance.[6] Often one is Tongan and the other Samoan. Typically, one is drawn to the other but upon reaching the goal, beauty, strength or love soon starts to dwindle because of homesickness, treachery or maltreatment. In some of the myths, the weakened party regains their former splendour by fleeing from a pursuing lover. In others, strength and beauty is regained only through death and revitalization by immersion in the 'Water of Life' (*Vaiola*), controlled by the deity Hikule'o. The many tales about Hina and Sinilau vary considerably – mostly with regard to where in a cycle of transformation the story commences and ends.

In the myth 'Hina and Nukuakakala', collected by Collocott in the early twentieth century, Hina is drawn to the magnificence of Sinilau:

> There was a virgin named Hina,[7] and she and the handsome man Sinilau heard reports of one another, and as time went on and they continually heard one another's praises Hina could rest no longer, because of her thought upon Sinilau. So one day she … leapt into the sea, and swam, and came to the land of Sinilau. (Collocott 1928: 359)

In another tale, Hina is brought from Samoa to Tonga by the chief Vaitokelau, who has heard about her beauty:

> One day Vaitokelau went to the pool, and addressing the rock, said, 'Oh, that you could bring Hinasioata from Samoa to be my wife.' He spoke at random, but the rock heard, and went to Samoa, and going ashore at night stood outside the door of Hina's

house ... Hina slept on the rock ... In the middle of the night the stone moved, went down to the sea, and set off on its return to Tonga. (ibid.: 28)

In yet another Hina myth, collected by Gifford, Hina is the beautiful daughter of the Tongan King Tu'i Ha'atakalaua and Sinilau a Samoan chief:

Hina was the daughter of the Tu'i Ha'atakalaua. She lived with her father in Tongatabu. News of Hina's marvellous beauty had spread far and wide, even to distant Samoa. Sinilau, who resided in Samoa, heard of the wondrous beauty of Hina and resolved to journey to Tonga to see her loveliness for himself. So launching his double sailing canoe (*kalia*) he and his brother sailed for Tonga. (Gifford 1924b: 187)

When Hina and her lover come together, the original attraction typically turns to repulsion as conflicts of interest produce misunderstandings and treachery weakens one of them. Thus, the Hina of the first myth who swam from her own land to come close to Sinilau was maltreated by the one who had attracted her:

Straightaway Sinilau bade two men, 'Go to the sea and bring the woman here' ... And Sinilau was filled with love [literally, was dead with love] for the maiden, and bade all his land go and gather food ... But when the morning came the food was finished, for Sinilau's wives had taken it and thrown it into the sea. And they told Sinilau, 'Lo, this woman is both spirit and human, She has eaten the food, and it is finished.' Then Sinilau bade his wives gather together ... ; and they took her and cast her into the pig yard, and fed her with left-over scraps of food. Then the maiden wept and remembered her land and parents, that she had come to dwell in such desolation and hardship. (Collocott 1928: 36)

Similarly, the Hina who was brought from Samoa to Tonga on the floating rock is turned away from Vaitokelau when his wives '... who were both spirit and human ... called their husband to them, and bewitched him, and he became foolish, so that the unfortunate Hina dwelt neglected in her compound' (ibid.: 29). The Sinilau, who had come all the way from Samoa because of Hina, fared no better:

He sidled up to her, but she turned and kicked him. Still Sinilau edged closer and she again kicked him and spat on him ... Immediately he left, climbing through the window. Hina saw for the first time that her lover was Sinilau. Infatuated with his handsome figure she at once climbed through the window and followed him ... but Sinilau thoroughly incensed over his rough treatment at her hands, cried out: 'You remain [Good bye]. I came across the ocean and I climbed eight fences and I extinguished one hundred watch fires, all for you. I entered your mosquito-proof room and I sidled up to you, but you spat upon me and kicked me. (Gifford 1924b: 188)

In some of the Hina myths, the two lovers come together gradually as they go through stages or overcome obstacles. Thus, in the myth of the Samoan Sinilau and the Tongan Hina, the lovers finally come together in the inmost room of a compound surrounded by eight fences:

> They proceeded to the place where Hina resided. They found it brilliantly illuminated, surrounded by eight fences or enclosures ... As they stood outside the walls, Sinilau said to his brother: 'Stay here. I will seek the girl and look upon her beauty, but, if I do not return by the second cock's crow, you will know that I am dead ... Sinilau climbed the fences and finally entered the house in which the girl was ... In his endeavours to approach the girl Hina, Sinilau extinguished all the one hundred watch fires. Then he went into the girl's room and tried to extinguish her lamp and after repeated efforts succeeded in doing so. (Gifford 1924b: 187)

Similarly, in the narrative about the Samoan Hina brought to the Tongan chief Vaitokelau on the floating rock, a trial involving the passing of eight fences is undertaken:

> Once there was a handsome young chief named Vaitokelau who had a large compound, surrounded by eight fences, in the midst of which was his chiefly house. He also had a bathing pool in which stood a rock. The spaces surrounded by the fences, the house, and the pool were all being kept for a beautiful girl in Samoa, named Hinasioata (Hina mirror) ... The girl was called Mirror (Sioata) because her skin was so fair and glistening that reflections could be seen in it ... Vaitokelau asked her to come with him to his home ... When they reached the outer palisade Vaitokelau called to the wardress Suamanu ... Let Atu-first-resting-place be opened that Drift-from-sea may sleep. But Hina replied 'Any woman who has erred will sleep in Atu-first-resting place' ... So they went through gate after gate. To the invitation to stay in the third enclosure she replied that a woman not right would stay there; at the fourth, that a woman without fame, at the fifth a woman who has done wrong (*hia*); at the sixth, a woman without prudence (*ta'eloto*); at the seventh, a woman who is wearied (giving in *fiu*) would remain in the various enclosures; until at the eighth she replied that a woman who has reached her goal (*kuo a'u*[8]) would sleep there. (Collocott 1928: 29)

The qualities describing the eight fences or enclosures of the spaces reserved for the Samoan Hina by the Tongan Vaitokelau as she approaches her 'goal' or 'completion' intriguingly recapture the qualitative nuances of a moon approaching one of the turning points of lunation. Thus, eight differentiated states of the moon bring it from the night that it is 'known by the spirits' (*'iloa 'e he fa'ahikehe*) to the night when the half 'moon stands in the evening' (*tu'u efiafi 'a e māhina*). Also, eight differentiated states would bring it from that of 'standing in the evening' to 'first moonrise', as well as from 'first moonrise' to the state of the 'weak moon'.

Likewise, the manner in which the Samoan Sinilau approaches Hina (by extinguishing the hundred watch fires of the eight enclosures of her brilliantly illuminated dwelling place) and then after several attempts succeeds in putting out the lamp of Hina herself recaptures with extraordinary accuracy the manner in which the sun reduces the magnitude and brilliance of the waning moon by 'approaching it' in the eastern morning sky. Eight states of diminishing illumination and very few states of 'weak moon' comprise the phase of waning from the night known as 'first moonrise', which occurs shortly after full moon, to the morning that the sun appears to extinguish the moon altogether on the eastern horizon. Thus, the countdown towards the culmination of the encounter between Hina and her lover so characteristic of these tales of attraction would seem to make sense in terms of turning points of lunation and the practice of counting the nights of the moon.

In the exploration of the tidal, diurnal and lunar dynamics, I have argued that the states of 'low tide' (*mamaha 'a e tahi*), 'day' (*'aho*) and 'full moon, reciprocal/mutual day' (*māhina katoa/fē'aho'aki*) were conceptualized in a parallel manner. Thus, they all appeared to share the quality of being a phase in an encompassing dialectical motion. The vocabularies of tides, the diurnal cycle and lunation all indicate that separation between sea and land, ground and sky, moon and sun was conceived as a temporary state. Thus, the diametrically opposed elements were referred to as ever merging into the inverted states of 'sea united with land' (*tau 'a e tahi*), 'day united with night' (*tau 'a e 'aho mo e pō*) and 'dead moon' (*mate 'a e māhina*) as the sun has overtaken and united with the moon in the eastern morning sky.

Engaging Tales of Attraction

The flow of events of the Hina and Sinilau tales of mutual attraction resonate strongly with the flow of events of lunation. So much so that the myths appear almost didactic. In some of the myths, it is as if Hina's adventures were modelled on the process of lunation as an elaboration of lunar transformations and apparent differences of sun-moon relationships throughout the lunar cycle. An approach to tales about gods and culture heroes as allegories of actual phenomena and processes in the environment of myth-making people would by no means be a novelty in the history of the study of myths. On the contrary, the notion that the fantastic elements of myths could have deeper meanings as allegories of natural phenomena and human qualities was fundamental in interpretive theories of myths and legends that developed with the growth of philosophy in Ancient Greece. Indeed, this was the dominant perspective on myths until the development of functionalist and structuralist approaches in the twentieth century. For Max Müller, for example, who was the author of *Comparative Mythology* (Müller 1856) and who was one of the founders of the discipline of comparative religion, Indo-European mythology consisted of allegorical stories about processes and features of nature such as the sky, the sun and moon, the stars, the dawn and so on. To his mind, these phenomena constituted original allegorical referents that in the course of time were lost as they (as a result of a 'disease of language') became detached from the phenomena and processes to which they originally referred. With the sociological turn of functionalism and the cognitive turn of structuralism, this approach to the interpretation of myths quickly appeared outdated, and in more recent interpretations of cultural meaning it mostly figures as a quaint and unsophisticated relic of a primitive perspective on myths and legends. Nina Witoszek's *Norwegian Mythology of Nature* (Witoszek 1998), where she attempts to interpret Norwegian fairy tales as 'ecological narratives', may illustrate just how outdated and unsophisticated this allegorical approach appears to contemporary students of culture: 'When I call [it] a thoroughly ecological story, it is not meant in Müller's (quaint) sense, with reference to the celestial sphere and stars …' (ibid.: 85). Witoszek clearly does not want to be identified with Müller's interpretation in which:

> the cannibalistic father who often appears in fairytales … is a coded sign for the sky which in a cyclical and alternating manner swallows the clouds and releases them. And children abandoned by their parents are really stars sent to illuminate the nighttime sky. (Ibid.: 85)

And indeed, Müller's perspective, in which an imagined original state of affairs represents the key for the definite meaning of coded signs, does appear quite unsatisfactory. Not least because it fails to account for why people whose cultural creativity caused them to take inspiration from phenomena that surround them to make up entertaining and meaningful stories should keep on repeating these 'coded' stories about natural phenomena or historical events long after having lost the key to their meaning. Still, very many myths from all times and from all over the world do have elements and narrative structures that with ease may be identified with phenomena of nature. This does indicate that the allegorical perspective may have pinpointed one very characteristic quality of myths that should perhaps not be rejected nor ridiculed; namely, the quality of *resonance* between what goes on in a tale worth inventing, remembering, retelling and listening to and what goes on in the lifeworld of those who invent it and enjoy listening to it. In other words, an allegorical perspective characterized by a quest for code-like denotation in the form of identifying *the* phenomenon for which the mythical stuff stands appears too simplistic. But as Von Herder emphasized a long time ago, it still might be quite useful to approach mythical narratives in terms of the components that surround myth-makers, storytellers and their audiences:

> In everything [on board ship] there is experience to illuminate the original era of myth ... Then, Jupiter's lightning was terrifying – as indeed it is on the Ocean ... There are thousand new and more natural explanations of mythology ... if one reads, say Orpheus, Homer, Pindar ... on board ship. (Von Herder, see Encyclopedia Britannica, 1999)

Thus, I hold that Tongan everyday modes of conceptualizing, experiencing and engaging with the environmental dynamics of tidal, diurnal and lunar cycles constitute an enduring basis for thinking about the world as well as for good storytelling and listening. The analogous relationship between the narrative structure and the way in which the process of lunation plays itself out and was conceptualized is not, I would argue, one that makes the tales of attraction simple allegories of what actually occurs in nature or society. Thus, Hina and Sinilau *do not* represent the moon and the sun nor are the narratives *about* qualitative shifts and changes of the lunar cycle. I do argue, however, that qualitative nuances with which people were familiar in many fields of everyday experience, including the dynamics of the relationship between sun and moon, constituted a kind of common sense underlying people's aesthetic appreciation. Such common sense may be tapped by myth-makers, storytellers and their audiences, who create, retell or appreciate a good tale. On this perspective, then, enduring everyday modes of conceptualizing, experiencing and engaging with environmental dynamics may continue to inform shared understandings and aesthetic sensibilities long after myths and tales embedded in the same dynamics have been forgotten. The myths and tales about Hina and Sinilau were no longer part of a living oral tradition in Tonga going into the twenty-first century. Thus, I never heard these tales during my fieldworks in Tonga. Tongans have been devout Christians for more than 150 years. This has had an undeniable impact on oral traditions in general and on the significance of pre-Christian myths and tales in particular. On the other hand, lunar dynamics, the 'counting of nights' (*lau pō*) and ideas about the significance of these qualitative nuances still constituted a part of the practical realities of everyday village living during my fieldworks on Kotu. The continuing practical significance of the moon was probably related to the fact that Kotu had not yet been electrified. By and large, fishing and farming were still subsistence activities, and the agricultural and marine regimes of resource use appeared to be based on techniques that had been around for quite a while. Modernization has not only affected different parts of Tonga differently but evidently also different fields of activities and ideas. This does not affect the theoretical significance of the discovery of resonance between the narrative structure of these myths and conceptualizations of lunar dynamics. It does, however, imply that some fields of activities and ideas change more slowly than others and that the exploration of such fields of experience offers rich potential for approaching enduring aspects of culture.

Engaging Aesthetics

In the last chapter, we have seen how dynamics discovered through an exploration of modes of conceptualizing and engaging the immediate surroundings within fields of everyday experience may constitute a useful context for appreciating the narrative logic of Tongan mythology. I am not suggesting that this is the only or ultimate meaning of these myths. Clearly, the symbolic forms of myths are multivalent and have several layers of meaning. The Hina myths address significant themes pertaining to the human condition and social life, such as: attraction between men and women; the strength of desire, jealousy, treachery, strife and struggle between men and women, co-wives or between ranked affines or sides of the family; and self-sacrifice, love and devotion to kin and homeland.

My reinterpretation of tales of attraction in the light of the moon of Tonga is part of a particular procedure of discovery that emphasizes the importance of paying attention to what goes on in everyday life and in particular to people's practical and routine involvements with the components of their environment. Thus, day-to-day dynamics of merging and separation discovered through an exploration of modes of conceiving and engaging the immediate surroundings have produced insights of relevance for understanding what may make a cultural expression, like a myth or tale, appreciated. And indeed, I hold that ethnography related to everyday practical engagements with the immediate environment offers untapped potential for discovering enduring and shared understandings about the world, why things happen and how to cope with it. In what follows, I shall go on to use the seemingly enduring understandings about the world that are implied by people's perceptions of environmental dynamics as a basis for analysing the dynamics of ceremonial aesthetics and everyday sociality and morality, both of which in their turn are essential for understanding why people responded as they did to the threats and environmental transformations taking place around them in the first decades of the twenty-first century. By exploring the many nuances that people read upon the surface of their surroundings on Kotu, we have seen that the rhythm of everyday life involved conceptions of surroundings constantly on the move between diametrically opposed states of the world. Over the next chapters, I shall turn to an exploration of how people coped with one another in a manner adapted to the dynamics of this 'given' world in order to create a society fit to live in.

Notes

1. Exactly how 'disorderly' is hard to know, but certainly the practice of burying people in one communal burial ground is relatively new. On the small island of Kotu, there are several old 'burial places' (*fa'itoka*) in the 'forest' (*vao*) and also plots in the '*uta* garden area.
2. Havili Hafoka, the author of the manuscript of the Palace Office in Nuku'alofa cited above, refers to this penultimate day of the 'month' as *māhina lekeleka mate* or 'tiny and dying moon'.
3. The altitude of the waxing half moon in the evening actually varies between a minimum of 40 degrees in March and April and a maximum of almost 85 degrees in October and November. Although the waxing half moon always *tu'u efiafi* ('stands in the evening'), it does not always *tu'u tonu efiafi* ('stand straight up in the evening'). Thus, in the period referred to as *tō ta'u* ('planting season') in the old Tongan calendar of yam cultivation, from May to November, its altitude increases steadily by each lunation, while in the period from November to April within the *utu ta'u* ('harvesting season') its altitude decreases steadily.
4. Several terms were used to refer to menstruation: *mahaki fakafefine*, lit. 'female sickness'; *mahaki fakamāhina*, lit. 'moon sickness' or 'monthly sickness'; and *fakakelekele*, lit. 'making dirt/soil'.
5. At least at the 'turning points' (*ngata'anga*) at which 'planting season' (*tō ta'u*), according to Hafoka's manuscript about Tongan modes of reckoning the passage of time (Hafoka n.d), turns into 'harvesting season' (*utu ta'u*) and 'harvesting season' turns into 'planting season'. These 'turning points' are sufficiently close to the solstices for the sunrise/sunset and moonrise/moonset to occur about as far apart as possible.
6. Some myths, however, start out from the other extreme of Hina and Sinilau being closely related, as for example full brother and sister originating from the same womb.
7. Hina figures prominently in Tongan myths and tales, very often in narratives of attraction to Sinilau but also other lovers, as well as attachment to her

family and homeland. Hina was associated with the beauty of the full moon *Māhina* and was sometimes referred to as *Hinasioata* ('Shining Hina') 'because her skin was so fair and glistening that reflections could be seen in it' (Collocott 1928: 27). In Tonga, it is said that Hina can be seen on the face of the full moon sitting under a tree making 'barkcloth' (*ngatu*).

8. *kuo aʻu* means 'to have arrived' and also 'to have culminated' or 'peaked'.

4

Creating Tableaus of Moving Beauty

◆●◆

In the exploration of basic rhythms of everyday experience, I argued that the conceptualization of dynamics characterizing important fields of everyday experience appeared to take the form of a motion of separation and merging that may be represented as a serial image of transformation (see Chapter 3). Such an image of transformation implied that states of the world elaborated in Polynesian cosmology and cosmogony should be viewed as temporary phases within an ongoing motion of growth and regeneration, produced by a process of merging, separation and re-merging. Mapping reconstructions of Polynesian cosmology (Gunson 1990: 15–16) onto a serial image of transformation, I found that they first of all resonated with the middle figure of the series (see Chapter 2) depicting a temporary state of optimal separateness.

Similarly, it is possible to map a spatial image of tableaus of ceremonial elaboration onto such a serial image. Thus, it would make sense to describe a kava ceremony, for example, in terms of the two halves of the 'group of kava-makers' (*tou'a*) and the position of supreme rank (*olovaha*) 'facing one another' (*fesiofaki*) across a 'gap/space' (*vaha'a*) upheld by the ranked positions of the kava drinkers (*'alofi*). Again, such an image would resonate with the middle image in the series depicting a state of optimal separateness, rather than the wider process of regeneration and growth produced by merging, separation and re-merging. Here, then, I shall make an effort to follow the threads discovered through exploration in the preceding chapters of rhythms dominating everyday experience. Thus I would argue for the value of making time a part of the context of interpretation by focusing on what may be called the ceremonial process of transformation rather than the 'ceremonial tableau' (which represents an important, meaningful instance or phase within a wider process of transformation). By ceremonial process, I do not wish to evoke the whole complex of concepts developed by Van Gennep and Turner to approach initiation rituals such as those of 'liminality', 'communitas-societas' and 'structure-anti-structure' associated with 'ritual process' and 'rites of passage' (Turner 1969). I use ceremonial process to refer to a chain of events moving along phases of anticipation, preparation, staging and performance. A process by which an occasion is brought to 'stand apart' (*mahuʻi*) as one of particular 'importance' (*mahuʻinga*) and by which a momentarily materialized order collapses again as that which constituted the ceremonial tableau flows back into or re-merges with the flow of everyday life. It seems to me that insight into important aspects of the meaning of a ceremonial tableau of unidimensional differentiation may be gained by opening up this 'frozen moment' in time to explore how it articulates with the diversity of activities that have been undertaken to create it. From the point of view of the numerous experiencing individuals who have gone out of their way to contribute to the whole transformational process of creating the ceremonial tableau, the meanings that may be constructed from the tableau itself may very well be insignificant in comparison with the meanings of this tableau as the realization of the capability to create it by common effort in order to achieve a common aim. In this chapter, then, I shall describe and undertake an analysis of ceremonial aesthetics, which lends its perspective from enduring perceptions of the world and its workings as discovered in everyday routines of engaging and referring to fundamental rhythms of the environment.

A Royal Visit

'Have you heard?' asked Melenaʻa, 'The Queen will come to Kotu next week and plans to spend the night here.' A royal visit was an extraordinary event. But she did not sound particularly proud or pleased that the Queen had chosen to spend the night on Kotu, out of all the islands of the Lulunga district. Later I asked Kotu's town officer, Heamasi Koloa, why people appeared to look forward to the visit with less enthusiasm than one might have expected. As *ofisa kolo* and steward of the 'King's Church' (Free Wesleyan Church of Tonga), he carried a great part of the responsibility for making the royal visit a success. Asked if a royal visit was not a happy occasion, he answered:

> That is true, but she comes on very short notice. Next week is the first week of the New Year, the 'week of prayer' (*uike lotu*) in our church. People are busy preparing the feasts of that week. Not so long ago we had the *misinale* (annual collection of money for the church), and then Amini died,[1] and much work was done to bring food and 'Tongan goods' (*koloa fakatonga*) for the funeral. Now it is said that the old

woman, Foli, is very weak. She is more than a hundred years old and has numerous kinsmen. Her funeral shall be very large. People are very busy preparing for the week of prayer as it is and exhausted by 'doing the duties/fulfilling obligations' (*fai fatongia*) and by 'carrying the burdens' (*fua kavenga*) of these things. The last time the Queen visited the Lulunga district, she stayed on Kotu, and it is a good thing that she has chosen Kotu again, but this has been a time of much work for us, and we are exhausted. It will be hard for people to become 'warm inside' (*loto māfana*) to do the work and the duties for the Queen's welcome.

So, initially people did not appear to anticipate the visit with great enthusiasm. Nevertheless, as the day of her arrival approached, people grew gradually more energetic and increasingly committed to the collaborative tasks of preparation. In order to make people 'warm inside' for the Queen's visit, Koloa decided to assemble an extraordinary 'village meeting' (*fono*[2]). At this meeting, he suggested that each '*api* or 'home' should bring 5 *pa'anga* (which equalled about 3.5 US$) so that the last large pig remaining on Kotu after the most recent funeral could be bought for 'Taufatōfua's basket to the Royal House' (*kato 'o Taufatōfua ki Loto'ā*[3]). Towards the end of the meeting, when Koloa had made his announcements, 'Atu Hē, a man in his forties, asked to be heard:

> It is good to bring money to buy the woman Lose 'Ilangana's large pig for the basket. But from the times of old the important thing in Taufatōfua's basket to the King is the *fonu* (turtle). It is said that the man Lotima down in *lalo* (the low end of the village) has caught a large turtle for the feast he shall give in the week of prayer. It would be right to bring the turtle for Taufatōfua's basket. If Lotima feels warm inside for this visit, maybe he will sell his turtle.[4] That is all.

Then Ana Afitu, a woman in her early seventies, asked to be heard:

> Taufatōfua's basket to the King is an important thing. But it would be very 'beautiful' (*faka'ofo'ofa*) if all the homes of this land brought food to the home of the town officer to prepare a 'board of food' (*kaipola*) for the welcome of the Queen's following here on Kotu. Another thing is the *ngatu* (barkcloth), the *fala* (plaited pandanus mats) and the *lolo tonga* (Tongan oil[5]). It is 'up to them' (*fa'iteliha*; 'to do as one pleases'), but it would be right for the women to bring out these from their 'beds' (*mohenga*[6]) for the Queen's visit.

Meletoa, Koloa's wife, then spoke:

> The Queen has been here on Kotu before. When she was here, she wanted to see the 'hidden burial mound' (*langi tu'u lilo*) and the 'pair of pools' (*ongo vai*[7]) of Veifua and

Tōkilangi behind *fa'itoka* (the village cemetery). These places are very 'overgrown' (*vaoa*). It would be good if these places were to be cleared to become 'nice and clean' (*ma'a lelei*) for the Queen's visit.

Finally, Koloa thanked people for the suggestions and said that it would be well if each home were to bring 10 *pa'anga* (about 7 US$) so that both the pig and the turtle could be included in Taufatōfua's basket to the King's House. He also told people to devote themselves to the task of cutting the grass of the village and to pay particular attention to the cemetery, the twin pools in the forest and the 'public roads' (*hala pule'anga*) leading to them. Everyone should do 'as they pleased' (*fa'iteliha pē*) and bring food and Tongan wealth for the Queen's welcome according to how 'warm they were inside' (*loto māfana*[8]). He also admonished people in general, and the youth in particular, to attend to their appearances during the Queen's visit. Thus, he said that no one must go out on the village roads without a *ta'ovala* (plaited matting worn around the waist), go outside their homes 'without a shirt' (*ta'e kofu*) or 'eat while standing up' (*kai tu'u*) in public. Such things, he emphasized, would show a 'lack of respect' (*ta'e faka'apa'apa*) for the important visitors. He reminded the elders of their duty to see to it that the young people of their households should keep the 'taboos' (*tapu*) so that the land would be 'orderly' (*maau*) for the Queen's visit:

> We all know that it is hard for 'the young people' (*kautalavou*; lit. 'the good-looking ones') to remember how to behave, but we must pay attention to their behaviour and keep on telling them what to do. 'Do not leave it to them to make them lead us all' ('*O'ua tuku 'ia ke nau pule kitautolu*). 'Let us all try to achieve orderliness in our living' (*Feinga ke tau maau he nofo*)!

Over the next few days, root crops were provided for the 'earth oven' (*'umu*). Small- and medium-sized pigs were slaughtered and carved up. Kava was pounded. Rubble was picked up and burnt. The grass was cut in the village, in the cemetery and along the public path to the twin pools in the forest behind the cemetery. Large amounts of barkcloth and mats were provided by village women to decorate the room in which the Queen would sleep, and a temporary house was erected nearby. Wooden columns were erected to make portals decked with fragrant flowers. A 200-meter path of barkcloth, on which the Queen was to walk, was laid out from *Fanga lahi*, the Great Landing on the beach, where she would first set foot on Kotu, to the Queen's quarters on the *mala'e*, the 'central village green'. The contrast between people's rather reserved initial response to the news of the visit and the later fervour of their commitment to the work of making Kotu a beautiful place, worthy of the important occasion of a royal visit, was very striking. It was evident that as people warmed to the project of preparing for the visit they came to enjoy very much the practical experience of working together to create an event of extraordinary importance and beauty. In contrast to what may have been expected on the basis of their initial sceptical response to the news of the Queen's visit, they appeared quite joyous. The sounds of joking, laughter and loud music filled the village. In short, people seemed to be having a very good time. When the Queen arrived, this atmosphere of industrious activity and humorous festivity of 'making happy' (*fakafiefia*) went on to be punctuated at certain points by short moments of solemnity, silence and immobility of which the *'ilokava* ceremony of the 'Queen's welcome' was the most marked one.

The Queen's Kava

As we waited to welcome Queen Mataʻaho, the kava drinkers were already sitting on the ground with legs crossed on the central village green, chatting, joking and smoking. When the Queen arrived and was seated at the head of the kava circle, it was like the introduction of a powerful magnet; immediately everything became oriented towards her. That the ceremonial occasion involved strict constraints on action was soon made clear in no uncertain terms. Koloa had some time earlier 'appointed me to the local talking-chief title *Fāhiva*' (*fakanofo ki he hingoa fakamatāpule ko Fāhiva*[9]), which entitled me to take part in the Queen's kava ceremony. When I took a picture of the Queen from my own position in the kava circle, one of the policemen who had accompanied her immediately came over and demanded that I stop disturbing the ceremony. This was the first and only time I met with photo restrictions in Tonga, where people were generally quite willing to be photographed. Having accepted a role in the task at hand, I was clearly obliged to abide by the constraints of the ceremonial occasion. I was told later that I could have 'done as I pleased' (*faʻiteliha*) and been free to take pictures of the ceremony if I did not partake in the kava. The attention of the kava drinkers should be exclusively directed towards the head of the circle, and any activity or, indeed, movement whatsoever should be directed at the partaking of her kava. For instance, smoking was not permitted during the ceremony, because it was perceived to divert the drinkers' attention from the shared task of celebrating this important occasion of hierarchical differentiation. After one round of kava, the Queen withdrew to the house that had been prepared for her. Once she had left, the kava ceremony seemed to lose its 'magnetic pole'. Attention shifted as it gravitated towards several visiting notables present. Later on, as other visitors of importance and rank excused themselves, the kava ceremony loosened up even more, becoming dominated by joking, smoking and drinking in a manner resembling that which had characterized it prior to the arrival of the Queen and her entourage of important people; proceedings steadily slipped back into a more informal mode of communication (for similar observations of 'ceremonial slippage' with regard to kava drinking, see Rogers 1975: 375–77). Early next morning, events peaked again as a procession of villagers brought root crops, a large pig, a turtle, barkcloth, mats and Tongan oil and presented it to the Queen, who was again seated at the head of her kava. The procession was led by some middle-aged married women with painted faces expressing their 'warmth inside' (*loto māfana*) by clowning around or 'making happy' (*fakafiefia*) at this occasion of lavish generosity.[10] The wife of the minister of one of the local churches presented the 'basket', asking the Queen to accept the 'tiny' pig and turtle and the rest of the 'rubbish' they were bringing as a small token of gratitude and respect.[11] The Queen, herself, remained silent and immobile, with the Queen's 'talking chief' (*matāpule*) thanking the minister's wife for the generous gift on her behalf. The Queen was taken on a tour of the island and shown the 'twin waters' (*vai māhanga*) and the 'Hidden burial mound' (*Langi tuʻu lilo*) behind the cemetery. When she left, most of Kotu's people escorted her to the beach of the 'Great Landing' (*Fanga lahi*) and remained there to wave goodbye and cheer until her boat left *Namolahi* Lagoon for another island.[12]

At the village meeting the following month, the town officer thanked people for having 'done their duties' (*fai fatongia*) and 'carried their burdens' (*fua kavenga*). He thanked them for making contributions to the presentation of food, kava and wealth and for making themselves and the land itself orderly and beautiful for the Queen's visit. He thanked the women, especially, for having provided the barkcloth and mats to make this possible. He then went on to ask them if they would start the work of weaving a 15-foot mat to be presented to the King on the next anniversary of his reign. On behalf of the women, Meletoa asked to be heard, saying that the women of Kotu would be quite happy to start this work immediately and would be able to finish it in a few days. A man in his fifties wanted to know whether the other women thought likewise about this. Ana Afitu asked to be heard:

> I do not think that the men should worry about this thing. The town officer's wife is quite right. It shall be no problem for us to do our part of the duty of this land to the King. I do not know why this man asks whether we are able to do our duties. It is not the women of this island who waste their time playing cards and sleeping off from too much kava drinking. Who was it that did the work of preparing this island for the Queen's visit? Who was it that prepared the house in which the Queen slept to make it beautiful? Who provided the mats, the barkcloth and the Tongan oil for her welcome and for the royal basket? And what did the men do? It should have been the duty of the men of this island to go out fishing to get the 'goatfish' (*vete*), both for the feast of welcome of the Queen's following and for Taufatōfua's basket to the

King's House, but this was not done. The men should not worry about the duties of the women of this island!

After the meeting, Koloa agreed that the woman had been speaking the truth: 'She is quite right ... It is the women who carry most of the burdens of doing duties of various kinds. The men have become more lazy.' A man in his early forties, however, did not quite agree:

> It is true. The women fulfil their obligations by weaving and by providing barkcloth as they have done from the days of old, but the men are not lazy. The large pig and the turtle for the Queen's basket was bought for money earned by men working hard on Tōfua growing the kava or night diving in the lagoon. The money for the annual *misinale* collections of the church, where does it come from? It comes from the selling of kava and fish. And matters of the family: housing, clothing, the children's education ... Where does the money come from for all these things? If you build a 'Tongan house' (*faletonga*), the women can help in the weaving of the ropes and mattings for the roof, the floors and the walls. Even the children can help by bringing the things used to build a 'Tongan house'. Much kava growing and fishing must be done by the men to buy the things needed to build a wooden European house. The truth is that men work more now because everybody wants the money.

Ceremonial Process

In the following, I shall approach the process of preparing and presenting the kava, the 'food' (*ngoue*) and the 'wealth' (*koloa*) during the Queen's visit as a realization of a motion towards a 'well-ordered' (*maau*) state of appearances and creating an event of extraordinary 'importance' (*mahuʻinga*) by the imposition of strict and 'beautifying' (*fakaʻofoʻofa*) 'constraints' (*tapu*) on behaviour. I shall argue that the creation of the many events of extraordinary beauty and significance that were so characteristic of Kotu sociality in the last decades of the twentieth century involved action that may be interpreted to remove that which spontaneously or 'haphazardly crops up' (*tupu noa ʻia pē*) in the flow of ordinary everyday events. Relatively frequent ceremonial occasions stood out in sharp contrast to ordinary and haphazard events of no particular significance. Instead of just cropping up, happening or appearing as a result of whims and personal preferences, ceremonial events of extraordinary significance involved bodies, food and behaviour all aligned in a particular direction by a common purpose and a common attentiveness to a centre of orientation.

The imposition of strict constraints on action was very striking during the Queen's visit to Kotu. This was most obvious at what stood out as peaks in the ceremonial process of the Queen's visit; the kava drinking and gift presentation, where everything that happened was oriented towards the Queen. But attention to details, on how to proceed, on protocol and rules constituted an important theme throughout the process of preparation. One way of approaching the constraints of the Queen's *'ilokava* is to concentrate on the spatial organization of the kava ceremony as a tableau of ceremonial elaboration (Biersack 1991). According to the Tongan noble Ve'ehala, important occasions of kava drinking may best be characterized by the fact that: 'You can't move around freely;[13] you have to move according to this or that; there are regulations' (see Biersack 1991: 246). I would have been 'free to do as I pleased' (*fa'iteliha*), move about and take pictures, if I had not been sitting in the circle of the Queen's *'ilokava*. But in partaking, I was bound to the task at hand and immobilized by strict constraints. This makes it possible to view the constraints as increasing as events proceeded towards the pivotal point of the ceremonial process and as a characteristic of the inside as opposed to the outside of the ceremonial tableau. As proceedings move towards a pivotal point in the flow of events, a ceremonial tableau may be interpreted to come temporarily into being; a materialization of a highly differentiated order in which one criterion of ideal differentiation is elaborated to the exclusion of several other potential criteria of social differentiation: 'In the kava ceremony the principle of stratification by titles is marked off as clearly as possible from all other forms of social differentiation' (Bott 1972b: 217; see also Perminow 1995).

More than the momentary reality[14] of frozen order and importance, what intrigued me about the Queen's visit to Kotu was the process of transformation from the day when rumours about her visit first started to spread until she arrived, five days later, to head the kava ceremony of welcome. The 'Queen's visit' illustrates well what I perceive to be a general characteristic of ceremonial processes; events moved from the relatively disoriented practices of everyday interaction, via frequent, idealized instances of unambiguous orientation. These ideal orders were 'frozen' by constraints too demanding to last and, thus, soon lost their ideal orientation in favour of the practical and ambiguous realities of everyday life interaction. To me, the frozen moment of unambiguous orientation of the ceremonial tableau makes sense; first of all, in terms of the dramatic movement of a wider process of transformation. It may be that to Tongans, who consistently used the terms *maau* ('orderly') and *faka'ofo'ofa* ('beautiful') to describe the quality of occasions of unambiguous orientation, the value of such an occasion was precisely that it realized an ideal (or even unrealistic) state of affairs, defying the muddled realities of everyday life. Achieving such an unlikely occurrence, even for an instant, demands the strict constraint of other orientational potentials. It also demands a lot of creative effort aimed at making the land, its bodies, its provisions and other materials presentable. Aesthetics clearly played an important part in this achievement, and as Kaeppler does in her examination of the relationship between art, aesthetics and social structure in Tonga, I too shall focus on some 'cultural forms that result from creative processes that use or "manipulate" words, sounds, movements, materials, and spaces in such a way that they formalise or intensify the formalisation of the non-formal' (Kaeppler 1990: 60). I would agree with her proposition 'that aesthetic experiences in Tonga are realized when fundamental cultural principles are made specific in works of art (that is, when the deep structure is manifested in a cultural form resulting from creative processes that manipulate movement, sound, words, spaces, or materials)' (ibid.: 70). Like Firth, I would regard aesthetic experience to be produced by 'attributing meaningful pattern ... accompanied by a feeling of rightness in that order ... satisfying some inner recognition of values' (Firth 1992: 16). And also as Firth does, I would emphasize that aesthetic experience 'is never a purely passive condition; it involves some degree of ideational and emotional engagement with the relations suggested by the object' (ibid.).

The Force of Beauty

The strong emphasis on beautification, which characterized ceremonial processes on Kotu, may be approached in terms of the imposition of strict constraints: containing, masking, removing, isolating, separating and channelling forceful elements of human existence. The aesthetic value of the most important materials of personal beautification and public decoration in Tonga (as elsewhere in Polynesia; Gell 1995) may seem to be inextricably interwoven with their capacity to keep things apart. Thus, a part of what makes barkcloth decorative is that the potential capacity of the 'skin' of the tree (*kili*) to delimit has been potentiated by being worked upon according to strict procedures of production, transforming the grey 'skin/bark' (*kili*) of tiny trees that would appear to be of 'no account' (*noa*) into huge, colourful tableaus of outstanding order (*maau*) and significance. For instance, when 'Ahokava Lātū, the president of the Constitutional Church of Tonga, came to the funeral of his kinsman Amini Laukau on Kotu in 1991, a *ngatu* ('barkcloth') was placed on the ground at the head of the feast of welcome to emphasize the superiority of his position. Likewise, the superiority of the person of the highest ceremonial rank (*fahu*) at the same funeral seemed to utilize the power of *ngatu* to 'uplift'. The *fahu* was said to be free and liberated from restrictions to 'do as they pleased' (*fa'iteliha*) and had the privilege of sitting by the head of his deceased kinsman on the *ngatu* upon which the body of the deceased rested and that was *tapu* to all others. That *ngatu* was perceived to have the capacity to elevate was further indicated by the fact that the *fahu* additionally had the privilege of sitting on a chair, whereas all others sat on the floor. This capacity to elevate or achieve vertical differentiation, however, may seem to be an instance of a more fundamental capacity to keep things apart.

The perceived capacity of *ngatu* to isolate or keep things apart may be illustrated by its use in burying the dead. Kotu people agreed that it may be harmful for a person to be exposed to the bones of his or her patrilateral relatives of the first ascending generation. These bones were said to be 'taboo' (*tapu*). Since most graves are used several times on Kotu, the bones of those already buried in a grave were normally exposed during the digging of a grave. Before the body of the dead was lowered into the grave, persons to whom the bones were taboo were protected by those liberated from this taboo to 'do as they pleased' (*faʻiteliha*). Holding the edges of a large *ngatu* and raising their arms above their heads, they formed the *ʻā kolo* or 'village fence' of protection by encircling the grave. Only those free from taboo should be 'inside the fence' (*loto ʻā kolo*) during the burial. The protective capacity of *ngatu* was replaced by a 'village of people' (*kolo tangata*) when the number of kin 'free from restraint' was high enough to make it possible for them to form an 'enclosure of people' (*ʻā tangata*), standing shoulder to shoulder around the pit.

As for the dead body itself, it is first 'wrapped in a piece of *ngatu*' (*kofukofu he ngatu vala*), extending from the feet to the armpits. It is then encased, cocoon-like, in a larger piece of *ngatu*, treated with scented Tongan oil. The *ngatu*, itself, is made from the 'inner bark' (*kili maʻa* or 'clean bark' as opposed to the *kili ʻuli* or 'outer/dark/dirty bark') of the Paper mulberry tree (*hiapo*), referred to as its 'skin'[15] (*kili*) (See also Fanua 1986; Kaeppler 1990; Van der Grijp 1993: 61–62). The bark is beaten with a wooden mallet into paper thin strips that are pasted together by the use of parboiled 'arrowroot' (*mahoaʻa*) to form wider strips. The strips made out of the inner bark of the wider ends of the trunks are joined together to become a long sheet making up the 'upper layer/surface' (*lauʻolunga*) of the *ngatu*. Bark sheets made from the narrow ends of the trunks become the 'lower layer/underside' (*laulalo*) of the *ngatu*.

The body of the dead, then, may be said to receive several layers of extra skin of *ngatu*, separating the bones that remain from their underground environment when the body deteriorates. Although more resilient than the skin of the deceased, the *ngatu* eventually breaks down. The 'Tongan illness' (*mahaki fakatonga*) known as *akafia* ('full of roots'[16]) was widely held to be caused by the breakdown of what protects the remains of the human body from contact with underground forces of wild growth. Lea, the middle-aged son in my *ʻapi*, explained:

Sometimes the 'roots' (*aka*) of trees and bushes that are close to the grave grow into it and penetrate the *ngatu* in which the body of the dead has been wrapped. If the roots penetrate the bones of the deceased, this may cause pain or weakness for living kinsmen that may not be cured by Western medicine or those Tongan healing practices that treat the body of the one who is ill. If the leg bones are pierced by the roots, then it is the legs of the living that hurt or become weak. If the head is pierced by roots, it causes a headache that will not go away. Roots piercing the back cause chronic backaches.

I asked if anything could be done to cure such an illness. 'It can be cured,' claimed Lea, 'by going to the grave at night, opening it up and caring for the bones'. He continued:

> The bones must be unwrapped. Destroyed barkcloth must be replaced, and the roots that have penetrated them must be removed. Then the bones must be cleaned, treated with Tongan oil and properly wrapped in new *ngatu*. The grave must be inspected to make sure that the bones of the different persons that have been buried there have not shifted. One must make sure that they lie separately, not on top of each other.

Lea informed me that such a task was not the job of the person who is ill:

> When *akafia* is suspected to cause illness, the afflicted must tell some relative who is 'free/can do as one pleases' ('*atā/faʻiteliha*) to unearth the bones and care for them. Do you remember my mother's brother (*faʻētangata*) who lives on Tongatapu? He became very ill. His legs hurt and he was hardly able to walk. The illness did not pass, so he went to a soothsayer who could read cards and who told him that the cause of his pain was *akafia* of his father's bones buried here on Kotu. Since I am his sister's son ('*ilamutu*) and 'unrestrained' to the bones of my 'grandfathers' (*kuitangata*), he phoned me to ask for help. One night I and my son went to the grave and tended the bones properly. Immediately the pain went away, and he was healed.

Roots of Pain

To the best of my knowledge, the *akafia* syndrome remains unexplored. Whistler does mention it, however, in the glossary of his exploration of Tongan herbal medicine and defines it as: 'A type of headache thought to be caused by the growth of tree roots into the skull of a deceased relative. The cure is to exhume and carefully rebury the bones. This is probably what Churchward and Parsons called *haukivaʻe*'[17] (Whistler 1992: 111). In greater detail, *akafia* and its cure were related to processes and qualities pertaining to the substances of bones, roots, *ngatu* and Tongan oil. The processes that seemed to cause the sickness were wild growth and decay, while the cure consisted of weeding (the area close to the grave), removing roots from the bones, renewing *ngatu* and oiling the bones. Put differently, sickness seemed to result when the resilient 'skin' of protection, separating the most enduring remains of the body from its underground environment, gave way to the encroaching potency of wild growth. In all the cases referred to on Kotu where chronic illness was thought to result from *akafia*, the genealogical distance between the bones and the one who was sick was very short. There seemed to be no limit to the effective geographical reach of *akafia*; people who had left the *fonua* ('homeland/island') for other peripheral islands or for Nuku'alofa – or people who had settled overseas – who became the victims of *akafia* had to recruit the assistance of relatives who had remained on the *fonua* in order to regain health. Pain, then, seemed to be incurred by neglect of the relatively recent dead; in the course of letting their names slip from memory and thus dropping their names from everyday communication in the local community, their graves were no longer kept free of weeds as the multiple demands and possibilities of the present turned people to other tasks and other places. As the dead receded still further out of mention and memory, their bones seemed to become less bothersome, although persons of particular rank or local reputation seemed to linger on 'below the land' (*lolofonua*) and affect the living in the shape of 'beings of the other side/kind'.

A conversation about what happens when people die contained numerous 'ghost stories' about the dead of Kotu. As *tevolo* ('devils', 'spirits') or *fa'ahikehe* ('beings of the other kind'), they were known to leave their underground dwellings in the cemetery to roam about the wild bush and enter the village at night. Some held that the *fa'ahikehe* sometimes punished disrespectful behaviour by causing untimely death in the village. But most people felt that these beings were just 'naughty/evil' (*pau'u*) in nature; they often caused problems by entering someone's body, causing him or her to behave in a weirdly uncontrollable and unpredictable manner ('*āvanga*; 'sickness caused by a *fa'ahikehe/tevolo* spirit'; see also Cowling 1990b; Whistler 1992: 53–55; Gordon 1996).

The unease with the inevitability of the process by which the dead tend to be crowded out of mention and memory by the multiple urgencies and mobilities of the present may also be illustrated by the local practice of 'naming' (*fakahingoa*) children after a namesake. As Rogers reported from Niuatoputapu (Rogers 1975: 267), the naming of a child is considered to be an important formative event on Kotu because it represents one of the earliest efforts to 'build/construct/assemble' (*ngaohi*) the child by attaching it to the one choosing the name and the one after whom the child is named. The naming thus opens up for the child the possibility of forming a lasting bond with his or her name-giver, and the child is expected to develop a personal style resembling that of its namesake. Quite often, one of the elders of the 'father's side' (*faʻahi ʻo tamai*) is asked by the parents to be the name-giver. Several of the elder name-givers on Kotu felt that one of the good things about being asked to choose the name of the child was that it allowed them to stop personal names from slipping out of mention and memory by reviving names of persons from the past. Thus, one old man on Kotu expressed his satisfaction at having done a beautiful thing when he chose the name of a man 'that had been old and weak in my youth, so that this name shall not disappear from the land.'

The practices and possible meanings of 'naming' and 'root penetration' make up rich fields of exploration in their own right. I touch upon them here to illustrate the constitutive aspect of aesthetics; beautiful and shapely things (like a *ngatu*) and beautiful and orderly proceedings (like 'building a child' or drinking kava) constitute 'important' (*mahuʻinga*) events and contribute to counteract, harness or channel the strength of 'wild growth' (*tupu noaʻia*) or the muddled and manifold urgencies of everyday social living; the undergrowth from which important events stand out.

The Beauty of the *Lohu Loa* Harvesting Stick

The interrelatedness of the conceptions of beauty, order and importance came out clearly in the way people talked about the value of particular events. The terms *fakaʻofoʻofa* ('beauty', 'beautiful') *maau* ('well ordered', 'orderly') and *mahuʻinga* ('important') were often used as more or less interchangeable synonyms, all sharing the antonym of *noa/noaʻia* ('nought/ without value/ haphazard/insignificant/dumb/un-ordered/good for nothing/of no account') used by people trying to describe the aesthetic and functional significance of specific events. When witnessing or referring to kava party procedures, the proceedings at a funeral, the planting of the 'first yam' (*tokamuʻa*) or the kava, events of 'child building' (*ngaohi fanau*), the 'construction of a speech' (*ngaohi lea*), a 'dance' (*taʻolunga*) well-performed, a 'song' (*hiva*) well sung and so on, people would often shake their heads slowly, touched or moved by what they saw, and exclaim: '*Mālie ʻaupito! Ko e meʻa mahuʻinga ʻeni. Sio ai, fakaʻofoʻofa eh? … maau ʻaupito* ('How pleasing! Here is an important thing. Look, it is beautiful, isn't it? … very well ordered').

Having made the exclamation, people evidently felt that they had said all that was needed and were generally not inclined to elaborate further on the worth and meaning of the act or occasion. Being asked what it is that makes a funeral an 'important occasion' (*meʻa mahuʻinga*), however, Koloa elaborated:

One of the things that makes the funeral an important thing is that it makes clear to the young the 'manner of the land' (*anga fakafonua*) and the 'manner of the family' (*anga 'o e fāmili*). Things do not just happen 'aimlessly' (*noa'ia pē*) at the funeral but according to this or that making things that happen 'very well ordered' (*maau 'aupito*). The duties of the mother's side are different from the duties of the father's side; the 'leader of the funeral' (*tu'utu'uni 'o e putu*) is different from the 'ceremonial chief' (*fahu*); the 'working people' (*kau ngāue*) are different from the 'kava drinkers'; and those 'outside the funeral' (*tu'a 'o e putu*) are different from those of the 'body/substance of the funeral' (*sino 'o e putu*). All these different things are made clear because people perform different duties and must act and dress in different manners in the funeral. The dress and the *ta'ovala* ('plaited waist matting') of those 'outside' the funeral (*kautu'a*), the 'low side' (*mā'ulalo*), like the children and the 'younger brother's' (*kautehina*) of the dead … they must wear 'black colours' (*teunga'uli*) and the *motumotu* ('coarse plaited mat covering most of the body'); they must 'work at the fire' (*ngāue he afi*) to prepare the food 'outside the place of the funeral' (*'i tu'a mala'e*). The 'high side' (*mā'olunga*) … those of the 'body of the funeral' (*sino 'o e putu*) like the 'grandchildren' (*mokopuna*), the 'fathers' (senior relatives on the father's side), the sister's children; they are unrestrained and may stay close to the corpse 'inside the place of the funeral' (*'i loto mala'e*). They do not work and may wear 'white clothes' (*teungahina*) and a small and comfortable *ta'ovala*. At other times, it is difficult to know the manner of the land and the family because things happen haphazardly as people want to have this or that and 'twist and turn' (*'āmio*) in the manner of their living, but the funeral makes things clear. That is why I think the choice of the *tu'utu'uni 'o e putu* ('leader of the funeral') who receives and 'distributes' (*tufa*) the food and the *fahu* ('chief of the funeral') who receives the 'wealth' (*koloa*) is an important thing. Do you remember the funeral of Amini? Epalahame was the *fahu* in that funeral, and that was a very beautiful thing. Amini's father was Kilione, and the sister of Kilione was Hingano. Epalahame is the son of Hingano's daughter. Epalahame comes from the sister of Amini's father. According to my thinking, it is most beautiful to choose the *fahu* like that: 'according to the long harvesting stick' (*lohu loa*[18]); because then people may see the manner of the family and remember the people who lived on the land before. But often the *fahu* is chosen according to 'the crop and its harvesting stick' (*to'u kai mo hono lohu*[19]). At Amini's funeral, his 'sister' (*tuofefine*) wanted her own son, Amini's 'sister's son' (*'ilamutu*) to be the *fahu* of the funeral. When Amini learnt that his sister wanted her own son to be the *fahu* of his funeral, he did not like it and refused her. It is true; he is Amini's 'chief' (*'eiki*) and unrestrained, and important to Amini's 'generation' (*to'u*), but it would not be 'a long harvesting stick' (*lohu loa*). Also, Amini was the eldest, older than this sister (*tuofefine*) and the 'leading mother's brother' (*fa'ētangata pule*) of his sister's son. No, I think that choosing Epalahame was better. The long harvesting stick is 'more beautiful' (*faka'ofo'ofa ange*) …' more well-ordered' (*maau ange*). And the *tu'utu'uni* ('leader') of that funeral … was Tevita Fanua, and it was 'the long harvesting stick' (*lohu loa*). His father's father was the 'oldest brother' (*taʻokete*), and the father of Amini was among the 'younger brothers' (*kautehina*). In the manner of 'the harvesting stick of this year's crop' (*toʻu kai mo hono lohu*), Amini was Tevita's 'father' (*tamai* i.e. 'father's brother'), but in the manner of 'the long harvesting stick', Tevita is the 'head' (*ʻulumotuʻa*) of this 'family' (*fāmili*[20]) because he 'comes here' (*hoko mai*) from the oldest brother (*taʻokete*), while Amini comes here from a 'younger brother' (*tehina*). But during the funeral Tevita became very angry (*ʻita*) because one of Amini's younger brothers took away from Tevita the task of distributing the food of the funeral on the people. That was not a good thing; not in the manner of 'the long harvesting stick' (*lohu loa*). It did not make known to people much about the 'manner of the family' (*anga ʻo e fāmili*).

The intimately interrelated capacities of 'beauty' (*fakaʻofoʻofa*), 'order' (*maau*) and 'importance' (*mahuʻinga*) to create moments of optimal separateness from a general flow of 'aimless' events that are of 'no account' because of things happening *noaʻia pē* ('haphazardly') may also be illuminated semantically. The core of the term *mahuʻinga* ('importance', 'important'), *mahuʻi*, may seem familiar from the foregoing exploration of tidal and diurnal dynamics. Thus, it was first encountered in the exploration of the conceptualization of the tidal motion of ebb tide – that is, the motion of separation from 'high tide' (*tau ʻa e tahi*) to 'low tide' (*mamaha ʻa e tahi*); *mahuʻi ʻa e tahi ke mamaha*. *Mahuʻi* means literally 'to wrench, tear apart or separate forcefully' (a branch wrenched from a tree, a child weaned away from the mother's breast and so on). The noun- forming suffix *-nga* pertains to 'the thing that achieves', the quality described by the semantic core or 'the grounds/reason for this quality'. For instance, according to Churchward (Churchward 1953: 239), *mālohi* signifies 'strong' while *mālohi-nga* signifies 'that which strengthens'. Thus, it is possible to interpret the term *mahuʻi-nga* to signify 'that which forcefully wrenches apart', 'the grounds on which something is separated' or, in other words, a powerful criterion by which something is thrown into relief by causing other things of potential prominence to melt into the background. This is, no doubt, to some degree how 'importance' must be constituted everywhere, but 'importance' is not everywhere so strongly and consistently coupled with what constitutes 'beauty'. The strong linkage between the conception of *maau* ('orderly', 'well ordered') and moving events evoking pleasurable feelings was first of all made clear by the look of satisfaction and admiration on the faces of those who made these exclamations. But this linkage may also be illuminated semantically. Thus, the writing of Tongan poetry, utilizing the evocative potentials of Tongan linguistic imagery most fully, is referred to as *fatu maau* or *faʻu maau*, meaning to 'create/make/build/compose/construct' (*faʻu/ fatu*) 'order/orderliness' (*maau*).

The Force of 'Warmth Inside'

The term *faka'ofo'ofa* ('beautiful', 'beauty'), itself, may be interpreted in terms of the capacity of events and things to evoke states of internal motion, the perception of which appeared to touch people 'inside' (*'i loto*); to strike a chord calling forth people's capacity to engage one another in events of social cooperation. The morphological core of the term *faka'ofo'ofa* ('beauty/beautiful') is *'ofa* ('love/compassion') reduplicated for intensification (-*'ofo'ofa*) and prefixed by the causative *faka-*. *Me'a 'ofa* or 'thing of love' is the Tongan expression for a concrete 'gift/present', but the emphasis is on the act of giving more than the thing given. The point is that generous deeds of giving may be seen as acts that express and evoke *'ofa* ('love/compassion') as a state of being that has moved beyond the confines of self-sufficiency and self-interest to engage the surrounding world. A possible semantic interpretation of the term *faka'ofo'ofa* ('beauty/beautiful') would be 'causing internal *'ofa*' or, simply, 'intensely moving'. A related term *faka'ofa*, consisting of the morphological core *'ofa* and the causative prefix *faka-*, but without the intensifying reduplication, is by Churchward interpreted to mean precisely 'moving/stirring (to pity)'. This interpretation of the constitutive force of 'beauty' to cause internal transformation in terms of being 'stirred' or 'moved' seems consonant with the description of engagement and deeply felt commitment in terms of being 'warm inside' (*loto māfana*[21]).

I realize that the interpretation of 'love/compassion' as moving or stirring to break out of isolation and self-sufficiency presupposes the existence of a notion of a human desire or predisposition to withdraw from the world and remain isolated and self-sufficient. This may seem to contradict some conventions of thinking about the difference between the 'West' and the 'Other'. Indeed, individual isolation and self-sufficiency seem often to have been thought of as characteristic traits of 'Western ways of life' as opposed to those of the 'Other'. As Bradd Shore claims also to be the case for Samoans, Tongans 'live most of their lives in a very public arena' (Shore 1982: 148), as 'powerful norms of social life … keep people in almost constant social interaction' (ibid.: 148). Like Samoans, Tongans would rarely claim that they like being by themselves. As social isolation is generally understood 'to encourage antisocial urges and acts' (ibid.: 148), such a claim would be morally questionable. Thus, the ideological emphasis on visibility and participation in the public arena did not seem to be produced by notions of inherent desirability but by notions of moral necessity. A perceived human disposition to withdraw and the general desirability of being self-sufficient and of being left in peace from demands of intense socializing, in general, and 'open- handedness' (*nimahomo*) or generosity, in particular, indeed seemed to constitute an undercurrent in most moral discourses on Kotu. A Western couple moved to Kotu in 1990 and decided that the village was too crowded and noisy and so arranged to live by themselves in the plantation area. People seemed to have no problem understanding that they found it desirable to do so. Several did, however, question the morality of their choosing to withdraw from the social intensity of village living, and they frequently asked one another, 'What are they talking about up there? What are they eating on their own? What secret things are they up to out there in the bush?'

People did not treat the chronic demands for intense socializing and generosity that characterized everyday village living as something inherently desirable, to be taken for granted, and they were very conscious that it involved both a strong resolve and an effort to defy an understandable desire for withdrawal and self-sufficiency. The very acts of taking part in the proceedings of a funeral, 'composing a speech' (*ngaohi lea*) or going to a kava party and presenting a 'novel/original' (*fo'ou*) or 'entertaining' (*mālie*) story were treated as generous 'gifts/things of love' (*me'a 'ofa*). Thus, a man who very seldom went to kava parties on Kotu was, when he made one of his rare appearances, received with the ironic greeting *malo 'e fakamotu*; literally, 'congratulations on coming away from your island' (i.e. isolation). People would sometimes, during streams of events involving particularly numerous or strenuous 'duties' (*fai fātongia*) and 'solicitations' (*fai kole*), exclaim: '*Fakahela mo'oni 'a e anga fakatonga eh!*' ('The Tongan way is in truth exhausting, isn't it!'). One generous fisherman, coming ashore with a nice catch after having spent several hours spear-diving, made this same exclamation when he returned to his *'api* with about a fourth of the catch intact, the rest having been given away in response to fish-less villagers' 'solicitations' (*kole*). Likewise, this exclamation was sometimes made by my companions to express sympathy on days when particularly numerous solicitations demanded my own attention. People all agreed that it was a 'good thing to beg' (*sai kole*) for things and assistance. But they evidently also felt that it represented exhausting work, taxing their personal 'strength' or 'energy' (*ivi*) to 'respond to solicitations' (*tali 'a e kole*). Comments about the 'exhausting Tongan way' were not only, or even primarily, made with reference to materially costly demands but with reference to a concentration of numerous solicitations for material trifles of everyday consumption that disturbed one's peace or contributed to distract one from whatever one was doing. Again, the desirability of not being disturbed, of not being distracted from one's purpose and of holding onto whatever assets one might control by declining to respond positively to acts of solicitation did seem to be highly understandable to all, albeit morally questionable, to say the least.[22]

Wild and Cultivated Growth

I have emphasized that the efforts of beautification characterizing ceremonial processes in Tonga may be described in terms of the imposition of strict constraints, containing, masking, removing, isolating, separating and channelling constitutive forces. The aesthetic value of the most important materials of personal beautification, such as the *ta'ovala* ('plaited waist matting'), used to cover up parts of the body, and scented 'Tongan oil' (*lolo fakatonga*) and 'garlands' (*kahoa*) of fragrant flowers, used to create a mask of scent, may be approached in a similar manner to that used with reference to the significance of *ngatu* above. One of the things that was emphasized regarding scented oils, 'Tongan soap' (*koa fakatonga*[23]) and fragrant flowers was their 'nice smell' (*namu lelei*) in situations that would otherwise be dominated by odours emerging from within the body. Thus, several persons on Kotu accounted for the custom of giving away garlands of fragrant flowers at leave-takings for their capacity to create an atmosphere of *namu lelei* during an uncomfortable voyage that might otherwise be dominated by the 'reek/putrid smell' (*namu palaku*) of seasickness. Similarly, fragrant flowers were always used to create an atmosphere of *namu lelei* at sick- or death beds by being placed in the containers into which those who were ill spat or vomited.

Noa/noa'ia[24] ('of no account/worthless/aimless/disarrayed/insignificant/haphazard') is a central concept in the context of kava ceremonies and other ceremonial processes involving efforts to beautify and establish occasions of importance. The interrelated concepts of *faka'ofo'ofa* (beauty), *maau* ('well-ordered/orderliness') and *mahu'inga* ('importance') all exist in opposition to things that are *noa/noa'ia*. All of these qualities appear to be what mark extraordinary occasions or that throw them into relief against a background of unmarked events. According to Johansen, who studied Maori everyday religiosity in the 1950s, 'The term *noa* does not mean "polluted", but rather "free", "nothing", "unmarked", and "unconstrained." It suggests action that is unguided, without purpose or destination. The profane, *noa*, thus characterizes everyday life, in which everything happens more informally and freely, but also more casually and haphazardly' (Johansen, see Shore 1989: 166). ' ... If these associations are accurate, then *tapu* conversely means "contained" or "bound", suggesting the creative (and hence sacred) containment of *mana*, and the concomitant subordination of humans to its divine wellspring' (ibid.).

In the everyday flow of communication on Kotu, however, *noa* was not usually used as the antonym of *tapu*. In most contexts, the first choice of antonym for *tapu* was *fa'iteliha* ('to be unrestrained' or *'atā* ('free')), while people used *maau* (well-ordered, orderly), *faka'ofo'ofa* and *mahu'inga* to describe opposite qualities of *noa/noaʻia*. Thus, young men on Kotu sometimes returned dejectedly from an unsuccessful search for available kava parties exclaiming: 'Ko fonua taʻeole moʻoni ko Kotu! ʻOku tapu pē ʻa e touʻa kotoa pē he poʻoni' ('Kotu is in truth a boring place! All the kava girls are taboo tonight'). One of the most consistent behavioural aspects of the brother-sister relationship of mutual 'respect' (*fakaʻapaʻapa*) was that a man should not join a kava party at which his cross-sex sibling prepared the kava. The form and content of communication at kava parties was understood to be at odds with the restraint that should characterize brother-sister interaction (Rogers 1975, 1977; Perminow 1993a, 1995). When, on the other hand, women referred to as 'new kava girls' (*touʻa foʻou*) prepared the kava (that is, women who are not siblings), the young men would say: 'Ko touʻa foʻou ai. ʻOku atā pē ʻe tamaiki ki ai' ('There is a new kava girl there. The boys are free to go there').

Thus, *ʻatā* ('free') and *faʻiteliha* ('to do as one pleases, to be unrestrained') seem conceptually linked to *tapu* ('constraint/constrained') by strongly implying the liberation from potential or specific 'constraints' (*tapu*). *Noa/noaʻia*, on the other hand, did not seem to presuppose *tapu* or constraints in the same way; it pertained to a state produced by acts neither explicitly nor implicitly constrained by, nor liberated from, a purposeful procedure. Thus, it referred to things that just crop up from within the dim reaches of whatever it is that constitutes the source of personal desires and motivations, much as wild weeds crop up to grow *noaʻia pē* (*tupu noaʻia pē*; 'grow/crop up aimlessly/all over') from within the dim reaches of that which constitutes the source of growth. Given the way these terms were used on Kotu, *noa* may perhaps best be understood to pertain to a kind of natural, untamed potency undifferentiated and unrefined by purposeful procedures. *Tapu* ('constraints'), personal beautification and decoration involving the use of materials and procedures isolating and separating elements from each other may perhaps best be understood as a purposeful channelling or harnessing of undomesticated *noa* qualities always threatening to spill indiscriminately out of a melting pot of wild potency. In this perspective, *tapu* (constraints) and 'beauty' (*fakaʻofoʻofa*) may be said to make kava ceremonies or food presentations marked or 'outstanding/important' (*mahuʻinga*) occasions because they effect a transition from a state of affairs of *noaʻia* to a state of affairs of *maau* (orderliness, being well proportioned). I perceive the process of transforming human existence from states of *noa* to states of *maau* as a very persistent theme of Tongan ceremonial aesthetics and sociality and one that certainly engaged people on Kotu in the last decades of the twentieth century. It appears to go more or less without saying that social realities might easily come to be wholly dominated by qualities of *noa*; unpredictability, uncertainty, aimlessness, haphazardness, lack of respect, disobedience, self-sufficiency, greed, unchecked strength, wild growth and aimless creativity. It was as if such a 'natural' and chaotic state of affairs may only be escaped by staging, again and again, events that transformed states of *noa* into states of *maau*, albeit as momentary glimpses of exemplary orderliness. This was, in a sense, an unrealistic, unidimensional orderliness that demanded so much effort, so much unitedness of purpose and such strict constraints on personal conduct that it could not but collapse. Thus, the peaks or pivotal points of ceremonial processes were always quite quickly done with before cross purposes, variations in personal preferences and an inherent desirability to be liberated 'to please oneself/be/free' (*faʻiteliha/ʻatā*) returned things to a default state dominated by a flow of events of 'no account' (*noa*).

Dumb Truths about Human Nature

At one point I discussed with one of my Tongan friends what may be called the *noa* aspect of being Tongan in terms of conceptions of personhood. I argued that Tongan conceptions of personhood seemed to involve a conviction that people share an unlimited capacity for deceit, greed, violence and sexual aggression. He did not seem to think that this represented an extraordinary insight or that this was peculiar to *Tongan* conceptions of the person. To his mind, it was not a truth about Tonga or Tongans at all but rather a general truth about human nature. I have not met any Tongans who did not take for granted that this rather pessimistic view of human nature constitutes a natural reality and thus a fundamental challenge for morality and sociality.

These 'truths' about human nature may be described as the *noa* aspect of the person, not only in the sense of being 'without order/chaotic' but also in the sense of being 'dumb', 'nought' or 'good for nothing' (all of which *noa* signifies) as a theme of discourse. The relevance of dumb truths was indicated in another discussion with Koloa, when a friend came to visit me during fieldwork on Kotu. Koloa complained that my friend was not *malimali* or 'smiling'. For Koloa, the main criterion of not being *malimali* other than facial expression is that no effort is made, actively or responsively, to look others in the eyes. As a guest, he said, one should wear a 'lively/attentive face' (*mata moʻui*). When I objected that people's faces vary and that some may look more melancholy than others, he said that everybody is able to 'compose a good face' (*ngaohi mata lelei*) if they wanted to and made an effort. I retreated to another line of defence on behalf of my visitor, saying that it could be a rather overwhelming experience to come all the way around the world to a Pacific village where everything is different and new to you. I argued that this may have made my friend tired, insecure and withdrawn. I went on to argue that, according to our customs, it may sometimes be considered insincere to 'put on a happy face' if this does not correspond with how you feel 'inside' (*'i loto*). He laughed then, saying that the *anga fakapālangi* ('European way') was not good for much if it did not make you realize that the relationship between the 'inside' (*loto*) and how you act is the other way round: 'When you compose a happy face you change what you feel inside, making it the same as your face.'

Like Samoans, then, my Tongan informants appeared to take a Hobbesian view of 'human nature' (Shore 1982: 157). Thus, one may perhaps characterize the Tongan conception of the dim reaches of private experience as related to: ' … a conception of forces that are understood as an ineradicable residue of destructive energy or will, against which social life is set' (ibid.: 148). The relationship between this 'ineradicable residue of energy or will' – what I have called a 'melting pot' of personal capacities and desires – and social conduct may in my view be seen as analogous to the relationship between the indispensable phase of merging in the procreative motion of growth, regeneration and cultivation – that is, if nothing is done to channel or work with the force or growth potentials generated by this motion, weeds or plants 'of no account' will 'crop up haphazardly' (*noa 'ia pē*) to crowd out the 'important' (*mahu'inga*) cultivated plants on which humans depend for survival. My findings indicate that people shared an assumption about the existence of reaches of personal (emotional, creative, destructive) potentials 'within' (*'i loto*) that were patently 'unfathomable' and 'chaotic' (*noa*) as well as 'useless' or 'nought' (*noa*) as a topic of discourse. In a sense, perhaps, being *malimali*, or 'composing a happy face', and other efforts to create a bright and shining visage can be viewed as a personal process (or ritual) of transforming human existence from a state of *noa* to a state of *maau*. The analytical significance of focusing on the whole process of personal and spatial beautification and ceremonial elaboration, rather than the end product of beauty and order, is that the moments of beauty and order may be seen to gain constitutive potency from people's energetic and enthusiastic commitment, steadily increasing as procedures of preparation force a wedge of order, beauty and enlightenment (*maau/faka'ofo'ofa/maama*) into an inherently unfathomable, unpredictable, changing and murky existence (*noa/fakapo'uli*). This focus involves a perspective on ceremonial aesthetics and personal beautification not first of all as frozen tableaus, celebrating or expressing a particular state of social or personal order, but rather as active ingredients in processes constituting and reconstituting the person, as well as the social relationships that constitute and reconstitute community, by people's active commitment to rework and refine the raw materials of human existence into resources of human sociality. The rare occasion of a visit by the Queen of Tonga to Kotu represents a dramatic example of ceremonial transformation. Less extraordinary sequences of events, in which people nevertheless seemed to dedicate themselves to create moments of 'beauty'/'order'/'importance' (*faka'ofo'ofa/maau/mahu'inga*), frequently occurred to break the monotonous flow of everyday village life. The most illuminating example of constitutively powerful processes of transformation (apart from the frequent occasions of kava drinking; see Perminow 1993a, 1995), by which quite concrete raw materials of human existence may be said to be transformed into resources of personal and social (re-) constitution, was perhaps the frequent staging of feasts; *kaipola* or *kai fakaafe*. In order to pave the way for an interpretation of the constitutive significance of feasting in the local community, it is first necessary to present local eating practices in general against a background of which the *kaipola* and the *kai fakaafe* stood out in sharp relief.

Everyday Eating

On Kotu, everyday meals did not seem to have a fixed time of occurrence, although meals were loosely referred to as *kai pongipongi* ('morning meal'), *kai ho'atā* ('midday meal') and *kai efiafi* ('afternoon/evening meal') (See also Rogers 1975: 328). The actual timing of meals was, first of all, influenced by the accessibility of *me'akiki*; the ingredients of a meal that complemented the staple *me'akai* of manioc, taro, yams, sweet potatoes and breadfruit to make up what was considered a complete and satisfying meal. Since fish was the overwhelmingly predominant *me'akiki* of the main everyday meal on Kotu, the availability of fresh fish was a sort of timekeeper of everyday eating. The importance of the availability of seafood for the timing of the meals on Kotu is well illustrated by a statement made by a visitor from Tongatapu in 1991: 'The sea decides when to eat here on Kotu!'

As a first rule of thumb, everyday eating moved to the rhythm of the tides. It did so because most fishing activities followed the tides and people generally preferred to eat as soon as possible after the fish had been brought ashore. However, everyday eating was made more complex by the rhythm of other natural phenomena of varying periodicity. First of all, as we saw in the previous chapter, the amount of natural light during the night varies over the four quarters of the moon. This in its turn affected 'night fishing' (*ama uku*). *Ama uku* involved the use of an electric torch and spear. On dark nights with no moonlight, the fish, which were said to be sleeping, 'stayed put' (*nofo maau*) when the torch was shined upon them and were most easily speared at low tide. If, on the other hand, the moon was up to illuminate the *Namolahi* Lagoon, the fish were said to be awake and would dart about much as they would during the daytime, making them hard to catch. In the second quarter of the moon, the conditions for night fishing were said to deteriorate with a waxing moon staying up increasingly far into the night. As we have seen earlier, sunset and moonrise coincide around full moon and alternate to provide illumination throughout the diurnal cycle. 'Reciprocal day' (*fē'aho'aki*) was said to leave no part of the night with conditions suitable for night fishing. During the third quarter, moonrise lags increasingly behind sunset, leading to a growing number of early nights, referred to as the 'dark ones' (*kaupo'uli*), in true darkness. Around the fourth quarter of the moon, the period of darkness comes to encompass the occurrence of low tide to again provide optimal conditions for night diving. These conditions last for at least the last quarter of one lunation and the first quarter of the next.

The basic significance of these natural rhythms for everyday eating was that they decided exactly when fresh fish was available and thus when it would be time for the main meal of the day. During the first and last quarters of the moon, night fishing would often make fresh fish available from the early morning, and so the main meal more frequently occurred well before noon. For some of the men, it even occurred before sunrise, as returning from a long night of kava drinking they would have a meal of fresh fish before going to sleep. During the second and third quarters, on the other hand, fresh seafood would normally be acquired through daytime 'net fishing' (*kupenga*), 'hook and line fishing' (*taumata'u*, 'octopus lure fishing' (*maka feke*) and 'shellfish/seaweed collecting' (*fingota*) whenever the tide was suitable during the day. Thus, the main meal would more frequently occur in the afternoon or evening during those quarters of the moon. Also, there are natural seasonal variations influencing the level of activity of night diving. The temperature of the sea drops markedly during the 'cool season' (*taimi momoko*), making night diving less attractive in the months from May through September. Thus, the range within which the occurrence of the main meal varied was not constant over the year. Additionally, natural occurrences of a more haphazard nature influenced eating times, first of all by periodically reducing the availability of fish. As may be recalled, the conditions referred to as *loka 'a e namo* ('the lagoon is on the move/astir') transform the *Namolahi* Lagoon into a troubled seascape of forceful currents in the lagoon to make fishing impracticable. Sometimes, strong winds or stormy weather make the sea too rough for fishing, leaving people to complement the staple components of the full meal with corned beef, occasionally available mutton flaps, an occasional chicken or whatever meat they could lay claim to.

Occasions such as funerals involved huge amounts of meat or fish often served to detach everyday eating from the rhythm of the marine environment. When a person died, a significant amount of food was 'distributed to each home' (*tufa faka'api*) in the village and eaten over the next week or so. Also, when Kotu people participated in the funerals of deceased relatives on nearby islands of Ha'apai, they would bring back their share of the funerary food presentation and redistribute it to neighbours, friends and relatives. Thus, funerals and other occasions where food was presented and distributed trickled into the flow of everyday eating as an unlooked for albeit welcome opportunity to include in the everyday diet high status food like yam, pork, horse meat, turtle, skipjack tuna and so on. Events of everyday eating, then, may be said to occur in an ad hoc fashion, being influenced by multiple movements, combinations and coincidences in the natural and social environments. Everyday eating appeared to be *noa'ia pē* ('of no account', 'insignificant' and 'good for nothing') in the sense of not having a specific purpose or aim (apart from that of reconstituting oneself by regaining personal strength[25]), cropping up 'haphazardly' (*noa'ia*) as a result of the unpredictable combination of other events. It may be described as 'non-ordered' (*noa'ia*) in the sense of not being dominated by specific procedures oriented around a pivotal point of reference producing a specific order of differentiation. People seldom sat down together but ate their food by themselves at different stages of preparation and according to their personal preference, their whims and fancies. Some would merely grab a piece of boiled manioc, roasted breadfruit or sweet potato and a fish and sit down under a tree, or eat standing up somewhere in the *'api*. Some would have the fish raw; others would bring their fish to the fire to roast it before eating or wait until the fish had cooked in boiling water.

One might think some of the constraints pertaining to the imperative of behaving with respect and deference towards sisters, fathers and elder brothers would remain at meal times, to give all occasions of eating a specific order, but the ideal that the father of the home should have his food before the children was very seldom realized. On the contrary, most children ate before their parents because they were usually simply given a piece of root crop and a raw fish, while grown-ups generally had the patience to wait for the fish to be roasted or boiled. Similarly, the ideal that a brother and sister should not eat together was seldom put into practice because of the general absence of commensality at everyday events of eating.

To sum up, then, the timing of everyday eating was influenced by the rhythm of surrounding dynamics and events for making *me'akiki* (a non-starchy food source, such as fish) available. In its organization, it was relatively unordered, characterized by a lack of commensality and dominated by individual tastes and preferences with regard to preparation and whether to sit down or eat standing up.

Ngaohi Pola; 'Building Boards of Food'

Some eating events and/or food presentations stood out sharply against the backdrop of everyday eating routines. Such extraordinary feasts were referred to by the terms *kai fakaafe* ('eat by invitation') and/or *kaipola* ('eating the board of food'). A third term *kai 'umu* ('eating the earth oven') primarily referred to the family meal that routinely followed the main 10 AM church service on Sundays. This did not involve a prolonged and elaborate process of preparation and collaboration between a large number of kinsmen, neighbours, friends and fellow worshippers. To the extent that it did involve cooperation between 'homes', it was in the form of 'mutual help' (*fetokoniaki*) from close kin and neighbours to achieve a well-balanced meal (see also Rogers 1975: 339). The most salient characteristic of the *kai 'umu* seemed to be that of communion and sharing. In contrast, the *kai fakaafe* and the *kaipola* had a more public profile and involved a much stronger emphasis on a protocol involving differentiation and separation.

Kai fakaafe, according to Churchward, refers to feasts to which specific persons have been invited. On Kotu, it was mostly used to refer to food presentations involving prominent members of the church and congregation during the 'week of praying' (*uike lotu*) at the beginning of the year, as well as other feasts related to the church schedule, such as 'quarterly church district meetings' (*kuata*), the annual 'congregational missionary collect' (*misinale*) and the annual 'church conference' (*konfelenisi 'o siasi*). Finally, the term *kaipola* was used as a general term of reference for a variety of events of food presentation and eating that accompanied occasions on which persons were installed to social positions or that constituted or reasserted social relationships. Thus, *kaipolas* were prepared as 'feasts of welcome' (*kai talitali*), as 'feasts of goodbye' (*kai fakamavae*), as feasts marking the first and twenty-first birthday (*fai'aho*), when a person was admitted to the group of preachers in the congregation (*hū ki he kau malanga*), and so on.

To understand the significance of these events in a manner that may do justice to their importance for the people who created them, I shall approach the culinary tableaus of 'beauty', 'order' and 'importance' in the context of their making. Rather than focusing on the *kaipola* at which food has been placed in an orderly fashion as a fixed and stable tableau, I shall first of all focus on the 'building/assembling of the board of food' (*ngaohi pola*). Moved by a 'warmth inside' (*loto māfana*) to commit to the task of 'building' (*ngaohi*) such a tableau, people seemed to generate yet more 'warmth' within themselves and others. By the 'warmth' of their mutual commitment, people devoted themselves to utilizing their common creative capacity to stage stable moments of unidimensional 'separateness/

importance' (*mahu'inga*) 'torn loose' (*mahu'i*) from the flux of multiple contingencies of ordinary everyday life.

The 'building/assembling of a board of food' (*ngaohi pola*), then, may be said to stand out as the achievement of a momentary glimpse of clear, single and definite order by people using their joint capacity to separate and differentiate. Thus, the process may be described in the following way. From the point of view of persons accepting the responsibility to 'build a board of food', resources must be marshalled and ingredients must be collected by utilizing any connection that may contribute to presenting a 'well proportioned' (*maau*) and 'beautiful and moving' (*faka'ofo'ofa*) *kaipola* to mark an 'important' (*mahu'inga*) event. 'Close kinsmen' (*kāinga ofi*) in the community, 'neighbours' (*kaungā'api*) and 'fellow worshippers' (*kau lotu*) were said to 'just offer assistance' ('*ō mai pē ke tokoni*) out of 'love/compassion' ('*ofa pē*) or as a part of more or less stable relations of 'mutual assistance' (*fetokoniaki/fe'ofa'ofani*) (Rogers 1975: 143; Decktor Korn 1978: 407). People did not generally account for the help they received or offered in terms of kin relationships, although one of the strongest ideals of kin interaction in Tonga is that kin should help one another (Cowling 1990a: 192). People emphasized that *fetokoniaki* was a matter of doing something out of a feeling of '*ofa* more than of having the 'same blood' (*toto tatau*). 'Blood'-relatedness seemed to be one among several potential relationships to be utilized in assembling a 'board of food' and was of particular significance when it came to acquiring choice ingredients that were hard to obtain locally. Thus, the Kotu phone booth[26] was very busy with people calling relatives who had moved to Nuku'alofa. Although not among the obligatory ingredients (being pork and yam, and extra-local and imported food such as melons, onions, corned beef chop-suey), boxes of soft drink and sweets were, when possible, incorporated into the food tableau to make it an outstanding presentation. Such sweet and colourful elements were referred to as *teuteu*, signifying 'decoration'. And indeed, such ingredients laid out neatly on the *pola* was perceived to add to its 'beauty'.

The next step involved 'building an earth oven' (*ngaohi 'umu*) by placing firewood and stones in a hole in the ground and 'lighting it up' (*faka'afu*; lit. 'make hot and steamy'). The 'red hot stones' (*kakaha*) were then 'spread out' (*ū*) in the hole and 'covered with leaves' (*lepo'i*) before the 'wrapped' (*kake'i*) and unwrapped ingredients were 'placed' in the pit (*ta'o*), 'covered with a layer of plantain leaves' (*tau*) and 'buried' with earth (*tanu*). Most foods were placed indiscriminately or without a particular order (*noa'ia pē*), but some were placed in close proximity to the stones. Once the food was 'cooked' (*moho*) in the 'steam and heat' ('*afu*) of the 'oven' (*ngoto'umu*), it was 'opened up' (*fuke 'a e 'umu*) by removing the earth and the 'leaf covering' (*tou-mohomoho*). The 'cooked food of the oven' (*fei'umu*) was then 'lifted out' (*hiko*) carefully (it was not to be handled haphazardly). The food was then first placed in separate heaps according to its kind and then placed on the *pola* according to its rank and worth. Thus, the most prestigious or most highly-ranked food was placed towards the 'frontal/preceding end' (*muʻa*) of the *pola*, with food of decreasing worth or rank placed down the length of the *pola* and hence 'following after' (*mui mai*) the food 'leading the way' (*muʻa mai*) towards the focal position at the 'front of the board' (*muʻa ʻo e pola*).

The individual pieces of the *kahokaho/tokamuʻa* ('first (early) yam') and other prestigious root crops (the 'frontal/head' (*kongamuʻa/ʻulu*) 'middle' (*kongaloto*) or 'posterior' (*kongamui*)) were examined to determine where they should be placed on the board. The 'chiefly' *kahokaho* yam was also referred to as *tokamuʻa*, signifying a 'preceding/foundational' crop. The *tokamuʻa* was recognized as a key crop with a capacity to mature faster than other kinds of yams and root crops and was planted in a small section of the garden referred to as the *maʻala*. It was often described by elder farmers on Kotu in terms of precedence; '*Toki muʻa mai ʻe tokamuʻa hoko mui mai pē ʻe tokamui/tokalahi*' ('The first crop leads the way here and then the late/big crop follows in its wake'). Elsewhere (see Perminow 2001), I argued that the '*inasi* presentation of 'first fruit' to the *Tuʻi Tonga* and his son, which was witnessed by Captain Cook on Tongatapu at the beginning of July 1777, made good sense as part of a year cycle ritual related to the growth of the *tokamuʻa* crop 'leading the way' (*muʻa mai*) so that the *tokamui* crop that was about to be planted might 'follow in its wake' (*mui mai*).

As a crop 'leading the way', older farmers felt that it was important that the business of planting the *kahokaho* yam in the *maʻala* should not be done 'whimsically' or 'without order' (*noaʻia*), as may be recalled. Koloa described just which planting strategy should be followed in order to make the *maʻala* an 'important/outstanding' (*mahuʻinga*), 'well-ordered' (*maau*) and 'beautiful' (*fakaʻofoʻofa*) thing. One should differentiate between the 'frontal section/head' (*konga muʻa/ʻulu*), the 'middle section' (*konga loto*) and the 'posterior section' (*konga mui*) of the 'mature yams/seed yams' (*ʻufimotuʻa*) set aside from the previous crop to be 'cut up' (*matofi*) and multiplied for planting.

> Do you see the small piece that is attached to the 'head of the yam' (*ʻuluʻi ʻufi*)? That is the piece of the 'old yam' (*ʻufi motuʻa*). The 'son' (*foha*) originated from it. By that you know what is the 'head of the yam' (*ʻuluʻi ʻufi*). You should not plant the *kahokaho* yam 'haphazardly' (*noaʻia pē*) but plant the pieces in separate rows according to which part of the seed yam they come from. The 'sons' of the old yam 'originating/growing/emerging' (*tupu*) from the pieces of the front grow faster than those of the middle, which in their turn grow faster than those of the last part of the yam. This

makes your *ma'ala* 'well proportioned' (*maau*) and very 'beautiful' (*faka'ofo'ofa*). You can see in it the 'nature/manner of growth' (*anga 'oe tupu*).

Among meat, pork was described as having the highest rank, but modes of carving up the slaughtered pig as well as the resulting pieces of pork were also ranked among themselves. Thus, Koloa set apart as a 'more important thing' (*me'a mahu'inga ange*) the mode of 'carving up the pig along the throat' (*tafa puaka fakakioa*), by separating all of the 'underside' (*lalo*) of the pig, from the joint of the 'upper jaw' (*loungutu 'olunga*) and the 'lower jaw' (*loungutu lalo*) to the area between the tail and the anal opening. After dividing the pig, the 'upper side' was separated into four sections of decreasing rank: *tu'a 'i puaka* ('mid-back'), *'ulu* (head and neck), *hiku* ('lower back') and *mui'ulu* ('upper back'). Except for the liver (*ate*), which should be 'passed forward' (*ate ki mu'a*) to the chief (during the process of preparing the feast), and the rectum (*lemu*), sexual organs and bladder (*tangai mimi*), which should be buried (to prevent the dogs from eating them), the 'entrails' (*to'oto'onga*) should be eaten by the 'working people' (*kau ngāue*). The fat around the 'intestines' (*ngakau*) was said to be very 'tasty' (*ifo*) and particularly important for 'renewing strength' (*fakafo'ou ivi*) spent on the hot and exhausting work of preparing the feast. The 'turtle' (*fonu*) and the 'skipjack tuna' (*'atu*) stood out from among the species of the sea as 'food' (*me'akiki*) of particular importance.

Often a *kaipola* presentation would consist of several 'boards' (*pola*), with the most prestigious *pola* at the 'front' (*mu'a 'oe pola*) and physically elevated by being placed on a low table (10 to 20 centimetres high) while the rest of the 'boards' were placed on the ground. The process of laying out the food on the *pola* was normally closely supervised by the 'leader of the work' (*pule ngāue*), the 'master of the earth oven' (*tu'utu'uni 'o e 'umu*) or another person (generally an older man) familiar with 'matters of respect/protocol' (*anga faka'apa'apa*). Instructions included: '*Ave 'ufi ko ia ki hē. 'Ulu pē ki mu'a 'o e pola*' ('Bring that yam over there with its "head" towards the "front" of the *pola*').

Elsewhere, I have shown how the distribution of essential qualities of plants along a continuum between frontal and posterior ends appears to be a part of an enduring perspective on qualitative differences in Tonga (see Perminow 2011). Thus, every growing plant was understood to have an end that 'leads the way' (the *mu'a*) and an end that 'follows behind' (the *mui*). And the essential qualities of all plants were quite consistently described to be concentrated towards the 'preceding/leading end' (*mu'a*). Thus, it appeared to go without saying that, for instance, the preceding end of the 'sugar cane' (*tō*) is its sweetest part. Likewise, everyone knew that the preceding end of the intoxicating kava root produces the strongest kava.

People familiar with housebuilding knew as a matter of fact that the preceding end of a tree – used as the 'central roof beam' (*toʻufūfū*) leading from a 'chiefly' (*ʻeiki*) 'frontal end' (*tāmuʻa*) to a 'commoner' (*tuʻa*) 'posterior end' (*tāmui*) in traditional 'Tongan houses' (*fale tonga*) – would have the hardest wood. Thus, recalling the days when it was still common to build such houses, Koloa described how builders decided which was the 'leading end' by the feel of the wood as they worked it with their tools. Likewise, in carving objects designed to last, wood carvers would describe a piece of wood from the *muʻa* of the 'ironwood tree' (*toa*) (the Casuarina) as most 'suitable' (*aonga*), albeit offering particularly fierce resistance to those working with it. During fieldwork among Tongan woodcarvers in 2004, the significance of the qualities of the *muʻa ʻo e toa* ('the preceding end of the ironwood') was brought home to me as I complained about the hardness of a particularly unforgiving piece of ironwood, which I was struggling to carve into a 'headrest' (*kali*). The woodcarver Feʻao Fehoko explained the challenge of shaping a piece of *toa* wood that was 'frontal' or *muʻa*: 'The *toa* is a tree that fights. When you strike it with the chisel, it strikes you right back! The first headrest you carved was "still young/later" (*kei mui*), but this one is "from before/old" (*muʻa pē*).'

So the qualities of sweetness, strength/bitterness and hardness were all clearly understood as increasing towards the *muʻa* end of a plant or crop. With the *kahokaho* yam, the emphasis was not on any substantial quality of size, taste or texture; rather, it was on the difference in reproductive speed and rate of growth of the preceding end and the part of the yam following in its wake. The quality that appeared to be emphasized, then, was vitality, its very capacity to regenerate and grow. It was this capacity that made it the *tokamuʻa*; the crop that leads the way. The end that leads the way was also perceived to be the oldest part of the plant, the reason for the existence of the parts that follow in its wake. Thus, the broad base of the coconut palm, for instance, is known by the term *tefito*, signifying, according to Churchward, 'basis or centre, principal or most essential part, or cause or reason' (Churchward 1959: 475).

Other scholars of Tongan culture and society have been struck by the extent to which the conceptual pair *muʻa* and *mui* appears to produce characteristic expressive forms (linguistically, materially and socially). Thus, the linguist Giovanni Bennardo has used precisely the conceptual opposition between *muʻa* and *mui* to identify what he hypothesizes as a foundational model of radiality in Tongan cognition, characterizing Tongan perceptions of spatial, temporal and social relationships (Bennardo 2009). He argues that radiality constitutes a 'cognitive molecule' that in Tonga plays a role in the 'generation and organization of a variety of knowledge domains' (ibid.: 173). My own findings, like Bennardo's, indicate that the opposition between *muʻa* and *mui* indeed does operate across a wide variety of skills and practices in Tonga in the composition of beautiful, valuable and useful things by differentiating essential qualities of components of the environment (see Perminow 2011). Like his linguistic material, my own ethnography indicates that the relationship between *muʻa* and *mui* is a relationship between origin and result, cause and effect. In contrast to Bennardo, I have no ambition to locate 'cognitive molecules' and foundational cognitive schema. Rather, I approach the constitutive significance of the relationship between *muʻa* and *mui* through what Tim Ingold, influenced by James Gibson's ecological approach to perception, refers to as people's creative involvement with components of the environment (Ingold 2000: 2–3).

We have seen that the yam's presentation in differentiated sections on boards of food mirrored or recapitulated the manner of its growth. Thus, the tableau of 'beauty, order and importance' constituted by hierarchically differentiated food increasing in worth with proximity to the 'chiefly position' at the 'front' (*muʻa*) at the same time may be interpreted to incorporate the process of growth itself. In Fox's terms of the relationship between Austronesian notions of precedence and growth, the 'board of food' laid out between the 'frontal' (*muʻa*) and the 'posterior' (*mui*) end may be said 'to move here' (*muʻa mai*) from the 'source', 'root', 'base', 'trunk' (Fox 1995: 218; 2008) of that which 'follows after' (*mui mai*).

Consuming such culinary tableaus of exemplary order was generally done rather quickly, often not taking more than 30 minutes. During the meal itself, 'conversation' (*talanoa*) was not common. The 'words' (*lea*) spoken were rather 'assembled/composed' speeches (*ngaohi*) to fit the occasion and were presented in turn. The persons to whom the *pola* was presented were usually unable to make more than a slight dent in the heaps of food laid out, and when they left the table, the 'working people' usually replaced them. This second seating along the *pola* was much more informal. Speeches would give way to conversation. Silence and solemnity would give way to laughter, joking and moving about. Food and words would be passed along those seated along the *pola* and on to those sitting (or even standing[27]) nearby, blurring the border between the tableau of the *pola* and its environment. Food would also be 'distributed' (*tufa*) by being put in small baskets and tins to be carried by children to the homes of those who had contributed to the work of building the board of food or to homes towards which the feast givers' 'door was open' (*ava ʻa e matapā*[28]) and from where food would be sent onwards across Kotu. Most of the food that had for a short time constituted a tableau of outstanding beauty and unidimensional order of precedence would thus trickle into the flow of everyday consumption. And to my mind, it was against such a backdrop that the creation of momentary glimpses of 'beauty' stood out and gained constitutive potency.

The Constitutive Potency of Merging and Separation

The serial image used to describe the characteristics of environmental dynamics explored in Chapter 2 and 3 may be used to understand what makes the frequent building of tableaus of order and emotionally moving beauty experientially meaningful and constitutively potent. Indeed, the image of a motion of merging, separation and re-merging coming out of the exploration of perceptions of environmental dynamics is very well suited to describe both the mode in which these tableaus were 'constructed' (*ngaohi*) and the way such feats of creativity articulated the multiple flows of everyday events. The 'bringing together' of food (*tokonaki*) of different kinds and from a wide variety of local and extra-local sources to be placed together beneath a 'layer of leaves' (*tau*[29]) to be transformed by a heat that brings it to a 'well-cooked'[30] (*moho lelei*), 'soft' (*molū*) and 'easy to swallow' (*folongofua*) state may be interpreted as an analogous recapitulation of the regenerative phase of merging. The significance of the foods in the context of 'building' a *pola* may lie in their transformation in being baked more than in 'any inhering qualities of the foods themselves' (Pollock 1992: 32). This does not mean that the general quality of Tongan foods was not classified 'according to its reputed effect on the body' (Manderson 1986: 127, see Leivestad 1995: 101). Thus, Rogers discovered that Tongans of Niuatoputapu ranked foods 'according to their innate and comparative energy giving qualities':

> Amongst kiki foods which give *ivi*, 'power, influence, energy', pork is the strongest. Pork and turtle (because they are too fatty) and raw fish and octopus (because they are too 'strong') are unsuitable for very sick or pregnant people ... Meʻakai foods give strength (fakamālohi). The strongest is long yam generally considered the best meʻakai for the hardest work. (Rogers 1975: 300–1)

Clearly, any 'innate and comparative energy giving qualities' are of constant significance in the 'biological event' (Pollock 1992: 32) of eating. Additionally, in 'building boards of food' that stand out from other events of eating, the human capacity to utilize and harness this energy becomes very important in making some social events of eating occasions of particular constitutive potency.

The 'opening of the earth oven' (*fuke ʻa e ʻumu*) and the 'separation' (*mavahevahe*) of types and parts of food stuffs by a specific order of precedence, orienting and placing them along an axis of hierarchical differentiation that recaptures their 'manner of growth'[31] (*anga ʻo e tupu*), may be interpreted as an analogous recapitulation of the regenerative phase of 'coming apart' (*māfoa, mahuʻi*). Finally, the moment of separateness, made to stand out as a tableau of 'importance' (*mahuʻinga*), 'order' (*maau*) and 'moving beauty' (*fakaʻofoʻofa*) by the imposition of strict constraints or taboos on speech and motion does not endure but in reality very soon re-merges with the environment from which it was momentarily 'torn' (*mahuʻi*).

As was true in the conceptualization of tidal, diurnal and lunar dynamics explored in previous chapters, everyday routines in which events may just crop up 'haphazardly, without significance' (*noaʼia pē*), or be staged as an occasion of 'importance, order and beauty' (*mahuʻinga, maau, fakaʻofoʻofa*) by the imposition of strict 'constraints' (*tapu*) do not exist in a stable oppositional relationship but as phases in the dynamic realities of the world. These dynamic realities will be useful as I, in the next chapter, turn to everyday sociality and morality by exploring the characteristics of establishing and re-creating social bonds in such a world. The ethnography of local sociality produced on the perspective of such enduring dynamics will in the concluding chapter be key in solving the puzzle of responses and attitudes to the ongoing environmental change presented in the introduction.

Notes

1. Amini had worked as a steward of the Kotu congregation of the Constitutional Church of Tonga for many years and was well respected. Many people had attended his funeral, making it a very demanding, albeit important, event on Kotu a short time before the Queen's visit.
2. *Fono* means 'to command, to direct, to give instructions' and is the term for the general village meeting that was normally held the first Monday of each month. At the *fono*, the town officer, representing King and Government, would inform villagers about public events or important undertakings in the upcoming month and instruct or encourage villagers to contribute to fulfil the obligations of the island. The town officer of Kotu also used these meetings to address specific instances of conflict and moral breaches that had occurred since the last *fono*. He also advised people on where they should concentrate their farming activities over the next month in order to make the island prosperous and bountiful.
3. *Kato* means 'basket/container', and *kato ʻo Taufatōfua* refers to the tribute brought by the chief of Kotu and Tōfua on behalf of the people of his territory. *Lotoʻā* means 'inside the fence/enclosure', which is a term that refers to the Tuʻi Kanokupolu title of the current Royal rulers of Tonga.
4. Lotima agreed to sell his turtle for 200 *paʻanga* (equalling 140 US$). This was considered to show that he was really 'warm-hearted/warm inside' (*loto māfana*), both because everyone knew that he had planned to make his own feast in the upcoming week of prayer memorable and also because the market price of a turtle in Nukuʻalofa would be higher.
5. The main ingredient of Tongan oil is coconut oil, but wild nuts growing in the 'uncultivated forest' (*vao*) and parts of other plants and flowers are added in varying

measures to create a great diversity of differing scents and viscosity. Tongan oil was used on Kotu as part of the everyday routines of personal hygiene for all, both to soften the skin and because it 'smells nice' (*namu lelei*). For festive occasions, it was used in generous quantities to make the hair shine and the skin glisten. It was also used to renew the shine and luster of painted 'barkcloth' (*ngatu*) and to enhance the smooth, black appearance of basalt pebbles (*kilikili*) used to decorate the graves of someone recently buried. Women usually had one or a few favorite recipes. The different Tongan oils enjoyed varying degrees of popularity and were generally referred to by the names of the women who made them.

6. *Mohenga* is the general term for a bed but also refers to bridewealth and the repository of 'Tongan wealth' (*koloa fakatonga*) in the form of barklcloth and mats, which generally made up a significant part of the beds of married couples in Kotu homes and which was extracted from when need arose to make a presentation at funerals or other ceremonial occasions.

7. *Vaitupu* means literally 'emerging/growing water' and usually refers to ponds or wells dug out to gain access to fresh water consisting of rainwater that has filtered through the soil and floats on seawater reservoirs.

8. *Loto* signifies 'inside' as well as 'heart', and the expression may be translated as 'warmth of the heart' as well as 'warmth inside'.

9. *Fāhiva* signifies the number 49 but was also the name of a location in the *Namolahi* Lagoon associated with turtle fishing. According to Koloa, an uncommonly light-skinned man named Matei had held the title in the past, and he thus felt that it was a particularly appropriate title for a 'white foreigner' or *pālangi*.

10. On any occasion involving strong encouragement to contribute generously for some greater communal good, as with, for instance, the annual collection of money for the churches (*misinale*), middle-aged and elderly female 'clowns' contributed to make the occasion a 'happy event' (*me'a fiefia*) by acting in ways that would otherwise have been considered 'silly' (*laupisi*) and disrespectful. According to some informants, the clowning around of women resulted from the belief that women are more easily moved by projects of cooperation that demand extraordinary generosity and more often express their 'warmth inside' (*loto māfana*) by 'making happy' (*fakafiefia*) and by shedding tears (*tangi*).

11. The conventions of making presentations of foods and goods routinely consisted of the person handing it over elaborating on the poverty of the gift in terms of quality as well as quantity. This communicative mode of selfabasement is known as *fakatōkilalo* and is considered to show respect for and 'uplift/praise' (*hiki hake*) the receiver of the presentation. Thus, the language of presentation transformed pigs and yams of extraordinary size to small and insignificant trifles and barkcloth and mats of extraordinary beauty to worthless rubbish. This practice of self-depreciation was extremely common at ceremonial presentations of food and wealth and is referred to as *heliaki* ('to say one thing and mean another') in Tonga.

12. In contrast to the characteristic laments of grief accompanying leave takings among close kin, this leave taking was characterized by a festive atmosphere of cheers and laughter. People seemed pleased with a job well done and were quite happy to devote themselves to the task of making the upcoming 'week of prayer' (*uike lotu*) a memorable one.
13. It is not clear whether he made this statement in Tongan or English, but the Tongan expression that would most likely be used to make the statement 'You can't move around freely' would be either '*Oku 'ikai ke 'alu noa'ia pē*, which may be translated as 'There is no whimsical/haphazard moving about' or '*Oku 'ikai ke ngofua/tapu 'alu noa'ia pē* ('It is not allowed/it is forbidden to move about whimsically') (without purpose in terms of the task at hand).
14. In an examination of the significance of the cross-cousin relationship in Fiji, Christina Toren interprets Fijian 'ritual practices' precisely in terms of their transitory reality in a wider regenerative dynamic: 'In their ritual practice Fijians succeed momentarily in the struggle to contain the equal, competitive relation between cross cousins, and the threat of disorder it sometimes represents, within the bounds of hierarchical kinship. That this struggle is in principle unending is a product of the fact that all dynamic, fertile and affective processes are founded in the relation between cross-cousins' (Toren 1995: 76).
15. The different parts of Tongan plants and trees are referred to by terms that are also used for, or are easily associated with, parts of the human body. Thus, the trunk of the tree may be referred to as its 'body' (*sino*), the bark as its 'skin' (*kili*) and the plant mass as its 'flesh/meat/substance' (*kakano*).
16. *aka*; roots (Churchward 1959: 3) *fia*; suffix forming adjectives and intransitive verbs (Churchward 1953: 244) denoting 'full of'.
17. The term *hau-ki-va'e* consists of a word pertaining to sharp objects/piercing and foot/leg. If Whistler is right, the term may seem to indicate a specific kind of root penetration (*akafia*) by describing which bones have been pierced. Conceivable terms like *hau-ki-'ulu* ('piercing the head'), *hau-ki-tu'a* ('piercing the back') may perhaps be other meaningful labels for specific kinds of the general syndrome of *akafia*. Also, according to Churchward, the term *haukiva'e* may refer specifically to a 'throat disease' (Churchward 1954: 214) rather than an affliction of the head or legs.
18. *Lohu loa* means, literally, 'The long harvesting stick' (*Hako loa* means, literally, 'a trunk growing long before the boughs branch off' or, metaphorically, 'a long line of descendants') and is used to describe the strategy of tracing genealogies to the original pair of siblings that constitute the source of a kin relationship, to establish relative worth or appropriate behavior in later generations.
19. The Tongan proverb (*leatonga*) *To'u kai mo hono lohu* means, literally, 'The crop and its harvesting stick' or 'Each crop has its own harvesting stick' and is used to express the notion that 'each generation has its own people of prominence or strength'. In the context of establishing kin relations, the expression describes a

strategy of concentrating the search for consanguinal links among contemporaries within the most immediate environment of your own generation.
20. The term *fāmili* was used in several different senses in different situations on Kotu to refer to 'nuclear family', 'bilateral kindred' (also referred to as *kāinga*), as well as 'shallow patrilineage', sometimes referred to as *faʻahinga* in the literature of Tongan kinship and sometimes referred to as *haʻa* on Kotu. The expression *tokonaki fakahaʻa* (but not *tufa fakafaʻahinga*) was sometimes used to describe the bringing of uncooked food to a funeral by groups of kinsmen recognizing common patrilineal ancestry to a constellation of eldest (*taʻokete*) and younger (*kautehina*) brothers in some previous generation in the relatively recent past.
21. *Loto momoko/loto mokomoko*, meaning literally 'cold/cool inside', was used to refer to an inner state of being unmoved – uncooperative about engaging in a task. The term *loto vela*, on the other hand, means literally 'burning inside' and refers to an inner state of wanting something too much, lusting for something or being consumed by desire for self-gratification, generating a need to 'cool down' (*fakamokomoko*).
22. The Samoan novelist Albert Wendt has captured the desirability of withdrawal and isolation produced by the multiple demands of village life in Samoa very well in his novel *Poʻuliʻuli*. The novel starts with a prominent member of the local community, a family head, fed up with the constant demands made on him and resolving to remain in his room. He refuses to engage in village affairs or, indeed, even to speak to the members of his family (Wendt 1987). A sudden refusal to cooperate is otherwise associated with the Samoan term *musu*, signifying extreme non-cooperativeness born of social pressure. This is primarily associated with Samoan youths frustrated with a lack of autonomy (Freeman 1983).
23. *Koa fakatonga*, or *mātuitui*, is made by chewing (*mama*) to a pulp 'candlenuts' (*fua tuitui*) and the small tubers (*foha*) of 'nut grass' (*pako*) with the 'flowers' (*matalaʻi*) of the 'Perfume Tree' (*Mohokoi*; cananga odorata or Ylang-ylang, see Whistler 1992: 86). This scented pulp is then smeared onto the body, with dust and grime coming off in rolls as it is rubbed along the limbs with the palm of the hand, leaving 'nice smelling' (*namu lelei*), 'clean' (*maʻa lelei*) skin. The advantages of this soap were said to be that it demands no water to work and is thus good if you want to freshen up during voyages at sea.
24. *Noaʻia* consists of the semantic core of *noa*, pertaining to a lack of orderliness, worthlessness or aimlessness, while, according to Churchward, the suffix *'ia* serves to emphasize or intensify the quality of the thing, act or state referred to.
25. This does not imply that everyday eating was considered to be 'of no account' in an absolute sense. On the contrary, the anthropologist Rogers has described Tongan conceptualization of food in the following manner: 'An important dimension concerning the quality of foods is their energy giving (*ivi*) and strength giving (*mālohi*) qualities … Weariness (from physical exertion) is immediately banished by eating even a meal of *meʻakai*; it is transformed into a feeling of

strength and energy potential by eating *kiki*. Consequently to give a person food in Tonga is to give him life and strength, food becomes the direct key to physical and sexual performance' (Rogers 1975: 300).

26. Kotu first became linked to the rest of the world by means of telecommunication, with a phone booth installed at the government primary school (*'api lau tohi*) in 1987. In 1991, telephone numbers to try in order to marshal resources for 'building of boards of food' could be seen scribbled on the inside wall of the booth.
27. The exchange of things or words between one seated at a *pola* and one standing 'outside' the *pola* was considered extremely inappropriate during the first serving of the *kaipola*.
28. The expression *'oku ava 'a e matapā* means literally 'the door is open' and was used on Kotu to describe persons willing to help (*fetokoniaki*), reflected in a flow of support and food/items.
29. The term *tau* refers to the green plantain or banana leaves, with the suffix *aki* meaning 'to cover the food with green leaves' (*tau-aki*). Thus, *tau*, here, refers to that which contains rather than 'to be joined with' as in the strong union between land and sea at high tide and day and night in the phase of stable darkness.
30. Although Tongans, like other Polynesians but in contrast to many other seaboard Austronesians, eat raw fish (see Leivestad 1995: 85), they very much prefer meat that is 'well cooked' (*moho lelei*). Food, including fish, coming out of the *'umu* should be 'well-cooked' and 'soft' (*molū*).
31. This recapturing of the manner of growth may also seem to be involved in the presentation of kava to a chief. A kava should be presented to a chief by placing the 'peeled' (*kava tele*) but uncut kava on the ground with the 'frontal part' (*mu'a kava*) closest to the root of the kava plant pointing towards the 'talking chief' (*matāpule*), who will be sitting next to the chiefly position and 'performing the duty' (*faifatongia*) of directing the preparation of the kava (*ui kava*).

5

Nurturing Flows between Hands That Let Go

◆●◆

Through an exploration of understandings related to everyday practices of referring to and coping with an ever-changing world, we have seen the outline of an enduring and largely taken for granted perspective on the relationship between the natural and the social world. With this perspective, cultivation, orderliness and beauty are closely interrelated. We have seen that although what spontaneously crops up in and around people was perceived as essential for growth and vitality such natural force needs to be channelled and refined through cultivation in order to reproduce a society worth living in. Importantly for the current puzzle of people's attitudes and responses to unfortunate environmental changes, such a perspective strongly implies that a society worth living in cannot be expected to happen on its own accord but demands continuous efforts of cultivation and refinement as well as self-discipline. To my mind, then, the social and moral ramifications of the enduring perspective on the relation between the world and its workings and the human condition discovered in the foregoing ethnography is key to solving the puzzle of local response and attitudes at hand. In this chapter, then, I shall go on to explore how this perspective affected local sociality and ideas of morality, in order to produce an ethnography that finally enables us (in the conclusion) to understand why people responded as they did to the threats and environmental transformations taking place around them.

'The Doorway Is Open'

The food laid out on this table is the 'farewell meal' (*kai fakamavae*) for the 'foreigner' (*pālangi*) who has come here from afar to become familiar with the 'manner of the land' (*anga fakafonua*). He shall return to his own land far away, but we have lived together here on Kotu, and he has become familiar with the people of Kotu. I believe that he shall remember this meal in the future. We have all had a 'strong fellowship' (*'oku tau feohi*[1]) during the time of his stay. We have 'helped one another' (*fetokoniaki*). This is why I think that he shall not go abroad to disappear altogether from this land. There are such things as the mail and the telephone. Although he goes to live very far away, 'the doorway remains open' (*'oku kei ava 'a e matapā*).

Koloa's farewell speech was a not too subtle statement that our relationship of 'mutual love' (*fe'ofa'aki*) and 'mutual help' (*fetokoniaki*) should not end abruptly; that the flow of mutual interchanges between us in the form of giving and receiving 'assistance' (*tokoni*) and 'gifts' (*me'a 'ofa*; lit. 'things of love/compassion') ought to endure separation. It may also serve as a point of departure for exploring motions constituting social relationships in the course of daily life interaction. Ideas about common origin and ideals about sharing, giving and mutual caring in the form of compassionate *'ofa* and a willingness to 'carry burdens' (*fua kavenga*) and 'do duties' (*fai fatongia*) in favour of people of precedence were clearly cornerstones of both kinship ideology and social hierarchy. But more than identifying and characterizing kinship or exchange systems, I am out to understand the generative mechanisms and constitutive dynamics of sociality. Thus, I shall approach the issue of social relatedness in terms of *what people did* to constitute and renegotiate social relationships by whatever means they found appropriate and effective, rather than in terms of being related by kinship or holding positions in a system of exchange.

In this context, the significance of Koloa's farewell speech is that, because the option of speaking about our relationship as one produced by common origin was closed, the moral obligation to keep on reciprocating and thus to contribute to reproducing our relationship was elaborated solely in terms of our common experiences of engaging one another in acts of 'mutual assistance' (*fetokoniaki*) in our short history of 'companionship/fellowship' (*feohi*). To gain a foothold for the understanding of the ongoing processes whereby social relatedness was produced, the image of the 'open doorway' will be central. Koloa chose this as an appropriate analogy to speak about the nurturing of social relationships in his words of farewell, and I shall examine it in some detail. Thus, I shall explore the practical significance of doorways on Kotu, as well as the wider semantic field in which the concept of the 'doorway' (*matapā*) may be meaningful.

Using the Doorways of Kotu

The 'public road' (*hala pule'anga*) of Kotu enters the village from the beach of the *Fanga lahi* ('Great landing'). After crossing the central 'village green' (*mala'e*), it turns sharply to the right and then runs to the 'low part' (*lalo*) of the village. The *'apis* or 'homes' were spaced neatly along this L-shaped road. Houses usually had two doorways: a 'frontal doorway' (*matapā 'i mu'a*), also referred to as 'the door facing the road' (*matapā ki hala*); and a 'posterior doorway'[2] (*matapā 'i mui*) facing the 'cooking area' (*peito/afi*). In terms of everyday practices, these entrances were not indiscriminately used.[3] People who were frequently involved in 'mutual assistance' (*fetokoniaki*) with those living in an *'api* ('home/homestead') preferred to 'enter from the back' (*hū mei mui*). 'Solicitations/requests' (*kole*) for things and services as well as offers of small gifts related to everyday consumption constituted much of everyday village socializing. 'Close kin' (*kāinga ofi*) or those who had gained a 'strong fellowship' (*feohi*) with the occupants of an *'api* would often make such requests through the back door; people who were on less intimate terms, coming to exchange news or make 'requests' (*kole*), would be expected to enter by the front door for everyone to see. The use of the back door by those expected to enter openly from the front would be considered somewhat suspect and would imply a 'disposition to twist and turn' (*anga 'amio*) away from obligations to reciprocate by attempting to keep the visit and/or the act of solicitation out of the public eye. Similarly, the use of the front door by someone with whom the people of the *'api* had a 'strong fellowship' (*feohi*) through frequent exchanges of 'mutual help' (*fetokoniaki*) was said to be avoided out of 'shame' (*mā*) because it might be understood to imply a questionable attempt to give oneself the 'appearance of importance' (*fie lahi*; lit. 'wish to be big') by using the higher-ranked 'door of honour' (Toren 1990: 84). Secondly, it could give rise to shame by making public, so to speak, the balance sheet in one's dealings with the people of an *'api*. The main point, however, is that the use of the different doorways of a house by persons differently related to an *'api* was not neutral but charged with moral significance, making the doorway an appropriate idiom in a moral discourse related to the constitution and reconstitution of social relationships.

From Face to Interface

Some of the properties of a doorway may seem well suited to make it an effective analogy of bounded social units' modes of relating to one another. First of all, a doorway may be described as an interface; a boundary through which something must pass or flow to establish and keep up a connectedness between what's 'inside' (*loto*) and what's 'outside' (*tu'a*). Indeed, the term *mata-pā* ('doorway'), itself, may perhaps best be translated as 'interface between a bounded entity and its environment or between bounded entities'. The last part of the compound word, *pā*, according to Churchward, signifies boundary in the form of 'fence, wall, enclosure' (Churchward 1959: 339). The first part, *mata*, has a great range of significations, most of which have in common what may be described as potentially permeable *contacting surfaces* and penetrable or penetrating *points of contact* in the relationship between bounded entities. *Mata* refers to 'face', 'eyes' and also to the act of perceiving by eyesight, as well as to 'front' (as in 'seafront'; *matātahi*, and 'front of the land'; *matāfonua*), 'top', 'point' (of a spear; *mata-tao*), 'edge' (of a knife; *mata-hele*), 'biting edge' (of the teeth; *mata-nifo*) 'battlefront/vanguard' (*mata-tau*), 'wound' (*mata-lavea/mata-'i-lavea*), 'boil', 'ulcer' (*mata-lava*), 'bud mark' (of a tuber) and 'sprouting point' (of a coconut).

The argument that a great number of the wide range of usages of *mata* may be semantically related by referring to an interface between bounded entities would seem to be consonant with Barnes' argument that the multiple meanings of the Austronesian term *mata* may be regarded 'as corresponding to a significantly interrelated family of concepts' (Barnes 1977: 302). According to Barnes, the multiple applications of *mata* seem to show 'persistent connections with the idea of transition … the word often expresses ideas of spiritual influence, growth and the general movement of life' (1977: 302). Although Barnes doubts that the extreme variety of Austronesian uses of the term may be united by one single unifying idea, he notes that 'one or another connection with boundaries' (ibid.: 309) seems to relate to a wide range of uses in which *mata* figures. The double association of *mata* to a general relationship between entities facing one another along a wide borderland or contacting surface *as well as* to specific relational points of contact is important in my approach to the ways Kotu people related to one another, and I shall examine it in some detail. Thus, it is my argument that such an examination may profitably be undertaken in terms of the dynamics of merging and separation that has been explored in the previous chapters.

Fuzzy Borderlands and Sharp Points of Conductivity

The term *matātahi* refers to the 'beach' or the 'seafront' from the perspective of the land, while the term *matāfonua* refers to the 'shore' or the 'face of the land' from the perspective of the sea. The intermediate littoral zone may be described as an ever-changing borderland; a wide contacting surface. This borderland is where 'sea and land unite' (*tau 'a e tahi mo e 'uta*) as the 'sea flows here to unite' (*hu'a mai ke tau e tahi*) and where 'land and sea separate' (*mahu'i e tahi*) as the sea recedes to produce an 'empty/almost empty' (*maha/mamaha*) lagoon, with many significant features in the space that has opened between land and the 'deep sea' (*moana*). Likewise, the 'front of the reef' (*matahakau*), referring to its outer perimeters from the perspective of the *moana* ('deep sea') along which the 'sea inside the lagoon' (*lotonamo*) meets the 'sea outside the lagoon' (*tuʻanamo*), may be described as a contacting surface, the properties of which change with the changing tides. The sea that flows indiscriminately between the lagoon and the deep sea around high tide, making it possible to enter and exit the lagoon *noaʻia pē* ('without consideration'), flows strongly through 'channels' or 'openings' (*foʻi ava*) closer to low tide, knowledge of such points of contact being essential. *Mata* also refers to salient or particularly significant points or parts of a bounded entity that are potential openings or points of enhanced conductivity. Fishermen, for example, detach clams clinging to the coral formations or imbedded in fissures on the reef by way of piercing the *mata ʻo e fingota*[4] ('the eye/opening of the clam') with a long sharp instrument like a 'spear' (*tao*) (the *mata ʻo e tao* or 'point of the spear' thus penetrating the *mata ʻo e fingota*) in order to pierce the strong muscle deep within the clamshell. Trying to pry it loose from the outside or missing the vulnerable spot of this 'eye/opening' at first thrust allows the clam to seal up, making it all but impossible to cut it loose from its coral environment. Such particularly significant points of enhanced conductivity, or interfaces in the relationship between bounded entities, may perhaps best be described as relational points of intensified exchange or communication. As may be recalled, the 'face of the person' (*mata ʻa tangata*) may, according to Koloa, be 'built, composed' (*ngaohi*) to make what you feel 'inside' (*ʻi loto*) correspond with outward appearance. Likewise, the points of enhanced conductivity of the 'eyes' (*mata*) were clearly understood to be a privileged interface in the communication between persons. Koloa claimed: '*Lahi ako ai he mata pē ʻa e kakai Tonga*' ('Tongans mostly learn by seeing'), such as when addressing someone hard of hearing, or in contexts where it was either very noisy or where silence was required.

Similarly, some important cultivated plants such as coconut, taro and pandanus are furnished with a *mata*, referring to points or parts of particular significance for achieving plant regeneration by establishing contact between a plant and its medium of growth. The *mataʻi niu* of the coconut refers to the indentations from which its new shoots sprout; *mataʻi talo* refers to the top of a taro tuber used for planting, while *mataʻi tofua* refers to the suckers/slips used for pandanus planting. That *mata* may describe a conductive interface, point of contact or source of a constitutive flow seems particularly well illustrated by a term such as *mataʻi huhu*, which signifies 'teat/nipple'. *Huhu* signifies 'to pierce', 'to sting', 'to inject', as well as the child's act of sucking. The expression referring to the 'interface', or the point of primary contact between a new person and the person with whom it was originally physically united and from whom it has recently emerged as a separate being, includes the whole relational interchange between mother and child by which well-being and growth is produced. *Mata* as a borderland – like that of the littoral zone along which sea and land meet – or a point of enhanced contact – like 'a nipple' (*mataʻi huhu*) an 'eye', a 'face' or the 'top of the taro' (*mataʻi talo*) – may both be described as interfaces in facilitating interchanges between interrelated but bounded (or periodically bounded) entities. But the *mata* as a wide borderland differs significantly from *mata* as a sharp point of contact by being a zone in which boundaries periodically break down in favour of merging. *Mata* as point of contact, in contrast, may be described as a channel or passage that facilitates interchanges that link bounded entities without a breakdown of the boundary between them or their total merging.

A perspective informed through the relational dynamics of everyday environmental engagements that were discovered in the previous chapters may be used to approach acts aimed at cultivating plants as well as nurturing and rearing children or to establish and reproduce social bonds as efforts feeding on and refining primary processes of nature. Such acts transform exchanges occurring 'spontaneously' (*noaʻia pē*) and along a fuzzy zone of contact into 'well-ordered' (*maau*) interchanges occurring at outstanding points of contact. A perspective informed by environmental engagement invites us to see all of these constitutive activities as efforts to order, focus or concentrate interchanges at certain (temporal and spatial) points of contact, by feeding on and potentiating a regenerative force produced by an all embracing 'natural' motion of merging and separation while, at the same time, retaining a certain degree of autonomy from the regenerative rhythm of this motion. With this perspective, it would seem reasonable to expect such efforts of transformation, refinement or the channelling of constitutive force to represent characteristic themes of cultural elaboration. Thus, the mode in which the building of 'boards of beauty, order and importance', explored in the previous chapter, was argued to be meaningful in the context of the dynamics of growth and regeneration and the multiple contingencies of everyday life may very well be described in terms of enhanced conductivity and concentration around specific points of contact. After all, the building of 'beautiful' (*fakaʻofoʻofa*) tableaus of extraordinary 'order' (*maau*) that stood out against a backdrop of 'ordinary, good for nothing, haphazard' events 'of no account' (*noaʻia*) involved precisely a radical narrowing down of potential modes of relating and capacities in which to interact by the application of strict 'taboos' (*tapu*).

It is perhaps not surprising with this perspective that the doorway as an interface between a house and its environment should take on particular significance as being well-suited to speak about the establishment and nurturing of social relationships. But a doorway may be 'closed' (*māpuni ʻa e matapā*) or 'open' (*ava ʻa e matapā*), in the sense of allowing or denying flows of interchange through them. This interface, then, may be described to exist in two possible states that either facilitate or bar the passage or flow necessary to establish and maintain the interconnectedness between what is inside and what is outside. Thus, the state of the doorway definitely has moral implications on Kotu. During the time when people were awake, a closed front door was usually a reliable sign that the 'api was empty. Thus, it was considered bad form to stay at home behind a closed door.[5] A closed front door would be interpreted as questionable in expressing a desire to withdraw. In terms of the current argument, then, it would be quite antisocial. It would be an attempt to stop up the passage between the 'inside' and the 'outside', barring the flows that constitute links between those whose 'strong fellowship/communion' (*feohi*) creates a sociality not wholly dominated by the 'dumb' and 'good for nothing' (*noa*) qualities of existence 'cropping up like wild weed' (*tupu noa 'ia pē*). As exemplified in the case of the *pālangi* couple who chose to withdraw to live peacefully in the plantation area, an individual's desire to close the door and refuse 'to come away from one's island' (*fakamotu*) seemed well understood on Kotu. But that was precisely what made keeping the door open a social imperative.

Tauhi Vahaʻa/Vā: 'Nuturing the Space In-Between'

Several students of Tongan society and culture have over the years used the Tongan expression *tauhi vā* or *tauhi vahaʻa* to approach the characteristics of establishing and maintaining social relationships. The expression *tauhi vahaʻa/vā* means, literally, 'to nurture/care for the space between' and has been used by scholars to approach the significance of reciprocity and networking in the reproduction of Tongan kin relations (see Kaʻili 2005; Leslie 2007; Poltorak 2007; Thaman 2008; Perminow 2018). *Vā* or *Vahaʻa* is a term referring to the space/void between any two entities regardless of scale and whether the entities are people, objects or land masses. It can be used to refer to the void or deep space between the earth and the moon, the deep sea between two landmasses, the open ocean separating Tonga from New Zealand or the space or gap between groups of people or between one person and the next. Thus, the *vā* or *vahaʻa* refers to the space in-between that separates things but also potentially connects them. In its sense of paying attention to decorum the use of the term 'nurturing/caring for the space' illustrates how not only material substances but also words and visual appearances are perceived to issue forth and flow in social spaces (see Perminow 2015: 129). The other part of the expression, '*tauhi*', signifies 'to feed', 'to nurture', 'to nurse' 'to tend' and 'to care for'. *Tauhi* is what you do in order to tend your garden to protect it from harm – that is, remove weeds and water it. It is what you do to assist and care for people who are getting too old and weak to cope on their own. It is what you do to nurse people back to health when they are ill. And most of all, it is what you do to nurture and feed infants so that they become strong and 'healthy' persons (*sino*; lit. signifying 'body' and 'fat'). *Tauhi* is strongly associated with motherhood, mother's brother and the mother's side in general in Tonga. Thus, people should be able to rely on mother, the mother's side and 'maternal uncle' (*fa'ētangata*) in particular to nurture and support them. The father, the father's side and 'father's sister' (*mehekitanga*), on the other hand, should be expected to chastise you and teach you to act with respect and decorum.

Tauhi may be described as the primary component of childcare in the sense of being the only acknowledged ingredient in the first phases of child-rearing until weaning. After weaning, *tauhi* should be complemented with the other main component of Tongan child-rearing known as *ngaohi*. *Ngaohi*, as may be recalled from the previous chapter, signifies 'to build', 'to put together', 'to compose', 'to construct', which involves instruction/commands combined with discipline aimed at making persons *poto* or 'competent' and which is strongly associated with fatherhood, 'father's sister' (*mehekitanga*) and the father's side in general in Tonga (see Perminow 1993; Morton 1996 for analyses of ideals and practices of Tongan child-rearing). I would argue that the primary significance of *tauhi* in ideas about child-rearing and a very strong emphasis on the strength of the primary attachment between mother and infant makes breast feeding an act of *tauhi par excellence* in Tonga. Quite enduring notions and practices exist related to the naval cord as a primal bond and an enduring source of personal well-being throughout life, which may be seen as further indication of the perceived significance of this primary 'natural' mother-child attachment. All Tongan parents I spoke to claimed that they take care of the 'afterbirth/placenta' (*fonua*) and the naval cord, often burying them at the roots of a tree in their 'town allotment' (*'api kolo*). People said that they should be put in a dry/warm place rather than in a wet/cold place in order for the person to remain in good health throughout life.

I have argued elsewhere (Perminow 2011) that there exists a very obvious and explicit cultural understanding of the higher status of father, father's side, and 'father's sister' (*mehekitanga*) in particular (which has been emphasized by several analysts of gender relations in Tonga (see Besnier 2004: 8)) that sits alongside a more implicit understanding of the 'natural' strength of the bond with the mother, the mother's side and the ever-supporting 'mother's brother' (*fa'ētangata*). Discussions with the Tongan carver Fe'ao Fehoko (with whom I worked as an apprentice in 2004) about parts of a tree in comparison with the stomach may illuminate the perceived natural strength and significance of this bond:

> This part [of the tree] is harder because it is 'in front/before' (*mu'a*), it 'leads the way' (*mu'a mai*) and the other parts 'follow after' (*mui mai*). It is just like the stomach, which is the most important part of the human body. It is the preceding part of the body because in order to be strong and to think well you first have to eat. Just like the stomach, the preceding part of the tree is the part which is closest to its 'place of origin' (*fonua*).

Here he used the term *fonua*, utilizing the fact that *fonua* signifies 'place of origin', 'land', 'territory', 'basis' as well as 'placenta' (Churchward 1959). Thus, he elaborated how the stomach's importance as the seat of vitality and strength was on account of its connection through the naval cord and the placenta within the body of the mother as both origin point and medium of growth. Finally, he emphasized how the mother and the mother's side as the original source of the human body and its well-being were the people you could really rely on for support and the ones you really feel love, compassion and gratitude for.

A nurturing space may be understood, then, as one in which primary, 'natural' bonds are transformed into, and lend strength to, other social bonds that are thus secondary but also more highly valued in a system of cultural evaluation that generally prizes cultivatedness above naturalness (see Perminow 2018). To 'nurture the space between' (*tauhi vaha'a/vā*) may be understood to involve paying attention to establishing and maintaining movements or flows that nurture and order the spaces between persons and groups. The Tongan description for living harmoniously within kin groups, neighbourhoods or churches is *vā lelei* (Leslie 2007), meaning literally 'good space', implying that 'the nurturing' (*tauhi*) turns spaces between social entities into something that unites rather than something that divides. Another metaphor – that of an 'open doorway', as illustrated by Koloa during my second fieldwork in Tonga 1991–92 – illustrates precisely the perceived importance of making an effort to maintain a 'good space/harmonius relations' (*vā lelei*) through long distance nurture.

Imagining the Tongan House

The significance of the image of the doorway to talk about socially constitutive flows may be illuminated by the way in which the image of the 'Tongan house' (*fale tonga*) was used by some of my informants to talk about challenges of achieving enduring social cohesion. Although few traditional Tongan houses existed on Kotu going into the twenty-first century and the ambition of most people was to build wooden or concrete European houses, some felt that the 'Tongan house' worked well as an analogy to talk about sociality; as Koloa stated: 'There is one thing that I find hard to understand about Europeans ... Why do they have so few children? If Europeans have two or three children they seem to think that is much/enough, but here, a family with only two or three children is considered very small and poor'. He continued:

> I can understand that if everything has to be bought for money, like the school-fees that we have to pay for the education of our children, then it must in truth be 'heavy/ expensive' (*mamafa*) to support a large family ... One aspect of development has been bad. It has made it more expensive to have children. But still Tonga is different. Here the children are the support of the parents.

He likened the individuals that make up a 'Tongan family'[6] (*fāmili fakatonga*) to the parts of a 'Tongan house' (*fale tonga*) and preceded to explain how Tongan houses are made:

> Several 'stakes' (*tokotuʻu*), 'posts' (*pou*) and 'rafters' (*kahoki*) are needed to carry the 'foundation of the house' (*toka ʻo e fale*), the 'loft' (*fata*), the 'inner ridgepole' (*toʻufūfū*) and the 'outer ridgepole' (*tumuʻaki*). If you have few stakes to use for 'walls' (*holisi*) and few posts to 'dig' (*keleʻi*) into the ground, then the 'encircling coconut that runs around the outside' (*ʻaoniu ʻoku lele ʻi tuʻa*) [or beams] will encircle a very small house. The distance between the 'curved beams' (*kautā*) of the 'front end' (*tāmuʻa*) and the 'back end' (*tāmui*) will not be very big, and the 'inner ridgepole' (*toʻufūfū*) running along the 'inside of the house' (*loto fale*) at the 'exterior summit' (*tumuʻaki*) will not be very long or stand very high. The inner ridgepole is very important and a 'chiefly thing' (*meʻa ʻeiki*) in the house. The position of the chief is directly below the 'front end of the inner ridgepole' (*muʻa ʻo e toʻufūfū*). There is only one inner ridgepole, and, like the important 'head' (*ʻulu/tefitoʻi*) of a large family, it is supported by many stakes and strong posts that are all united by the encircling coconut that runs all around the outside of the 'roof' (*ato*). That is why it is said that there should be two 'interior beams' (*apai*) running around the roof on the inside of the house, but just as there may only be one king in Tonga, there may only be one 'encircling coconut' (*aoniu*) encompassing all of the house on the outside. You know the church building that was destroyed during the hurricane Isaac in 1982? It was such a large and beautiful *fale tonga* ('Tongan house'). It was built by my great grandfather Paula Polata. Now all that remains of that house is the inner ridgepole into which the name of my great grandfather and the year of the building of the house is carved. It was finished in 1886 and 'almost made it for a hundred years' (*mei lava taʻu ʻe teau*). It is a pity, isn't it?

I agreed that it was a pity and asked why they had chosen to spend so much money building a European-style church instead of rebuilding a Tongan house; whether the technique had been forgotten. He answered:

There are still some who are competent, but it is much more exhausting to build a Tongan house, starting from choosing the trees that are 'suitable' (*aonga*) to use for posts and 'curved beams' (*kautā*), making the 'coconut ropes' (*kafa niu*) for the 'lashing' (*lalava*) and the *hulu* ('coarse palm mattings') and the *takapau* ('green palm mattings') for the 'floor' (*faliki*), and the *pola* ('palm mattings') for the 'walls' (*holisi*) and 'roof' (*ato*). Taking care of the Tongan house is much work. After a few years, the 'coconut leaves' (*louniu*) used for floor, walls and roof must be 'renewed' (*fakafoʻou*). If 'reeds' (*kaho*) and 'cane thatching' (*au*) have been used instead of palm leaves 'to make walls' (*holisiʻaki*) and 'to make roof' (*atoʻaki*) or 'to make rooms' (*lokiʻaki*) within the house, the renewal may perhaps wait for eight years. It is much quicker and less exhausting to build and care for a European house.

I asked him about the cost of the building materials for a European house:

> All the money comes from the work of men growing kava and fishing. I suppose that the women could also earn money by selling some of the mats that they weave, but they use the mats to 'exchange' (*feitongi*) for barkcloth. The building of a 'Tongan house' as church: all of the people of the congregation would have to work hard together to build it and also to take care of it. But the building of a European house: the burden is carried by those who earn money.

It seems, then, that the relationship between elements of construction of the house were made into analogies of social relationships. It would probably not be advisable to construct a Tongan house from the rough sketch below (Figure 5.1); it is useful, however, for understanding the imagery of Koloa's analogy. I drew the house under the direction of Koloa, who did not base his instructions on any existing Tongan houses nor from any observations of house building. Rather, the sketch resulted from his effort to visualize the old church that was blown away by Cyclone Isaac in 1982, in the context of elaborating on the analogy between the Tongan house and the *fāmili*. The choice of perspective and the strategy of committing the three dimensions of the house that he had in mind to the two dimensions of the paper were Koloa's, to the extent that I only gradually grasped the meaning of what I was drawing. Believing, for instance, that we were starting our reconstruction from the ground and building our way towards the summit of the house, I was slow to realize that the 'foundation of the house' (*toka ʻo e fale*), which served as Koloa's starting point, was the horizontal beams of the loft running lengthwise along the summit to carry the roof; the 'posts' (*pou*) and 'stakes' (*tokotuʻu*) were also elements of the roof construction. Koloa's approach thus appears to conform to what Fox has identified as an Austronesian mode of conceptualizing origin as a form of growth in terms of a ' … derivation from a "source", "root", "base", or "trunk"' (Fox 1995: 218).

Nurturing Flows 123

As we have seen in the Tongan variety of an Austronesian mode of conceptualizing origin as a form of growth, the idea of precedence appears paramount. With regard to the growth of plants, this order of precedence appears to stand trees on their heads, so to speak. Thus, the end that is physically lowest in the growing tree (*tefito'i*) (i.e. that which is below ground) proceeds that which is physically highest (i.e. the crown of the tree)

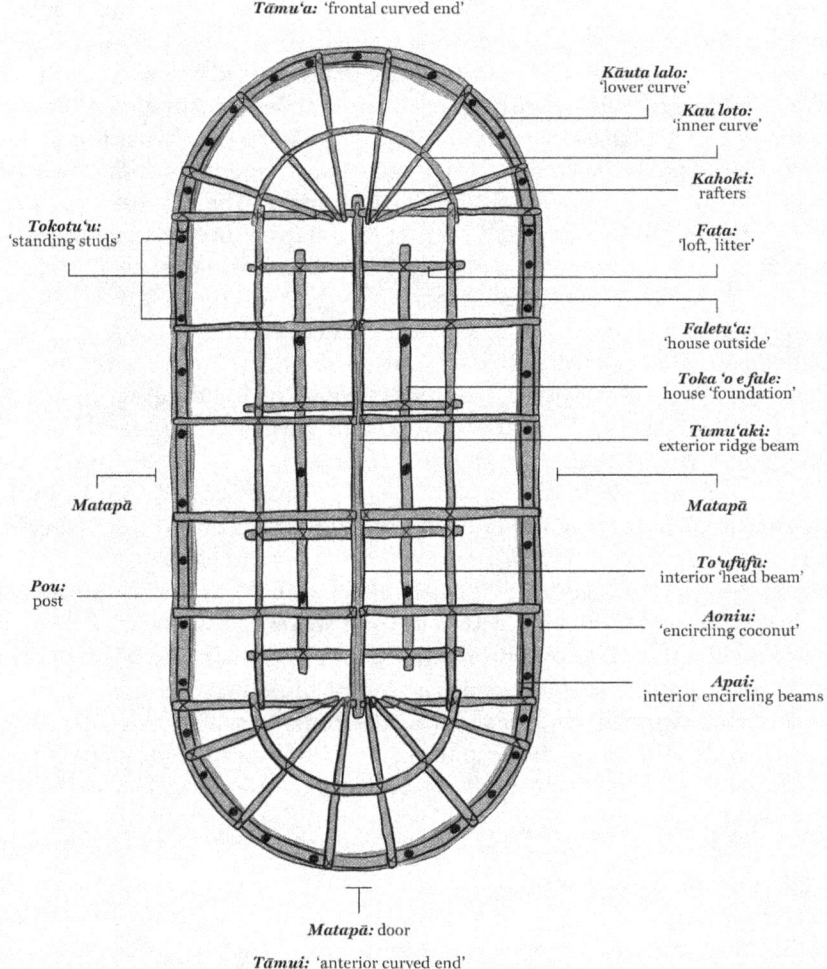

Figure 5.1. Plan of *fale tonga* ('Tongan house'). The plan was sketched by the author under the directions of Heamasi Koloa, based on his memory of the Free Wesleyan Church of Tonga on Kotu Island, destroyed during tropical Cyclone Isaac in 1982. © Arne Aleksej Perminow and Kristine Lie Øverland.

(referred to as its 'tail end' (*hiku*)) in terms of 'leading the way' (*muʻa mai*) and being closer to the point of origin. In Tongan terms then, natural growth is first of all referred to as an order of precedence whereby events or occurrences 'leading the way' cause later events to happen.

The Tongan House as an Analogy of Social Relations

One striking characteristic of Koloa's mode of elaborating the analogy between the elements of the material structure of the house and social relatedness is that the image of the house that emerged resonates strongly with Gunson's graphic image of Tongan pre-Christian cosmological beliefs (Gunson 1990). It also resonates with the graphic image of what I have described as phases of separateness in a regenerative motion of tidal, diurnal and lunar dynamics presented in Chapter 2 and 3. The process by which growth produces a strong and enduring tree may be incorporated into the structure of the house. The 'oldest' or 'senior' end of the 'chiefly' *toʻufūfū* ('inner ridgepole') that has grown closest to the roots or the tree's point of origin is the 'front' (*muʻa ʻo e ʻakau*) or the 'cause, centre, essential part' (*tefito*) and should be oriented towards the 'front end' (*tāmuʻa*) of the house. Thus, the essential property[7] (for the purpose of building an enduring structure that may last for a hundred years) of 'hardness/toughness' (*fefeka*) diminishes with the 'later' or 'younger' (*ki mui*) sections of the beam that 'follow' (*mui mai*) towards the 'softer' (*molū*) 'posterior end of the house' (*tāmui*). Koloa's imagery implies that the orientation of the chiefly beam, the 'inner ridgepole' (*toʻufūfū*), recapitulates the manner of growth of enduring things as the 'old head of the family' (*ʻulumotuʻa*), the 'cause/centre of the family' (*tefitoʻi fāmili*), with posts and stakes of the house analogous to later generations that are thus naturally obliged to support or 'carry' (*fua*) their cause of existence. The construction of the Tongan house may well be approached in the same manner as the construction of other tableaus of 'well-ordered beauty and importance' (*maau, fakaʻofoʻofa, mahuʻinga*). In contrast to the frequent 'building of boards of food' (*ngaohi pola*), for example, the 'building' (*langa*) and 'maintenance' (*tauhi*) of traditional *fale tonga* no longer made up a significant part of the practical life world on Kotu in the final decades of the twentieth century. Only a handful of small *fale tonga* remained in 1992, and none were built during any of my fieldworks on Kotu. Thus, I cannot, as I did with the 'boards of food' (*kaipola*), explore in detail the significance of the *fale tonga* in the experiential terms of its making.

In contrast to the important occasion of preparing a 'board of food' (*kaipoloa*), the building of a house obviously results in something more enduring and stable. Together with the interrelatedness of its constituent parts resonating with forceful regenerative dynamics, it is precisely the endurance and stability of the house (if properly maintained) that makes it appropriate to use as an analogy of the relatedness of social units. This is not because Tongan family groups, or groups at other levels of social integration, are inherently stable. Rather, endurance and stability seemed to be perceived as what makes some great or important families or groups stand out from other families or groups whose members (perhaps not being united by an overarching sense of a common purpose) might walk away from their positions as 'posts' and 'stakes'. People would quite often leave a house in order to be the 'inner ridgepole' (toʻufūfū) of a greater house. Just as the significance of the 'building of boards of food' (ngaohi pola) lay in its articulation with the dynamics of the multiple flows of events of everyday production and consumption, so does the Tongan house.

In terms of the puzzle of local responses and attitudes to ongoing environmental change the significance of Koloa's house analogy is also that it demonstrates a strong awareness that in reality stability and enduring orderliness is not something to be taken for granted. And just like the assembling of tableaus of beauty, order and importance in the form of food presentations, it may only be brought into existence by people committing to the task of achieving it by a common, focused and often exhausting effort. Such a perspective has very important moral implications for what people ought to do, what happens if they do not and why things go awry, which is key to an experientially grounded analysis of understandings of environmental events and developments. Thus, it is also key to solving the puzzle of local responses, which is undertaken in the concluding chapter of this book.

Intensifying Flows by Limiting Freedom

The 'door of the house' (matapā), then, is an image well suited to a discussion about the constitution of social relationships. It facilitates a flow interrelating what is inside and what is outside. Being a point of enhanced conductivity, however, the impenetrable quality of a house is emphasized at the same time. Thus, the door also denies the indiscriminate and haphazard flows by which boundaries dissolve. Attentiveness to strong or potent flows as well as impenetrable or strong boundaries seemed to run parallel through numerous fields of knowledge and interaction on Kotu and may be explored in terms of the dynamics discovered and discussed in the preceding chapters. For instance, Tongan ideals and practices of interaction among kin may be illuminated in such terms. Taboos constraining father-children, elder-younger, chief-commoner, brother-sister interaction may well be described as rules of respectful conduct that erect barriers against indiscriminate interchanges along a broad contacting surface in favour of intensified flows of communication at some points of contact, by radically narrowing down the 'freedom' (*fa'iteliha*) to act impulsively or 'haphazardly' (*noa 'ia pē*). For example, the so-called brother-sister taboo in Tonga restricts any form of intimacy among cross sex siblings and emphasises that crude words or deeds associable with hunger, anger or sexuality (Perminow 1993a; 1995) should not be communicated in their interaction. It was said to evoke a feeling of 'shame' (*mā*). Still, enduring ideals of mutual respect and support between cross sex siblings also emphasise that brothers and sisters should be strongly attached to one another. A brother should feel obliged to provide food for important events in the life of a sister, while a sister would often feel obliged to provide barkcloth, mats and 'Tongan oil' (*lolo tonga*) for her brother. Also, a brother and sister are strongly attached by having lasting and specific responsibilities and privileges as 'father's sister' (*mehekitanga*) and 'mother's brother' (*fa'ētangata*) at important events in the lives of their children. On the current perspective the relationship between Tongan brothers and sisters, may be said to be an intensely cultivated relation produced by taboos that restrict indiscriminate interchanges along a broad contacting surface in favour of orderly and appropriate interchanges at certain points of contact.

I am not primarily concerned with the ideals and practices of kin relations as something constituting a privileged principle of social organization; rather, these are some among several different kinds of ideals and practices articulated within a general dynamic of constitutive flows. In the previous chapter, I argued that the importance of building and presenting culinary tableaus of 'beauty, orderliness and importance' that momentarily materialized something that stood out in sharp relief against a backdrop of the ordinary flux of everyday living lies with an articulation of fundamental ideas about the relationship between wild and cultivated growth. In a similar vein, I would argue that a part of the significance of key kin relations was the clarity with which they stood out against a backdrop of the ordinary flux and multiple contingencies of everyday socializing. Thus, very strict demands to act according to the restraints of 'respectful conduct' (*faka'apa'apa*) rather than 'doing as you please' (*fa'iteliha*) may be argued to make certain kin relations stand out as particularly significant for achieving a sociality not wholly dominated by qualities understood by all to characterize human nature. My primary concern, though, is the constitutive potency of the flows by which people related to one another not just as kin but as friends, neighbours or members of the same church or congregation.

Slipping into the Flows of Everyday Living

The degree to which motility of persons and things dominated the quality of everyday living on Kotu can hardly be overemphasized. Indeed, allowing oneself to become an 'interface', so to speak, for the flows of everyday life exchanges represented the most challenging, exhausting but also rewarding aspect of doing fieldwork on Kotu. It was challenging not least because the relatively stable relationship between myself and my possessions, to which a life in Norway had habituated me, seemed under constant attack. Thus, it caused me to feel considerable discomfort as possessions on which I felt particularly dependent slipped out of my grip and into the flows of everyday borrowing. It was exhausting because of the energy demanded to respond to frequent 'requests' (*fai kole*) and because of the energy spent regaining access to things or getting hold of things to compensate their loss. Occasionally, the intensity of requests for the trifles of everyday life gave rise to an uncomfortable feeling of having lost control and my autonomy. Despite this, it was also quite rewarding to have things unasked for flowing through my own doorway from unexpected directions,[8] and I gained a degree of confidence that letting go of something need not mean having to go without and also the security of not being on my own; the trifles flowing out of my door connected me to networks of 'mutual support' (*fetokoni'aki*) extending from the *'api* in which I was staying far beyond Kotu and Tonga. The following episode illustrates the extent to which the motility of trivial objects may characterize the routines of everyday village living.

> Starting the day by drinking a cup of coffee was one personal routine that I was unwilling to forego. Thus, before going to bed, I always made sure that there was fuel in my stove, water in my cooking pot, coffee in my tin and a lighter nearby. Upon waking one morning, I went over to get the coffee going and, to my great disappointment, found that stove, cooking pot and lighter had all disappeared during the early hours of the morning. The only thing that remained was the coffee powder. Going over to our kitchen house, I found the stove and the cooking pot. But now it was just as empty of fuel and water as my can of kerosene and the rainwater tank of our *'api*. Having spent some time trying to locate water and fuel in our *'api* without result, I went over to our next-door neighbours with a jug and a bottle to 'make a request' (*fai kole*) to Koloa's *'ilamutu* ('sister's daughter') for some water (which was in very short supply on Kotu at the time) and some kerosene. The request for water was readily granted, but they were out of kerosene themselves. Luckily, our other next-door neighbours still had some left and were quite happy to part with it. So in about 1 1/2 hours I had assembled stove, cooking pot, water and kerosene and would have been all set to start making the coffee if I had been able to locate my lighter or a matchbox. After a short investigation, I learnt that the lighter had

been borrowed by one of the children of the *'api* – a son of Koloa – and taken to near the waterfront, so Koloa sent one of his children who had been adopted to our *'api* to reclaim it. About 30 minutes later, I was able to perform the comforting ritual of drinking my morning coffee. While doing so, I soothed myself by reflecting on the fact that although I had spent about two hours of effort to achieve a rather trivial goal, the time and energy spent were not wasted. I had at least contributed to keeping up the flows between our *'api* and three of the *'apis* with which we routinely had 'close fellowship' (*feohi*) – not really a bad return for the short delay of a trivial habit. Nevertheless, I reminded myself that it would be wise to keep some matches and kerosene stashed away somewhere in reserve (a notion not altogether foreign I believe, even by Kotu standards).

Clearly people on Kotu, having grown up with it, would feel somewhat differently about the intensity of everyday exchange. The idiosyncrasies of personal habits did not seem to involve the same kind of reliance on a stable relationship between persons and personal belongings. Nevertheless, impulsive statements that all essentially relayed that 'the Tongan way is in truth exhausting!' (*'Fakahela mo'oni 'a e anga fakatonga!'*) seemed to indicate among those born into it that a certain yearning for such stability may give rise to an ambivalence that makes some aspects of the realities of 'mutual support' (*fetokoni'aki*) seem rather demanding. Indeed, the keenness with which possessions, in a very wide sense, including objects, beings and knowledge, were desired and emphasized as being attached to persons seemed to run contrary to the strength of their generosity and condemnation of miserliness and withdrawal. People would not allow that which belonged to them to flow indiscriminately out of their grip, and they clearly considered it a great 'folly/incompetence' (*vale*) not to pay attention to the movements of their belongings. Few things seemed insignificant enough not to be attached to individuals of an *'api*.[9] Thus, among the numerous dogs, seemingly stray and moving freely around the village, there were none that did not belong to an *'api* by being named and possessed by specific individuals.

Some durable belongings were clearly given more attention than others. Men would pay very close attention to their fishing gear, like swimming goggles, flippers, spear, fishing net, fishing hooks and 'octopus lure/stone' (*maka feke*), and to their 'digging stick' (*huo*), axe, bush knife, paddle and other useful tools. Koloa claimed that he had inherited his octopus lure from his father and aimed to 'set it aside to pass on' (*tuku fakaholo*) to his own son. Similarly, when I returned to Kotu five years after my first fieldwork trip and asked to use the knife I had given as a present of farewell to one of Koloa's sons, he told me that he had 'paid close attention' (*tokanga lelei*) to its whereabouts and had not allowed the knife to be used outside his *'api* in these five years. These 'male things' (*me'a fakatangata*) were clearly among the most 'stationary' objects on Kotu and were only committed to the flows of mutual support with great reluctance. Typical 'female things' (*me'a fakafefine*) of everyday use like pots, pans, plates and other kitchen utensils were more often on the move, as were prestigious 'Tongan goods/valuables' (*koloa fakatonga*) of 'printed barkcloth' (*ngatu*) and 'plaited mats' (*fala/kietonga*) on occasions of 'outstanding importance' (*mahu'inga*). Finally, children understood to belong to particular persons and homes were also frequently objects of solicitation (*kole*) to 'have' (*ma'u*) or 'adopt' (*pusiaki*). Both in terms of how common various kinds of fostering arrangements were on Kotu and their role in constituting relations between people, a focus on such arrangements reveals quite fundamental qualities of sociality and understandings about how 'good spaces/harmonious relations' (*vā lelei*) may be achieved. This also makes an analysis of the role of children to 'nurture spaces' (*tauhi vaha'a*) between people key to an understanding of what people think, say and do when things threaten to go awry in the community, which is what the next, concluding chapter is all about.

Although children on Kotu were quite often 'sent away for adoption' (*ave ke pusiaki*), biological parents and children were clearly perceived to be strongly attached to one another. Indeed, as Firth claimed was the case on Tikopia (Firth 1936: 205–6), it would seem that precisely the perceived strength of this attachment made letting go of a child an event of extraordinary constitutive potency (see also Carroll 1970: 152; Levy 1973: 482–83). A Kotu father in his forties once explained:

> Granting a request 'to give up a child for adoption' is not easy you know. It really makes you 'hurt inside/suffer' (*loto mamahi*). It is not like giving up dog or something … Giving away *lī'aki* ('cast aside/sacrifice') a child is different; if I 'send away my child to be adopted' (*ave ke pusiaki*) by some other person, people will really understand that we are 'close kinsmen' (*kāinga ofi*).

I shall return to the use of the term *lī'aki* ('cast aside/sacrifice') in the context of adoption later to approach people's attitudes towards events involving a sharp decrease in the flow of interchanges between that which has been strongly connected or united. But this informant's use of the term *lī'aki* warrants a short comment here. Its meaning varies contextually between 'cast aside/neglect/ abandon', on the one hand, and 'lay down/sacrifice/devote' on the other, depending on the individual's prior experiences with adoption and the specifics of the situation at hand. There always remained a semantic ambiguity. This informant had himself been a *pusiaki* in his father's second cousin's *'api* and was now the father of five children. In 1986, all of his children lived with him and his wife, and he claimed to have refused numerous requests from people wanting to adopt them. He also said that he would deny such requests in the future. In 1991, however, two of the children had been adopted by his own foster parents. He emphasized that the main reasons he and his wife had granted their request was his gratitude that his foster parents had taken him in as a child and the fact that they were living in a neighbouring household so that the children would still be staying close by. Indeed, the amount of 'hurt inside/suffering' (*loto mamahi*) seemed generally to be perceived to increase proportionally with the distance between the 'child-giver' and the 'child-taker'. Thus, the reduction of the possibility for biological parents and children to impinge on one another's senses in the mutual flows of everyday communication of 'seeing one another' (*fēsiofaki*) and 'knowing one another' (*feʻiloʻaki*) and 'understanding one another' (*femahinoʻaki*) corresponded with an increase in the degree of 'hurt inside'. His use of the expression *loto mamahi* to emphasize how it 'hurts inside' to send away a child to be adopted by others serves also to stress the magnitude of the sacrifice; an act of ultimate devotion and generosity. For mothers who had given up children for adoption, the magnitude of the sacrifice and the *loto mamahi* was often described by other people, as well as by the mothers themselves, through statements like: '*Osi ave tama ke pusiaki, naʻaku tangi lahi pē*' ('When I had sent away my child for adoption, I cried a lot') or '*Osi ave ʻene tama ke pusiaki. ʻOku tangi pē e faʻē he taimini!*' (Her child has been sent away for adoption. Now the mother cries all the time!') People would expect mothers to express their sense of loss by 'crying' (*tangi*), but not for too long. Tears would be appropriate for expressing *loto mamahi* at such a great sacrifice for a week or a fortnight. If the *tangi* of the mother continued, it would be interpreted as negating the initial act of generosity nurturing a relationship between child-giver and child-taker.

The Way of the Hand That Lets Go

The understood desirability of keeping hold of one's possessions or persons whose existence one has caused, and the inherent strength of the attachment between the person and that which belongs to him/her or issues forth from him/her, constituted an important part of the background for ideological statements people from Kotu made about themselves. One Kotu woman once compared the *anga fakatonga* ('Tongan way of life/manner') and the *anga fakapālangi* ('European way of life/manner') precisely in terms of generosity:

> The Tongan way of life is the way of the 'hand that lets go' (*nimahomo*; lit. 'hand from which things easily slip'). It is not like the European way, which is the way of

'clenching the hand' (*puke 'a e nima*). Unlike abroad, things never stay for long in one place in Tonga but 'move about a lot' (*lahi 'alu*).

Although ostensibly about the difference between 'our way of life' versus 'the way of life of foreigners', her statement was clearly not made by one who had first become aware of the human capacity to act without generosity and to hold onto belongings by interacting with Europeans. On the contrary, it seems more reasonable to regard her understanding of the characteristics of a way of life with which she was not very familiar as one informed by her familiarity with a human capacity to act without generosity and a 'natural' human tendency to clench the hand around belongings. The Europeans of her statement, as in most statements involving the self-conscious comparison of the Tongan and the European ways of life on Kotu, seemed to serve as a prototype against which representational notions of what ought to characterize the acts of a 'true Tongan' could be elaborated (see also Perminow 1993a; 2003). Thus, for Kotu people, the lack of generosity and tendency to engage one another less extensively in 'close fellowship' (*feohi*) were prominent points of comparison when looking at other individuals on the island, from one island to another and from one *api* to another, as well as when comparing people from Ha'apai with people from Tongatapu and Nuku'alofa. Indeed, the woman who made this statement was herself talked about a couple of weeks later as one for 'clenching her hand' (*puke 'a e nima*) around valuable possessions. People felt that she was not 'distributing the Tongan goods' (*tufa he kakai 'a e koloa fakatonga*) that had been brought by most *apis* of Kotu to the funeral of her brother, stopping them from flowing on in order to secure these valuables for herself.

I would suggest that the combination of an understood human tendency to become strongly attached to things and persons, the natural desirability of holding onto possessions and the moral imperative to be generous lies the socially constitutive potency of the multiple flows by which people relate to one another. An exploration of practices of exchanging children indicates that the multiple relational flows were interconnected on Kotu. Thus, by focusing on local exchanges of children on Kotu we shall in the following explore how decreases in material and communicative flows running through primary bonds and points of contact may go with increases in material and communicative flows between bounded entities at other levels of closure and other points of contact. This analysis of the interconnectedness of relational flows is an important part of the puzzle at hand because it will be used to illuminate local perspectives on why things go awry and what to do about it when the final part of the puzzle is laid out in the final chapter of the book.

Composing Children

One of the routines of 'composing/assembling/building' (*ngaohi*) a child may be used to illustrate that modes of conceptualizing how important social relations may be established imply the interconnectedness of relational flows. The Tongan term for 'baby' (along with *pēpē* of English origin) is *valevale*, which signifies 'unable to think for oneself'. The first few months of a child's life were described in terms of a gradual development of the 'mind/understanding' (*'atamai*) in an existence dominated by *tauhi* or 'nurturing' through interchanges of *huhu* ('sucking') and *fakahuhu* ('suckling'). This gradual growth of awareness was said to consist of three phases or stages, indicated by the degree to which the child's 'face/eyes' (*mata*) shows signs of her being impressionable by responding to sudden movements close to the face. The child would be said to be *'atamai noa* ('of an undiscriminating mind') if she did not 'flinch' (*papaka*) when a 'sham thrust' (*fakapoi*) was made towards her face. This stage was said to be succeeded by a stage of *'atamai manu* ('animal mind'), when the child starts to flinch at sudden movements. Finally, the child is said to be *'atamai 'i tangata* ('of human mind') when it starts to cry when the mother leaves. Such a response was understood to show that 'the small child distinguished/knew its mother' (*'ilo 'e he tamasi'i 'ene fa'ē*). Although breastfeeding could continue much longer, several practical circumstances tended to combine to make most 'weaning' (*mahu'i*; 'to detach/wean away' or *mavae*; 'to be separated/weaned') occur during the first year. 'Breast inflammation' (*mahaki'ia 'a e huhu*), new pregnancy/birth resulting in 'undernourishment' (*fē'ea*), the 'sending away to be adopted' (*ave ke pusiaki*) and the child simply losing interest were all factors said to make weaning take place around the time when the child had become of 'human mind' (*'atamai 'i tangata*). Weaning was said to occur by physically removing the child from the presence of the mother: 'in order that it may no longer pay attention to its mother and her breast' (*ke 'oua 'e toe tokanga mai ki he'ene fa'ē pea mo 'ene huhu*). Sometimes this removal would be achieved by the child temporarily being looked after by 'grandparents' (*kui*), 'father's sister' (*mehekitanga*) or other close relatives. For numerous children, however, weaning would take place by being 'adopted out'[10] (*ave ke pusiaki*) to another *'api*, when they were between 6 and 8 months old. Either way, an important part of the task of separating mother and child (*faimavae*; 'to wean/bring apart') was said to be achieved by starting the work of 'composing/assembling' (*ngaohi*) the child by exposing its 'mind' (*'atamai*) to the presence of all the living beings of the *'api*. The person weaning the child would routinely encourage it to face away from him/her and try to make the child 'pay attention' (*tokanga'i*) to specific persons and animals of the *'api*. This was routinely done by softly repeating the proper name of persons, pigs and dogs as they entered into the visual field of the child, which was at the same time said to make the child stop crying for its mother.

This practice may be described as part of a process where the separation of that which has been strongly joined through a life-giving flow at the point of enhanced conductivity with the mother's 'teat' (*mata 'i huhu*) goes with the intensification of flows of impressions/communication at other points of enhanced conductivity such as the 'face/eyes' (*mata*), constituting new bonds. Using shared concepts about the development of the mind as a point of departure, I shall argue that it is illuminating to regard other acts and events particularly significant in the process of composing or assembling a child as involving a similar redirection of flows or interchanges.

In the context of child-rearing, the term *ngaohi* was used to refer to the forming of a child by making explicit the limits of the child's freedom to act 'haphazardly' or without considerations of appropriateness (*noa'ia pē*). Verbal instructions about how to proceed and behave, and scolding and severe physical punishment in contexts where it was felt that the child transgressed these limits, constituted everyday techniques of child-rearing. These limits clearly contracted as the child grew older. Behaviour described as *pau'u* or 'naughty' was perceived to stem from 'ignorance' (*kei vale*) in a 3-year-old child but would be described as *talangata'a* or 'insubordinate' if encountered in a 5- or 6-year-old child. The perceived transgressions of rules limiting the freedom to act *noa'ia* would often be described as resulting from a 'lack of building' (*ta'engaohi*). 'Naming' (*fakahingoa*) and 'teaching/educating' (*ako'i*) a child/youth were described as particularly important strategies for the 'composing/building' (*ngaohi*) of children.

Building by Naming and Teaching

Fakahingoa or 'naming' was described as 'an important thing' (*me'a mahu'inga*) in two ways. First of all, the named child was expected to be formed by receiving some of the characteristic qualities of the person after whom the child was named. Thus, a Kotu child named after my own son (who stayed with me on Kotu during my fieldworks) was quite consistently referred to in terms of being similar in behaviour and looks. The two were described as being *pau'u tatau, poto tatau mo e mata tatau* ('just as naughty, just as clever and of similar face'). They were even said to have the same food preferences. Secondly, the naming of a child was understood to open up the possibility for establishing a bond between the child and the one choosing its name, as well as between the child's parents and the name-giver. Giving someone the task of naming a child would thus imply that a future request by the name-giver to adopt the child would more likely be responded to favourably, the name-giver thus becoming child-taker. Similarly, consenting to name a child would imply that the name-giver might be expected to take on some responsibility for other important events of 'composing/building' a person, such as 'teaching' (*ako'i*) him/her a skill or helping to give him/her 'schooling' (*ako*) by contributing to pay the school fees for secondary education, for example. Quite often a name-giver would become a child-taker by paying the school fees for secondary education. Then the youth would be referred to as being 'adopted' and expected to stay with those paying the school fees when returning from Nuku'alofa for the school holidays.

These events of particular significance in the process of 'composing/building' a person – that is, 'naming' (*fakahingoa*) and 'teaching' (*ako'i*) – 'involve the increased intensity of some relational flow *at the expense* of other relational flows. From the point of view of biological parents, the best way of making sure that a child is 'composed' properly by receiving education often involved establishing points of contact between a child, a namesake and a name-giver. In terms of everyday 'close companionship/fellowship' (*feohi*), it would mean a decrease in communicative and material interchanges between a child and its original caretakers but would open up possibilities for the child through a 'close fellowship' (*feohi*) with new caretakers.

Doing a village census in 1991 to collect information about who had been asked to name a child on Kotu or who had had a child named after them, I became familiar with naming as a means of opening up a passage for flows of interchanges in the present as well in the future. One of the last *'apis* I visited to do the survey was one of our closest neighbours, whose youngest son had been born in 1987 a few months after my first fieldwork and who had been named after my own son. This fact had obviously not escaped me and had been emphasized on several occasions during our stay on Kotu. Nevertheless, I diligently enquired about the circumstances of his naming in my survey. I was told that I had written a letter to the 'family head' (*'ulumotu'a*) of their 'family' (*fāmili*), requesting that the child should be named after my son. Although I was unable to recall making this request, in accepting this story of name-giving, I clearly contributed to the child's biography as well as the history and flows of interchanges between us. I suspected that part of the significance of naming as an event of child-building was the potential it pointed to in the future. Therefore, I followed up by saying that I hoped his parents would encourage him to work hard at school so that he would be well prepared for secondary education away from Kotu and that I would offer to help with the school fees when that time came. This offer was well received and led to a marked increase in the frequency with which the little boy was encouraged to sleep in our *'api* and the number of occasions on which he moved between our *'apis* bringing and receiving food and other trifles of everyday use.

Although events such as these are perhaps most significant in terms of the child's future potential, they involve the establishment of contact points for flows of interchanges that may profitably be approached in terms of utilizing or 'sacrificing' something of unique and intrinsic value to achieve some other uniquely valuable good. Said differently, the establishment of any kind of relatedness or belonging may be approached as something feeding on or transforming other kinds of relatedness and belonging. Before going on, however, to elaborate further on the sense in which transactions involving children can be approached in terms of sacrifice, it is essential to provide a sociological outline.

Ad-option

The term *pusiaki* was used as a general term referring to the act of adopting a child, the act of adopting out a child and also to the child itself. This term was used indiscriminately to refer to acts and relations of adoption whether they involved transactions among people living within the same *'api*, next door, on different islands or in different countries. Also it was used indiscriminately to refer to both seemingly temporary and seemingly enduring or permanent arrangements. According to some students of Tongan culture (Gifford 1929: 26–27; Beaglehole 1944: 71; Urbanowicz 1973; Morton 1976), the two terms *tauhi* and *ohi* differentiate between acts and relationships involving the relocation of children much as the terms fostering and adoption do in English. The former refers to a less stable arrangement and a less total transfer of parental rights and duties, and the latter to a break between child and biological parents that is more fundamental and lasting. Although all of those with whom I discussed it felt that *tauhi* and *ohi* both referred to the same sorts of acts and relationships as *pusiaki*, they were unable to agree among themselves about the specific nuances of these terms. Some understood *tauhi* ('nurture/care for') to refer to a situation whereby someone takes on the task of nurturing and looking after a child, or alternatively where a child supports and takes care of an older relative. As the term *līaki* ambivalently connoted 'cast aside/neglect' as well as 'sacrifice/devote', *tauhi* would signify the kind act of taking in, nurturing and caring for a child for some people while for others it would mean the child's devotedness to support and serve someone to whom it had been given. The latter, however, would also potentially imply that the child may have to forego involvement with other constitutive flows of impressions such as secondary education. Because there was a general agreement on Kotu that formal education was of high value, the latter sense of *tauhi* would also potentially imply parental neglect.

The term *ohi* was generally described as synonymous with *pusiaki* but was never used spontaneously to refer to acts, persons or relationships on Kotu. When I proposed that there might be some semantic relationship between *ohi* and the term *fe-ohi*, used to describe close companionship/fellowship, Koloa disagreed. He felt that the term *ohi* when used to refer to children was related to the term used to refer to a banana or plantain plant, or its fruit, which has been developed by detaching a part of an old plant and transplant it. In principle, the terms *tauhi* and *ohi* seemed to be terms by which temporary arrangements of caring and nurturing and more enduring arrangements based on detachment and transfer may be elaborated respectively. The fact remains, however, that neither of the terms were much used on Kotu to refer to the transfer of children from one person or home to another or the moving children themselves. The formal registration of adoption was extremely rare, and the term *pusiaki* was used to refer to a wide variety of acts, relations and persons, both in terms of the extent to which rights and duties were transferred and in terms of the permanence of relationships over time. Still, the use of the term adoption in a very wide and open sense suits my purpose better than using the term fosterage or trying to differentiate between such transactions in a manner that people on Kotu seemed to avoid. Indeed, the term *ad option* or 'by choice' itself, without the other connotations of adoption produced by Western legal rules and practices of a permanent transfer of rights and duties with children, makes it particularly well suited to a very wide range of Tongan transactions involving children in motion. The events establishing adoptive relations were produced *ad option*, or by the multiple choices of differently situated persons. Furthermore, a general diffuseness in transfer of rights and duties and an uncertainty as to the permanence of the arrangement made the reproduction of adoptive relations the outcome only as long as the differently situated parties to the transaction kept on choosing in a manner reproducing that outcome. The fact that Tongan 'adoption' seldom involves a transaction done once and for all, establishing permanent relationships in a sense makes the term *ad option* better suited to refer to Tongan transactions in children than Western transactions of adoption.

In 1987, I did a census on Kotu showing that out of 139 persons under 28 years of age originating or staying in the 40 'homes' or *'apis* of Kotu, 36% were referred to as *pusiakis* or 'adoptees'. The sociological significance of adoption practices seems well illustrated by the fact that more than 90% of the *'apis* were involved in such transactions as either child-givers, child-takers or both. The remaining 10% of the *'apis* were quite young in the sense of being in an early stage of a cycle of household regeneration. Given the general extent of involvement in such transactions, there can be little doubt that the involvement of these *'apis* was only a matter of time. Sociologically, the material clearly indicates that one of the effects of the transaction of children was that it made for a remarkably equal distribution of children in the ʻapis of Kotu. At the time of the census, the mean number of children born to the child-givers' ʻapis was 5.8, with the number of children still referred to as belonging to the ʻapi (whether staying there or not) at 4.2. On the other hand, the mean number of children born to child-takers' ʻapis was 1.9, with children still belonging to the ʻapi at 4.3. These distributive effects were produced mainly by the fact that about half of the child-takers did not have biological children at all. Infertile married couples, as well as some single women, were able to ʻenlarge the ʻapi' (fakalahi ʻa e ʻapi), setting up and reproducing more or less autonomous ʻapis by adopting children of various ages and both male and female from their pool of potentially close relatives (transforming kāinga or 'kin' into kāinga ofi or 'close kin' in the process).

Although every pregnancy and birth on Kotu evoked several 'requests' (kole) for the expected child, and these requests continued to be made frequently during the first months after birth, biological parents were clearly much more reluctant to respond positively to requests to adopt the firstborn child/children than children with higher sibling numbers. The mean biological sibling number of children referred to as pusiakis was almost 5, whereas they became, in average, one of three children in the adopting ʻapi. Not surprisingly then, adoptions moved children from ʻapis in which there were many children to ʻapis to which fewer children had been born and/or in which few children were currently living. This sociological characteristic was further enhanced by the fact that older married couples who had 'sent away children to be adopted' in earlier stages of their married life and whose own biological children had moved away to other islands or had set up ʻapis of their own on Kotu were among the child-takers. Thus, the average age of child-takers on Kotu in 1987 was 50 years, while the average age of child-givers was 40 years.

The group of unmarried persons under 28 years of age consisted of 50.5% girls and 49.5% boys, while the group of pusiakis consisted of 55% girls and 45% boys. Given the limited extent of quantitative material, the preponderance of female pusiakis is too slight to indicate that gender was a significant variable at the level of aggregated outcomes. From the point of view of individuals engaging in such transactions, however, a consideration of gender was clearly significant for people wanting to 'enlarge the home' (fakalahi ʻa e ʻapi) by balancing the personnel of the ʻapi. Thus, would-be child-takers who had only male biological children (or who had previously adopted a boy or boys) would seek to correct the imbalance by adopting a girl, and vice versa. Similarly, child- givers would be far less likely to send away for adoption a child whose birth contributed to balance the personnel of their own ʻapi. The variety of compositions of child-taker and child-giver homes would thus tend to work against the preponderance of one gender among *pusiakis*.

On the other hand, one of the characteristics of the distribution of the ages at which adoptions were reported to take place clearly shows a considerable preponderance of transactions taking place during the first year of the child's life. More than half of the adoptions on Kotu were reported to have occurred before the child's first birthday. In contrast, about a third were reported to occur between age 4 and 11, with less than a tenth happening during the second and third year of the child's life. In general, there were clear peaks in adoption around the time when children are described as having attained a 'human mind' (*atamai 'i tangata*) and become receptive to 'building' (*ngaohi*), but adoptions were less likely to have taken place in the period between first birthday and the time when children had become more competent (*poto*) – that is, approaching another event of particular significance in the process of becoming 'well built' (*ngaohi lelei*), namely that of entering secondary school away from Kotu.

Finally, *pusiakis* predominantly moved among kinsmen. In 98% of the cases, child-giver and child-taker were relatives. In almost 3/4 of the cases, the kin relationship referred to as the basis of the transaction was patrilateral. Almost 2/3 of patrilateral child-takers were the *pusiaki's* 'father's sister' (*mehekitanga*) or 'father's brother' (*tamai/tamai'aki*), while another third were more distant relatives of the *pusiaki's* father. Of the remaining 30% of the cases, about 2/3 of the child-takers were the *pusiaki's* 'mother's brother' (*fa'ētangata*), 'mother's sister' (*fa'ē*) and 'mother's mother' (*kuifefine*), while another third were more distant relatives of the *pusiaki's* mother. All in all then, about 2/3 of the *pusiakis* belonged to the *'apis* of the siblings of one of their biological parents among whom the *mehekitanga* or 'father's sister' was the greatest taker, having adopted a little less than one third of all those referred to as *pusiakis* on Kotu. The pre-eminence of 'father's sister' as a child-taker seems to reflect a combination of her outranking her brother, according to Tongan kinship ideals, and the expectations that the youngest daughter should stay home to care for her parents when they grow old. For example, a single woman in her forties on Kotu claimed that she had not married because she was a youngest daughter and had stayed on to care for her parents. When her parents died, she stayed on in their house as the head of an *'api* to which belonged seven *pusiakis*, ranging in age from 3 to 24 years in 1987, four of whom were her brothers' children.[11]

The main aim of this exploration of the practice of adopting children on Kotu is to discover and foreground shared understandings about the natural force of primary bonds/attachments, which are redirected, cultivated and transformed into highly valued new bonds, making transactions of children constitutively potent. An ethnography sensitive to enduring and shared perspectives on how the world works (explored in the three first chapters), what is beautiful and valuable (explored in Chapter 4) and how to cope with one another (explored in this chapter) is quite essential in order to understand how people respond to whatever changes and challenges the world has to offer (which is the subject matter of the final chapter). Before laying out the final part of the puzzle, then, of local attitudes and responses to ongoing environmental changes and challenges, it is necessary to delve more deeply into ideas and values shaping everyday sociality and informing moral judgements as well as notions about what may be the best way forward when things go awry.

Constitutive Force of Mutual Sacrifice

As noted earlier in this chapter, the act of sending away children to be adopted was sometimes referred to by the ambiguous term *līʻaki*. This term signifies, on the one hand, 'devotion/sacrifice' and on the other 'casting aside/neglect'. I have implied that transactions involving children may profitably be approached in terms of sacrifice. But if the constitutive potency (to 'build persons' and to establish lasting social relationships) of flows of communicative and material interchanges related to moving children may be approached in terms of sacrifice, what is it that is sacrificed? I think it would be too simple to understand this in terms of adopted *children* being sacrificed to achieve something of greater value. Rather, I would suggest that it should be understood as one *relationship* of intrinsic value sacrificed in favour of other relationships as one constitutively potent *flow of interchanges* is transformed into other flows of interchanges constitutive of new relations.

The field of naming/building/adopting on Kotu was made up of a complexity of the aims, gains and losses of child-givers, child-takers and the children themselves. It would be misleading to identify the parties engaging one another in these flows of events as the one making the sacrifice, the one receiving the sacrifice and the sacrificed. Consensus among people in terms of losses and gains would be extremely rare and would depend on their personal experiences with adoption and how they were situated with regard to specific events related to adoption. Thus, some would emphasize the kindness of the one taking in a child to 'care for it' (*tauhi*), helping to 'build' (*ngaohi*) a child, paying for schooling etc. Others might accentuate the kindness of giving up a child to someone unable to have children of their own or of supporting (*tauhi*) someone in need. Also, as with the father of six who had sent away two of his children to be adopted between 1987 and 1992, views were not necessarily consistent or stable over time. What people did agree about, however, was that flows of events involving moving children turned 'relatives' (*kāinga*) into 'close relatives' (*kāinga 'ofi*[12]) and was accompanied by an intensification of other flows of 'mutual assistance' (*fetokoniaki*). Also, people shared an understanding of the fact that flows of interchanges related to moving children could stop quite abruptly if any of the parties involved failed to curb the understandable desire 'to close their hand' (*puke 'a e nima*) and thus ceased acting with the generosity of the 'hand that lets go' (*nimahomo*), which was needed to keep up the constitutive flows of social interaction.

I do not, then, understand the constitutive potency of events involving the movement of children to establish and reproduce social relations in terms of a clear-cut distinction between those making the sacrifice and those sacrificed. Rather, it should be approached in terms of what may be called *mutual sacrifice*. The establishment of adoptive relatedness seemed to demand that all the involved parties forego or let go of something of inherent value and was thus described as a mutual willingness to keep on making the sacrifices that reproduce adoptive relatedness. Vagueness as to whose interests were best served by the flows of interchanges whereby adoptive relatedness was established and reproduced characterized the discourse on adoption as long as the adoptive relatedness continued and all parties were 'satisfied/thriving' (*lata*). But in case of the discontinuation or redirection of flows of interchanges in the 'spaces between' (*vaha 'a/vā*), resulting from one of the parties refusing to keep on making the necessary sacrifices, this discourse of mutual generosity would be replaced by one dominated by the imbalance of the interests of the involved parties.

The socially constitutive potency of mutual sacrifice to transform primary bonds, or to redirect inherently strong flows of interchanges, may seem to constitute a cultural theme of quite general significance in Tonga. Reflecting on one of the most widely known myths of Tonga, that of the origin of kava, Queen Sālote once explained to the anthropologist Elizabeth Bott that: '... the myth expressed the *mutual sacrifice and understanding* between ruler and subjects that was essential to keep Tonga united and strong. It was this mutual sacrifice and understanding the kava ceremony was commemorating' (my emphasis) (Bott 1972a: 226). A Kotu version of the myth goes like this:

> An old couple living on the Island of 'Eueiki had a single daughter named Kava'onau ('their kava'), who was a leper. One day, the Tu'i Tonga came ashore on the island, but there was a famine, and they had no food to offer him. While the King was resting, the King's servant saw the parents kill their daughter and put her in the earth oven for the King to eat. The servant went to the Tu'i Tonga and told him what he had seen. The Tu'i Tonga was deeply moved by their generosity and told them to bury their child, instructing them to pay careful attention to the grave. After some time, two

plants grew up from the grave. A plant with bark like the skin of a leper grew from the place of the head, while a red plant grew from the other end. The plants were new in Tonga, and the old couple did not know their use. A little palm rat came to the grave, and it started to eat the plant growing at the head. The rat was not able to walk straight and zigzagged over to the plant growing from the other end. After having eaten from that plant it was able to walk straight again. The plant growing from the head was the kava. It is strong and bitter. The plant growing from the other end was the sugar cane, which is sweet. This is how they learnt that after becoming drunk from drinking too much kava it is a great help to eat sugar cane.

In the version of the kava myth quoted by Bott, the figure of Loʻau (turning up in Tongan legends at times of institutional establishment and change) comes along to instruct people to show their gratitude to the Tuʻi Tonga by sending him a part of the kava: 'And so kava was made for the first time and the rules and procedures for making it were established' (ibid.: 216).

The enduring potency of events of kava drinking to constitute social relationships has been explored in some detail elsewhere (Perminow 1993a; 1995). In the context of the current analysis, however, I would draw the attention to the significance of the mutual sacrifice, whereby connectedness constituted by a strong flow of interchanges between parents and that which has issued forth from them is transformed into another kind of social connectedness redirecting or feeding on the primary flow. The kava as a socially constitutive medium thus originates in a selfless act of giving up a relation of inherent, 'natural' and unique value and a willingness to forego the close, day-to-day 'companionship' (*feohi*) of engaging one another in 'mutual seeing' (*fēsiofaki*) and 'mutual understanding' (*fēmahinoaki*) that goes with it. This was reciprocated by the King's selflessness of foregoing to close his hand around what was offered by eating it. It may be argued that the act of killing a daughter to feed the King is a rather more demanding act of generosity than foregoing to eat her. However, just as producing children and having rights in them is what makes people parents, receiving tribute and being fed by the people may be said to be a fundamental part of what being a king is all about. Thus, the constitutive potency of kava may be said to have been produced in 'the gap' (*vahaʻa/vā*) or pipeline between the open hands of the King and his people.

To the extent that adoption produces transformation in two senses – the people intimately linked to the process whereby children are 'composed/built' (*ngaohi*) are changed as are the children themselves – it may be described in the sacrificial terms of the kava myth, in involving mutual sacrifices. Simultaneously, like the mutual sacrifice whereby Kavaʻonau was transformed to play a constitutive role in the establishment and reproduction of the interrelatedness of King and people, the *pusiaki* may be described to transform the interrelatedness between child-giver and child-taker by bringing them closer together through intensified flows of interchanges constituting 'close companionship' (*feohi*). Although the kava myth is about an original constitutive event of mutual sacrifice, it should be emphasized that the kava did not gain constitutive potency once and for all but is kept potent by continually involving mutual sacrifice in the frequent events of kava drinking. Similarly, the constitutive potency of the multiple and mutual sacrifices of adoption was not gained once and for all on Kotu but was kept potent by continuing to involve mutual sacrifice. As with regard to the kava myth, it may be argued that the act of 'sending a child away to be adopted' (*'ave ke pusiaki*) or 'sacrificing' (*lī'aki*) a child is a more demanding act of generosity than 'taking in a child in adoption' (*omi ke pusiaki'i*), and indeed the act of 'responding to a request' (*tali 'a e kole*) was described as a very open-handed act of 'love/compassion' (*'ofa*). But so was the act of making the request to 'care for' and 'build' a child as long as the child-taker refrained from 'closing the hand' (*puke 'a e nima*) around the child or other things that the flow of adoption had opened a channel for.

Refusing a *pusiaki*'s request to seek out the *'api* of its biological parents and siblings *noa 'ia pē* ('according to the child's whims and fancies') would be considered quite appropriate on Kotu. But refusing a child and biological parents 'to see one another' (*fēsiofaki*) and 'understand one another' (*fēmahinoaki*) altogether would be considered to be the 'unloving' (*ta'e'ofa*) act of someone 'closing the hand'. This does not mean that all *pusiakis* stayed in touch with their biological parents. Clearly, numerous events crop up to make this impracticable or undesirable. Additionally, people did sometimes act in 'unloving' ways. After all, the fundamental human capacity and the understood temptation to 'close the hand' is what makes it meaningful or even possible to talk about social relatedness in terms of an 'open hand' in the first place. If adoptive relatedness may be described as constituted by the intensification of flows in the gap between open hands (feeding on strong flows of prior existence), and if adoptive relatedness is not established once and for all, then the endurance of the relatedness demands that hands are kept open. This must necessarily put the stability of adoptive relatedness in constant jeopardy by the 'unloving acts' of someone 'clenching their hands' or 'closing their doors' that constitute the points of relational contact potentially facilitating strong flows of interchanges.

Indeed, one of the characteristics of adoption practices on Kotu was that numerous 'facts' of biography related to the complex of relatedness among name-givers, name-takers, child-givers, child-takers and children were continuously in the making. Some of the children living in *'apis* referred to as adopted in 1986–87 had moved back to their parental *'apis* in 1991–92. Not only were they no longer referred to as adopted but people were quite insistent that they never had been in the first place. Thus, givers, takers and children, as well as other Kotu people, would usually say about returned children that they/I 'just used to go there/come here a lot' (*na'a ne lahi 'alu ai/ha'u mai pē*) but that they no longer do so. People tended to refer to relational flows that had come to nought in a manner that reduced the significance of the history of that flow. Instead, they would concentrate on remaking relational histories and personal biographies in terms of flows of greater current potential. This does not, however, mean that the dilemmas related to increases, stability and decreases in relational flows were of no account. On the contrary, the complex of flows constituting relatedness among givers, takers and that which was given and taken in the field of naming and adopting constituted a moral and emotional minefield. Numerous conflicts of everyday interaction resulted as the intensity of some relational flow increased at the expense of others or decreased in favour of others.

One Kotu couple with no biological children of their own adopted a boy from the husband's brother's son in the 1970s. They made several requests to adopt a girl over the years, and it was finally granted in 1986 by the wife's mother's brother's daughter and her husband, from whom they received a girl six months old. At the same time, they were granted a request to adopt the 7-year-old son of the husband's mother's brother's son, who used to visit their *'api* a lot. In 1987, their 11-year-old *pusiaki* went with the husband to Tongatapu to enter secondary school. He stayed on Tonga for a fortnight while the wife remained on Kotu with the 7-year-old boy and the baby girl. In the absence of the husband and the 11-year-old boy, the 7-year-old *pusiaki* quickly started 'feeling homesick/discontent' (*ta'elata*) and stayed more and more in the *'api* of his biological parents and siblings. The adoptive mother kept sending for him. At first the boy reluctantly returned to sleep in his adoptive *'api* but kept returning to the *'api* of his biological parents and finally remained there. This was described as making the adoptive mother 'hurt inside/suffer' (*loto mamahi*) and making her 'cry a lot' (*tangi lahi*), but since the kin relationship on which the request to adopt had been based was one between biological and adoptive father, she did not feel that she could go and get him back and felt obliged to wait for the return of her husband. Upon his return to Kotu, the husband did go to his kinsman and returned with the homesick *pusiaki*. The boy kept on 'running away/fleeing' (*hola*) to his natal home, however, and was finally allowed to remain there. According to the adoptive father, the boy was obviously so set in his mind about wanting to return that forcing him to stay with them would perhaps 'destroy his mind' (*maumau 'a e 'atamai*).

During the flow of these events and for some time after, people voiced different opinions about the reasons, motives and morality of the acts involved. According to one theory, the boy's wish to return was a reaction to what was described as the adoptive parents' lack of 'sincere love' (*'ofa mo'oni*) towards the boy. Others felt that he had been adopted first of all to help look after the infant girl adopted at the same time, or that he had been 'taken' (*ma'u*) because he admired the 11-year-old adopted son of the *'api* and liked being around him; when the 11-year-old boy went away for secondary education, his motivation to stay on in the home might have been drastically reduced. Yet others felt that the reason why he returned was the sharp increase in chores and a corresponding lack of opportunities to play with the other children, resulting from the fact that he had to do alone the work he had previously shared with the 11-year-old boy who had left for school in Nuku'alofa. There were some who felt the problem was that the boy's biological father had been too 'receptive' (*tali lelei*) when the boy returned; they said that the biological father should have taken him back and encouraged the boy to stay, since the adoptive parents were more well-to-do and could offer better opportunities for secondary education. Others thought that seeing the way the work was heaped on the boy, the biological father probably doubted that the boy would be given the opportunity to go to secondary school anyway and thus felt more inclined to 'receive well' his returning son.

Four years later, the then 11-year-old former *pusiaki* was still staying in the *'api* of his biological parents and siblings, his career as a *pusiaki* being referred to in terms of his 'going a lot' (*'alu ai pē*) to the *'api* for some time and then 'just staying at home' (*nofo pē 'i 'api*).

Coping with One Another in a World of Movements

'Compassionate love' (*'ofa*) as the willingness to let something of inherent desirability slip out of your hand appeared to be understood as a fundamental requirement for achieving a beautiful, well-ordered and predictable society. From such a perspective, a sociality not wholly dominated by actions and events of 'no account' (*noa*) that 'crop up aimlessly' (*tupu noa 'ia pē*) as people grasp for and clench their hands around that which is desirable may not be taken for granted. It becomes an achievement of human collaborative creativity. But just as blurred phases of *noa* were conceived as inescapable (and essential) phases in the regenerative motions producing the growth on which people rely for their living, 'dumb, good for nothing' (*noa*) aspects of the person appeared to be understood as inescapable (and essential) facts of life, producing desires that may not be eradicated. The exploration of people's engagements with and understandings of the dynamics of the surroundings indicates that growth and vitality were perceived as the spontaneous outcome of a regenerative motion of merging and separation. The exploration of the aesthetics of ceremonial materializing practices indicates a conviction that growing things of particular significance and high social value do not come about spontaneously. They may not be achieved 'haphazardly' (*noa 'ia pē*) but according to procedures and regulations, making the manner of growth 'beautiful' (*faka'ofo'ofa*) and 'well-ordered' (*maau*). We also saw how the building of presentable boards of food may be interpreted as a further refinement of what was produced by engaging with the basic rhythm of merging and separation and subjecting the ingredients to particular procedures of separation, organization, orientation and distribution in order to create a tableau of 'order' (*maau*), and a tableau that stands out in terms of being detached from the multiple contingencies of everyday consumption and in terms of briefly materializing something that foregrounds an ideal order that mostly remains in the background in ordinary socializing. It is an order that recapitulates the significance of the relationship between that which leads or causes and that which follows or results. The symbolic significance of the Tongan house may similarly be approached in terms of the construction of a beautiful tableau of order that articulates the process of growth that produces *enduring* things in a world in which stability and endurance are difficult to achieve. Finally, the exploration of 'building/composing children', entangled in a wide variety of adoptive arrangements whereby people are engaged with one another through mutual sacrifice, indicates a shared assumption that the temptation to close the hand is constant. It also indicates an assumption that the decrease in one constitutive flow opens up for the increase in another flow of constitutive interchanges. The children were built, then, in a manner in which 'compassionate love' (*'ofa*) kept producing relations between child-givers, child-takers and children and in which such relations kept dissolving as people redirected flows of interchanges or simply closed their hands.

One dimension of the establishment and reproduction of adoptive relatedness, then, may be described in terms of the *intensity* of flows of interchanges, while another may be described in terms of the *endurance* of flows of interchanges. Of the two, endurance must clearly be harder to achieve, simply because it is produced by several people who must continually commit to the demanding requirements of 'compassionate love' (*'ofa*) and who may potentially opt out. As we have seen, Kotu people did not make this distinction, but the terms *tauhi* ('care for/nurture') and *ohi* ('transplant'), described to differentiate between temporary fostering arrangements and 'truly earnest' (Gifford 1929: 26) and lasting arrangements of adoption, seem to fit rather well with the differences of intensity and endurance. Thus, *ohi* arrangements may be said to have the beauty and strength of that which endures (like the Tongan house), but in real life endurance is rare, and it is very hard to know how enduring a *pusiaki* relatedness will prove to be. Also in real life, generosity is a difficult thing (and very 'exhausting' *fakahela*); it is fraught with dilemmas and ambivalence, both because people appeared to share Hobbes' pessimistic views on 'human nature' and because the flows by which people related to one another appeared to feed on one another so that the increase of one flow of interchanges goes with a parallel decrease of other flows of interchanges. This was consonant with a more general theme of channelling and transforming constitutively potent flows that characterized people's mode of relating to their environment and one another in several fields of experience.

Throughout the analysis, I have argued for the potential for discovering shared 'horizons of expectations' (see Shore 1996: 282) by taking seriously involvements with and conceptualizations of the components and dynamics of the environment that people engaged with on a day-to-day basis. Thus, I have explored the dynamics of people's understandings and involvement with their surroundings, their conceptualizations of natural qualities, their aesthetic sensibilities and their practices of relating to one another in the flow of everyday events. My emphasis on the potential for discovery in focusing on people's practical engagements is not an attempt to establish a unified grid of meanings that synchronizes individual strategies of personal goal achievement, producing homogeneity in individuals' understandings of their world and social stability. It does, however, represent an attempt to illuminate enduring 'culture themes'[13] embedded in everyday practices as persistent understandings that largely go without saying and that play an important part in shaping the multiplicity of statements, acts and responses to events in the world. These shared horizons of expectations of everyday life neither imply that Kotu people's attitudes were free from ambivalence nor that choices were free of dilemmas. Neither do they imply that people's coping with one another was, or has ever been, characterized by their agreeing with one another about the appropriateness of acts or the meaning of events. They do suggest, however, that the ambivalence, dilemmas and disagreements related to the flows of social interaction, produced by people trying to act appropriately and effectively, were embedded in fields of experience and meaning that tend to persist over time to make events meaningful. These insights about such shared and persistent understandings should be expected to prove quite helpful in trying to figure out why people responded as they did to changes taking place around them, the question that shall finally be answered in the next, concluding chapter.

Notes

1. According to Churchward's dictionary, *feohi* signifies '(to have) fellowship or communion or moral and spiritual comradeship' (Churchward 1959: 171). It is frequently used in a religious context, where it signifies achieving 'communion/oneness' by taking in and being taken in by God or Jesus.
2. Other ways of discriminating between 'frontal' and 'posterior/back' parts of the house were also common. Regarding the part of the house sectioned off as the 'bedroom' (*loki*), to which there was no direct entrance from outside, this was perceived as 'frontal' (*mu'a/tāmu'a*). One can note that specific events taking place in the house would sometimes involve the overruling of general criteria of orientation. A 'restriction' (*tapu*) consistently held to, even on everyday occasions of recreational kava drinking, was that a *faikava* must not be joined 'from the front' (*mei mu'a*), since this would mean entering the *faikava* from the chiefly end directly opposite from the kava-maker's end, the *tou'a*. The kava-maker would often sit with her/his back to the 'door facing the road' (*matapā ki hala*) so that potential kava drinkers would have easy access by 'entering from behind' (*hū ki he kava mei mui*). Thus, what was otherwise referred to as 'entering the house from the front' (*hū ki fale mei mu'a*) would be referred to as 'entering from behind' (*hū mei mui*) on occasions of kava drinking. Regarding the assembly of 'boards of food' (*kaipola*), the 'frontal end' (*mu' a 'o e pola*) would normally be positioned towards the 'front door' and thus the 'posterior end' (*mui 'oe pola*) would be close to the 'cooking area' (*afi*), affording the 'working people' (*kaungāue*) easy access when bringing the food to be placed on the *pola*.
3. For an interpretation of doors and doorways and their cultural significance in Fiji, see Toren (1990: 33, 35, 84).
4. Another term, *mata'i tofe*, refers to the pearl of a pearl oyster.
5. A significant exception to this public policy of open doors occurred during a certain phase of funerary procedures. During the 'preparation of the corpse' (*teuteu 'a e sino 'o e mate*) by those 'free of restraint' (*'atā/fa'iteliha*), the doors of the house would be closed and the windows (*sio'ata*) covered with 'barkcloth' (*ngatu*), entirely sealing the house off to keep those 'outside' (*'i tu'a*) from seeing what was going on 'inside the house' (*loto fale*) and to protect them from the naked corpse until it had been oiled with *lolo tonga* ('Tongan oil') and wrapped in *ngatu*.
6. Paul van der Grijp uses precisely the concept of 'house' (*maison*) to describe what contemporary Tongans refer to as *famili* – that is, ' ... a local group [that] stems from a number of brothers and their descendants ...' (Van der Grijp 1993a: 136). He claims to use this 'Levi-Straussian concept ... for purposes of clarity' (ibid.: 136).
7. 'Essential property' is used to refer to a property whose importance was emphasized by people describing the quality of specific plants for specific purposes. The essential property of 'sugar cane' (*tō*) for purposes of eating would be its

'sweetness' (*melie*), and this was described to be more 'at the frontal end' ('*i mu'a*), close to the roots, while the essential property of kava for the purpose of kava drinking would be its affective 'strength' (*mālohi*), similarly unevenly distributed.

8. Such unexpected material benefits were described by the term *tapuaki*, meaning 'blessing', 'good thing', 'benefit', 'advantage' and understood to be the unlooked-for reward of a generous attitude.

9. Medical recipes for making even some of the most widely known 'Tongan waters' (*vai tonga*), the ingredients of which were known by virtually all, were not used freely but 'asked for' (*kole*) and 'granted' (*tali*) by those said 'to have' (*ma'u*) a particular medicine. This would involve 'washing the hands' (*fanofano*) in a vessel of water to allow the ability to cure to flow from the one to which it belonged to the one who was granted to use it.

10. The durability of relations of fostering/adoption would vary enormously, but child exchanges taking place as the child was weaned would tend to result in more stable arrangements than exchanges involving older children. Certainly, the transfer of a 6- to 8-month-old child would be intended to result in a durable relationship between the child and the foster parent(s) and the other members of his/her new '*api*, as well as between child-givers and child-takers.

11. This home or '*api* was located between the homes of two of her elder brothers, who occasionally brought her food from their plantations, which happened to be partly cultivated by those staying in her '*api*. Thus, her '*api* was rather intimately linked to the '*apis* of her brothers and represented (as numerous other Kotu '*apis*) a not altogether autonomous household. Clearly, her capacity to run her own 'home' or '*api* and the 'close fellowship' (*feohi*) between her '*api* and those of her brothers' were brought about by the flow of children among these '*apis*.

12. Since about two thirds of the *pusiakis* were adopted by persons who would be referred to as 'close kin' or *kāinga ofi*, anyway, this interpretation must be qualified. The Tongan classificatory terms of kinship by which siblings with the same mother and father refer to one another with the same terms as even third cousins imply that there are some senses in which their relationships are the same. This does not mean that there are no senses in which the relationship between true siblings is quite different from the relationship between third cousins, particularly in terms of histories of sharing experiences of actual intermixing. Similarly, the histories of intermixing are different among even true siblings, some of whom are closer to one another than others and some of whom are brought closer together by precisely such experiences of intermixing as those involved in the practices of naming, adoption and 'child-building'.

13. The expression 'culture theme' is borrowed from James Fox, who has used the expression 'Austronesian culture theme' (Fox 2008) to approach the possible cross-cultural unity of Austronesia in spite of an obvious cultural diversity.

Conclusion

Calamity, Sacrifice and Blessing in a Changing World

━━━━━ ◆●◆ ━━━━━

Understanding and Coping with a Changing Environment

In 2012, two decades after the bulk of this ethnography of the relationship between perceptions of environmental dynamics and the character of cultural aesthetics and sociality was produced, people on Kotu Island built a sea wall to protect the lower part of their garden lands. As we saw in the introduction, people had not seemed too worried in 2011 by the potential destructive force of the 'red wave' (*peau kula*) moving in. Also, they had not seemed overly concerned about the loss of land on the 'weather coast' (*liku*), the dying trees, the transformation of the 'forest' (*vao*) into a swamp, or the loss of historical landmarks such as the 'twin pools' (*vai māhanga*) and the 'burial mound hidden in the forest' (*Langi tuʻu lilo*) associated with the high-ranked Tungī Manaʻia. On the contrary, they expressed confidence in being 'sheltered/protected' (*leʻohi*) from destruction by their staunch faith. Many appeared to turn a blind eye to the environmental changes, with some claiming that they had 'not yet gone to examine it with their own eyes' (*teeki ai fakasio*). People seemed reluctant to talk about what was going on and were apparently not thrilled by the idea of broadcasting the news about the sea eating their land. Thus, the very substantial and noticeable changes in the immediate environment became rumours further afield on the neighbouring islands of the Lulunga district, in the regional centre of Haʻapai, in the capital of Nukuʻalofa and overseas among migrants to New Zealand, Australia and the US.

By the end of 2011, however, such rumours had reached MORDI (Mainstreaming of Rural Development Innovation), a small NGO based in Nukuʻalofa. MORDI is stated as working 'towards aiding the rural isolated communities of Tonga [to] fight poverty' (MORDI 2016). With the growing awareness of climate change in recent years, MORDI's development projects have increasingly focused on environmental challenges. The NGO had previously been involved in development projects in the Lulunga islands of Haʻapai, where Kotu is located. According to its General Manager, Soane Patolo, MORDI took the initiative to conduct a survey aiming to find out what could be done to alleviate the problems of erosion and inundation on Kotu. In dialogue with the new town officer of Kotu, Halapua Puleʻanga, and a project committee from the Kotu community, it was decided that a voluntary work project would be established to construct a concrete sea wall where the encroaching sea was threatening the lowest lying part of the *ʻuta* garden lands. The new sea wall was completed by the end of 2012. By 2016, however, it was crumbling in places, and MORDI was planning to send another survey team to evaluate what future measures might be taken to strengthen this defence.

No one on Kotu in 2016 was averse to the idea of strengthening the wall built four years earlier, or to making it longer in order to stop the sea from eroding other parts of the *liku* coast. They were quite sober, though, with regard to expectations about the extent to which such a strategy might prove successful in keeping the sea at bay in the long run. The attitude of most people was that while it could not hurt to strengthen or lengthen the sea wall, reliable protection against the destructive forces in their marine environment was in God's hands.

Everyone agreed that the sea had encroached, with rising sea levels, higher flood tides and more powerful storm surges accompanying increasingly fierce and frequent tropical storms. People appeared divided, however, as to the underlying causes. Those considering themselves to be among the *kau lotu*, or 'the praying ones/faithful believers', did not hesitate to identify religious slackness as a very significant root cause for the current state of affairs. Thus, they were quick to point out how much more people went to church in the old days; how much more time and energy were spent 'worshipping' (*lotu*), 'doing duties' (*fai fatongia*) and 'carrying burdens' (*fua kavenga*) for the benefit of the local congregation, local minister, district minister and church president. Also, they would point out increasing 'sinfulness' (*faihala*) in terms of 'disrespectfulness' (*taʻefakaʻapaʻapa*), 'laziness/crookedness' (*fakapikopiko/ʻāmio*), 'deceitful/ false worship' (*lotu kākā/lotu loi*) and 'non-marriage cohabitation' (*nofo fakasuva*; lit. 'living together in the Suva manner'). Some people identified more with what was referred to as *kau poto* – 'the knowledgeable ones' (sometimes referred to as *kau saienisi*; 'the scientific ones') and were familiar with the idea that local sea level rise and 'changing weather' (*fēliuliuʻaki ʻa e ʻea*) might be caused by 'the air being made dirty' (*fakaʻuliʻi ʻa e ʻea*) by heavy traffic and industrial emission around the globe. No one, however, appeared to find the idea very credible – that something happening so far away could affect local conditions. Nevertheless, those identifying with a *kau poto* or 'educated/scientific' perspective tended to see ongoing environmental changes as a result of naturally unpredictable marine surroundings, rather than the result of religious slackness or moral decline. Thus, they would characterize the changes as '*me'a hoko fakanatula pē*', or 'things just happening according to nature'. With regard to what measures might be most reliable to counteract this and protect land and people from the destructive forces of an encroaching marine environment, whatever the root causes might be, people of *kau lotu* and *kau poto* persuasion appeared to be in agreement about one thing. Since God is almighty, they believed it must be in his power to control all forces of nature and thus felt it was prudent to seek his protection. Thus, in February 2016 as the category 5 tropical cyclone Winston was meandering through Tongan waters on its path from Vanuatu to Fiji via Tonga, *kau poto* and *kau lotu* alike were reported to have congregated in all the Kotu churches to beseech God for his protection with great fervour. After Winston had skirted and spared the islands of Ha'apai twice on its unpredictable path towards its devastating landfall in Fiji (where 44 people were killed), it was thought that *lotu mālohi* ('powerful/forceful praying') that was voluble and sincere had the capacity to gain God's graces and therefore that it might have been instrumental in keeping Winston at bay and diverting its course elsewhere. When asked whether they believed that the people on Fiji who had been less fortunate had not also 'prayed forcefully', all were sure that they had; however, informants of strong *kau lotu* persuasion questioned Fijian moral standards in general, and one volunteered that he had heard rumours that 'witchcraft' was common in the places where many had died during Winston. Thus, he felt that such a degree of sinfulness might reduce the efficacy of even forceful praying.

The significance of Christianity for Tongan sociality as what Frederik Barth in *Balinese Worlds* (Barth 1993) called a 'cultural stream' among '… other streams found within the broader flow of the civilization …' (ibid.: 177) and can probably not be overestimated. Attitudes to calamities, fortune, failure and success and ideas about the moral judgements underlying their cause as well as ideas about appropriate and effective responses and remedies cannot be understood without this 'cultural stream'. But as Redfield emphasized long ago in his perspective on the coexistence of 'great' and 'small traditions' (Redfield 1956; see also Barth 1993: 177), which inspired Barth in his effort to understand the dynamics of Bali sociality, 'Great Traditions', like that of 'intrusive' and historically recent Christianity in Tonga, may be '… a structure of ideas and practices that penetrates but does not encompass the lives of its practitioners' (ibid.: 177). In a similar vein, I would suggest that although the lives of contemporary Tongans have been thoroughly penetrated by Christian concepts, and although moral discourse is dominated by Christian terminology, Christianity is not all-encompassing. Rather, it should be seen as one of several 'streams of traditions' and kinds of knowing involved in shaping attitudes to calamities, strategies of coping and moral judgements in everyday sociality. To my mind, Christian doctrines and practices should be approached as a 'tradition' coexisting and combining with beliefs and certainties imbedded in fields of everyday experience and engagement to produce what might be called hybrid 'horizons of expectations' (Husserl, see Shore 1996: 282) as well as pragmatic strategies of coping with challenges appearing on this horizon. Thus, it is against the background of such a conceptual and moral blend that I seek to approach the puzzle of people's attitudes and responses to ongoing environmental changes encountered on Kotu in recent years. The relatedness between sinfulness, calamity, blessing and fortune to my mind lies at the heart of this puzzle; a relatedness that appears to remain central in the blend between a relatively recent Christian stream of ideas and enduring understandings and routines of engaging one another and the surrounds with a significant continuity with the older world view that Christianity replaced. Thus, it is my argument that the foregoing ethnography of such enduring understandings and routines of engagement will be key in fitting together the pieces of the puzzle.

This does not mean, however, that people's apparently laconic attitude and a marked reluctance to broadcast the ongoing changes were exclusively produced by this blend of world views. A general reticence motivated by a feeling of 'shame/shamefulness' or *mā* appeared to make people hesitant to call attention to their plight for fear of being ridiculed as 'incompetent/ignorant' (*vale*) and 'uneducated' (*ta'eako/ta'emahino*). This 'shame' may be related to a very strong emphasis in Tonga on the value of formal education and a corresponding stereotype of remote islands as backward and those remaining there as 'lazy' (*fakapikopiko*) and 'incompetent/ignorant' (*vale*). This stereotype appears to relate primarily to the value placed on social mobility, something first of all attainable by turning away from 'growing kava' (*tō kava*) on Tōfua, 'fishing' (*fangota*) in *Namolahi* Lagoon and 'plaiting mats' (*lālanga*) on Kotu in favour of 'looking for life' (*kumi mo'ui*) elsewhere in Tonga and ultimately overseas. The extent to which *nofo pē* or 'just staying' tends to be perceived as a socially stigmatized dead end may be illustrated by the following parental strategy of motivating a wayward son to 'look for his life' (*kumi ene mo'ui*) through formal education and by moving to new places rather than by following in his father's footsteps closer to home, as in the following story.

A man in his late thirties who grew up on Kotu moved to Auckland to 'look for life' in the last decade of the twentieth century when he was in his early twenties. By 2012, he had gained residency in New Zealand, had a permanent work contract within the construction sector and lived with his wife and children in a suburb of South Auckland. He had not been back to Kotu and Tōfua since leaving Tonga for New Zealand. In 2012, he recalled his last experience with the 'difficult terrain' (*tokakovi*) and the 'exhausting' (*fakahela*) conditions on Tōfua. He had moved away from Kotu to attend secondary school on Tongatapu, where he stayed with close patrilateral kin. Sometime in form 3 or 4, he and his cousin decided they were fed up with school, he recalled, and ran away to the island of 'Eua, where they spent the time relaxing, sleeping and drinking 'home brew' (*hopi*). One morning, however, they were woken up by the stern voice of their 'father', their *tamai*,[1] who had found out where they had fled; he beat them quite severely with a large piece of wood he found nearby. To their surprise, he did not bring them back to school on Tongatapu. Instead, he brought them back home to Kotu and from there to his kava plantation on Tōfua. Two decades later, he still vividly recalled how his father treated them like 'slaves/prisoners' (*kaupōpula*) over the next month or so; up before the crack of dawn, little food, long days of weeding and clearing new land for planting and having to carry heavy loads up and down the treacherous and steep footpaths of Tōfua. And every now and then, the angry and insistent question of his father; 'Is this the life you want!? For this is surely the life you will get if you "stay home from school" (*nofo mei he ako*)!' He recalled that it was just like a military camp. But two decades later, he described this experience as instrumental in turning him back towards formal education and away from kava growing and his home onto a path that gradually led him further from the place where he grew up. He also described his father's harsh measures as 'tough love' (*tā 'ofa*; lit. 'strike/punish out of love/compassion') that eventually led him to his new life overseas and for which he was now grateful.

It is likely that the social stigma of 'just staying' (*nofo pē*) and its association with backwardness may motivate reticence with regard to broadcasting misfortune, including the loss of land or environmental degradation. Thus, it is necessary to explore it as a separate part of this puzzle before delving more deeply into the general relationship between calamity and morality in the context of a Tongan Christian sociality that is a blend of 'streams of traditions' (Barth 1993: 177) or 'compromise culture' (Marcus 1980: 10).

What Happened in the Forest and Who's to Blame?

The two teachers at the Government Primary School on Kotu in 2011 were outsiders and very outspoken with regard to what might have caused the death of the forest between the village and the *liku* coast. On a revisit to Kotu, I approached them in order to film the schoolkids making their way through the swamp and the dead forest to reach the *liku* coast. I had filmed a similar expedition across Kotu in 1987 and showed them this so they could see the environmental transformation that had taken place in the twenty-four years that had passed. The schoolkids were first of all thrilled to see their parents, aunties and uncles as small boys and girls. In the film, they wear next to no clothes or are entirely 'naked' (*telefua*) and are seen diving into the pools in the forest from the thick boughs of the trees that then surrounded them. Although working on Kotu for more than a year, the teachers had neither heard much about the transformation of the forest nor 'examined with their own eyes' (*fakasio*) the state of the forest or the beach on the *liku* coast. Seeing the film, they were quite struck by the changes. One of them volunteered his opinion that it was people's own fault; that they were too 'lazy' (*fakapikopiko*) to go further than the uncultivated bush next to the village in order to get firewood. Thus, he was sure that the cause of the demise of the forest was local over-exploitation of its resources based on 'ignorance/incompetence' (*vale*) and 'lack of education' (*taʻeako*). While not denying that the forest had always been useful as a source of deadwood, wild fruits and nuts as well as bark and leaves for 'Tongan medicine' (*faitoʻo fakatonga/vai tonga*), Kotu people felt that there had been no intensification in the use of the forest for firewood in the period before the trees started to die. Some argued that the teacher had got it wrong; that it was only after the forest had started to die, they said, that it became more significant as a source of firewood because of the increasing amount of deadwood. It was also argued that there had been an overall decline in demand for firewood related to a marked population decrease on Kotu in the new Millennium. Thus, people claimed that compared to twenty-five years ago these days there were 'only a few people' (*tokosiʻi pē kakai*) living on Kotu: 'More *ʻapis* are now empty, and fewer people stay in those that are left', I was told. Finally, far more of the cooking was done on gas stoves during my visits in 2011, 2014 and 2016 than what had been the case in the 80s and 90s. Clearly, this had contributed to a reduction rather than an increase in the demand for firewood.

Thus, the outsider teacher's theory probably did not reflect realities of resource exploitation very accurately. His immediate readiness to account for the failing forest in terms of local 'ignorance', 'lack of education' and 'laziness' appeared to reflect a tendency of outsiders to assume that remote places are backward places. It also indicates that the harsh realities of shaming or blaming people for their own misfortunes might motivate people to be quite reticent about broadcasting unfortunate developments. Since achieving fortune and avoiding misfortune appears quite central to Tongan everyday religiosity, we will come back to this. But before doing so, we should see what other theories of what happened to the forest and who might be blamed emerged in the aftermath of its demise.

While rejecting the theory that over-exploitation was the reason why the forest had died out, some locals questioned why even the *tongo* or 'mangrove', which was the dominating species of the forest, should succumb to sea water inundation; 'that is strange', one person said, 'for the *tongo* is related to the sea. It is very much accustomed to seawater (*"Oku fāmili pē ki tahi 'a e tongo. Maheni 'aupito mo e vai tahi'*). Some said that it was rumoured that some years ago one of the elders of Kotu had started to pour out kerosene in the forest in order to kill off mosquitos breeding in and around the twin pools and increasingly plaguing villagers. This practice of poisoning the mosquitos' breeding grounds in the forest was said to have been dropped in favour of introducing *lapila* fish[2] imported from Nomuka island into the pools and the growing swamp that the forest was transforming into. The elder had since passed away, but his son confirmed that his father had indeed occasionally poured some kerosene into the pools. He emphasized, however, that the quantity used was very small and strictly limited to the two small pools themselves, since that was where the mosquitos were believed to breed. Thus, he doubted that the quantities in question could be sufficient to explain the transformation of the entire forest. Rather than environmental change being caused by contamination, he felt that it was salt-water inundation that had killed the forest and made it an ideal environment for mosquitos, which his father in turn made an effort to control. In response to the question why a *tongo* or 'mangrove' forest that many people described as *fāmili ki tahi* or 'related to the sea' should succumb to inundation, he claimed of the two varieties of mangrove on Kotu – the *tongo* and the *tongo lei* – the latter, which was the dominant species of the forest, does not thrive in very salty conditions. Others on Kotu agreed that only the *tongo* thrives in a saline environment and pointed out in 2016 that it was now reappearing in the forest between the village and the *liku* coast.

Environmental change and its relationship to global climate dynamics, regional geological events and local human agency is too complex to conclude with certainty what happened to the forest between the village and the weather coast on Kotu. What is most striking for the purpose of the current puzzle of people's laconic responses to the undeniable changes that had taken place, of a silence bordering on secrecy, is the local reticence and resistance to portray themselves as victims of misfortune, with the potential that there is for being ridiculed, shamed or blamed for their own plight. So far we have seen how a general association between success, social mobility and moving away, and an accompanying stigmatization of 'just staying' (*nofo pē*) as an expression of backwardness and 'ignorance/

incompetence' (*vale*), might make it preferable to let what had happened to the forest stay in the forest. But at an existential level, there may be more at stake for people than fear of derision and ridicule when powerful forces that surround people cause damage and the sea nibbles at the very ground on which they make their stand and work to re-create a community worth living in. In what follows, I shall argue that at an existential level the apparent complacency and reticence, nurtured by fear of blame, is related to a cultural complex of enduring ideas about the human condition – that is, their situation and challenges in a world where they routinely engage with the dynamics of forceful and unpredictable surroundings in order to survive and thrive. In order to discover the characteristics of this cultural complex, it is necessary, I think, to turn to what people themselves again and again described as their most invaluable asset and most important strategy for surviving and thriving with one another in such powerful surroundings: their faith. Through the three decades that I attended Methodist services in Tonga, one of the warnings most frequently and most forcefully repeated from the pulpit of the numerous churches on Kotu was: "*Oua teke falala he ivi 'o e tangata!*" ('Do not rely on the strength of Man!') As Rosaldo once pointed out in the introduction to *Culture & Truth* (Rosaldo 1993), there may be considerable 'force in a simple statement taken literally' (ibid.: 2). It is high time to take seriously Tongan Christianity as a means to make sense of and cope with the potentially overpowering and destructive forces of the surrounds; a 'weather-world', to borrow a concept from Tim Ingold, 'in which every being is destined to combine wind, rain, sunshine and earth in the continuation of its own existence' (Ingold 2011: 115). These are surroundings of multiple motions within which the qualities of the world change as tides go in and out, as night falls and day dawns, as the moon waxes and wanes, as things grow, as presentations are made, as substances and persons flow, as sociality unfolds and as moral judgements are made.

Tuku Kelekele; 'Placing the Land'

In Chapter 1, 2 and 3, about everyday motions of merging and separation, we saw how dynamics that were central in many Polynesian pre-Christian cosmogonical and cosmological narratives still characterized modes of referring to and engaging with environmental components and processes in the final decades of the twentieth century on Kotu. Thus, in spite of a marked discontinuity with regard to pre-Christian myths and tales in favour of Biblical narratives, it was argued that themes of world views that predate Christianity may be discovered in enduring ways of perceiving and engaging with environmental dynamics in many everyday life activities. In later chapters, it was shown how these discoveries may be used as a basis for an ethnographic analysis of Tongan cultural aesthetics and sociality. Christianity had clearly 'penetrated' (Barth 1993: 177) Tongan sociality long before my fieldworks, and churches remain the dominant arenas of sociality on Kotu as elsewhere in Tonga. Although a forceful stream or layer of culture, Christian ideas and practices do not, I have claimed, 'encompass the lives of its practitioners' (ibid.: 177). It is my argument that enduring ways of perceiving and engaging with environmental dynamics are also key to understanding Tongan everyday religiosity. Alfred Gell has argued that an 'existential anxiety' (Gell 1995: 50) related to a chronic threat of annihilation underlies a preoccupation with differentiating, separating and protecting that comes through strongly in the aesthetics and arts of pre-Christian Polynesia (Gell 1998). But as we saw in Chapter 4, about the enduring significance of creating tableaus of 'beauty' (*faka'ofo'ofa*), 'order' (*maau*) and 'importance' (*mahu'inga*), a preoccupation with creating orderliness by means of differentiation and separation has not gone away with Christianization. Neither, I would argue, has the need for insulation and protection from potentially overpowering surroundings. Thus, reconfirming an alliance with God to achieve protective intervention against misfortunes understood to chronically threaten human life and well-being appears to remain central to everyday religiosity.

While pre-Christian narratives about the world and its workings are not well known, then, and were never told on Kotu, the origin myth of Tongan Christianity itself is very well known and often retold. In order to explain the reason why the concept of *le'ohi/le'o*, signifying 'shelter, protect/guard', always figures so prominently in Tongan Methodist church services, in 2012 'Isikeli Lātū from Kotu relied precisely on the foundational story of Tongan Christianity. In 1986, he still lived on Kotu with his family as a respected member of the local congregation of the Free Constitutional Church of Tonga (*Siasi Tauatahina Konisitutone 'o Tonga*). This Methodist church was founded by his father's brother, 'Ahokava Lātū, when he broke from another Methodist church, The Free Chiefly Church of Tonga (*Siasi Tauatahina 'o Tonga Hou'eiki*) as a result of dissatisfaction with church leadership and allegations that the church leaders were 'eating the money' (*kai pa'anga*). In the 1990s, 'Isikeli had moved away from Kotu and risen from a position as *setuata* or 'church steward' up through the ranks of the church. Twenty years and several moves later, he had become first *faifekau* or 'church minister', then *faifekau pule* or 'head/leading church minister', and finally *faifekau tokoni* or 'assisting church minister' at the main church in Nuku'alofa and next in rank to the *'eiki palisiteni 'o siasi* or 'noble church president'. By 2012, the church president had passed away and 'Isikeli had become acting church president until a new president could be elected at the next annual church conference. In a conversation about the root causes of misfortune, he told the following version of the foundational story of Tongan Christianity:

> In 1845, a few years after Taufa'āhau Tupou I was baptized and made king of all of Tonga at Pouono in Vava'u, he decided to return there to make a covenant with God on behalf of Tonga. The King had brought his Bible to Pouono and bent down to scoop up a handful of soil from the ground. He placed this 'soil' (*kelekele*) on the Bible and lifted it up toward Heaven before saying: *"Oku ou tuku 'a e kelekele mo e kakai 'o Tonga ki he Langi keke pule pē ki ai'*; 'I place/dedicate the land and people of Tonga to Heaven so that you shall rule over it all.'

According to 'Isikeli, this pledge, covenant or act of dedication established a 'binding/dependable contract, covenant' (*alea pau*) between all Tongans and the Lord of Heaven that he would shelter Tonga from all evil as long as Tongans abided by his taboos and worshipped him. By placing the totality of 'land and people' in God's hands, 'Isikeli argued, the 'binding contract/ covenant' (*alea pau*) also included all of the 'Tongan manner' (*'ulungaanga fakatonga*) and made God the overseer of even traditional Tongan taboos of respect and avoidance related to the kinship ideology of 'compassion/ love' (*'ofa*) and 'reverence/respect' (*faka'apa'apa*). In a conversation in 2014, a Tongan Mormon bishop also emphasized the significance of this 'binding contract' in terms of the protection it produced for those abiding with the terms of the contract. Thus, he said:

> You know at that time there were many colonial powers offering protection to the islands of the South Pacific. But King Taufa'āhau Tupou I was 'very clever' (*poto 'aupito*). He refused to let Tonga become a colony under protection of any European power. Instead he 'placed/dedicated the land' (*tuku kelekele*) to God and thus gained the most powerful ally of all!

According to the many Tongans with whom I have discussed the root causes of failure and misfortune over the years, breach of this binding contract with God may lead to a loss of his protection or preventive intervention. Breaches of contract appear to be understood to open up vulnerability to all kinds of misfortunes and accidents pressing, as it were, against the perimeter of God's protection. Similarly, acts reconfirming the original pledge and the placing of the land and people of Tonga in God's hands appear to be understood to ward off misfortune by strengthening the perimeter of God's protection. Responding to a question of what he felt were the root causes of destructive events related to tropical cyclones, tsunamis and earthquakes, 'Isikeli thus characterized them as *me'a fakafafangu* or 'wake-up calls, warnings'; events that should remind people of the need to hold aloft the light that worship produces so as to keep away the darkness. So just like Koloa had done more than twenty years earlier on Kotu, 'Isikeli described *lotu* or worship as the most important source of 'light' (*maama*); words and actions operating to keep at bay the 'darkness' (*po'uli*) believed by most to have dominated Tonga in the 'dark times' (*taimi fakapo'uli*) before King Taufa'āhau Tupou I placed Tonga in God's hands through the Covenant of Land offering in Pouono.

As Mike Poltorak has noted in his analysis of stigmatization and contestation related to 'mental illnesses' in Vava'u (Poltorak 2007), morally inappropriate behaviour in the form of rumours and gossip quite often crop up in Tonga as explanations for such illness (ibid.: 16–18). But in the form of rumours and gossip explanations using morally inappropriate behaviour as true, underlying causes are by no means limited to discourse about mental illnesses. Root causes of a wide variety of abnormal, unfortunate events or conditions are very often identified in acts breaching the original covenant through which God's protection was granted and that is still earnestly and frequently reconfirmed through *lotu* or 'worship'. As may be recalled, those identifying with a *kau lotu* perspective perceived local environmental changes to be caused by a moral decline and lack of worship, while those identifying with a *kau poto* perspective tended to perceive the causes as *me'a fakanatula* or a 'thing of nature' (although agreeing that protection against destructive natural events was ultimately in the hands of God). Similarly, people of strong *kau lotu* persuasion would account for all kinds of illnesses, personal afflictions and accidents as caused by breaches of taboos and lack of faith. Those identifying more with an 'educated/scientific' (*kaupoto/kau saienisi*) perspective tended to explain fewer kinds of misfortunes by underlying moral breaches. Thus, only the diehard *kau lotu* would explain serious and sometimes fatal but common conditions related to *ma'olunga toto* ('high blood pressure'), *suka* ('diabetes') and *kanisa* ('cancer') in terms of *mahaki pē*; 'just illness' (i.e. with no hidden underlying moral cause). In 2011, a religious movement called *Kai manna mei Langi* (signifying 'Eat *manna* from Heaven'), with a particularly uncompromising belief in transgressions as a cause of illness and in God's power to heal, recruited a handful of followers on Kotu. Followers were strictly forbidden to seek a cure through Western medicine in favour of unfailing faith, ecstatic worship and treatment with an ointment of olive oil said to originate in the Holy Land itself. On Kotu, it was the beginning of the end for the movement when a woman in her forties suffering from a growing ulcer in the stomach finally broke with the movement to seek medical treatment at the Vaiola hospital in Nuku'alofa, where she soon after died from cancer. To most people on Kotu and elsewhere in Tonga, the faith of *Kai manna* was far too uncompromising, and the evangelical movement appeared to have died out by 2014.

With regard to sudden and totally unexpected accidents, however, rather than common and serious illnesses, *kau lotu* and *kau poto* alike appeared to agree that the cause was hidden or unconfessed moral transgression. For instance, serious or fatal shark attacks would always be accounted for in terms of the victim's hidden and unconfessed theft from church or a minister, leading to a loss of God's protection, which in its turn would expose the victim to the shark's natural capacity to maim and kill. Thus, a very common expression when unforeseen misfortune strikes is simply *uʻu!* or 'a bite!' – that is, a shark's bite. This may be illustrated by how people reacted to unfortunate episodes in the course of everyday events during my stays on Kotu.

In 1987, an 11-year-old boy died on the island of Fotuhaʻa when he was stung by a Red Firefish (*Pterois volitans*) (Randall 1990: 80) known as *houhau lā* in Tonga. The tragic death became a much discussed topic on Kotu; after a while, a consensus on the underlying cause of death was a past quarrel between the father of the boy and the father's uncle, with whom the boy stayed as an adopted child, about where to bury the boys grandfather who had passed away in Nukuʻalofa. The boy's father who had also moved to Nukuʻalofa was rumoured to have denied his father's brother the permission to bring the body of the boy's grandfather back to Fotuhaʻa for burial and had 'shaken his fist in the face' of his father's brother (*tuhutuhuʻi*; lit. shaking the index finger).[3] It was this immoral act of disrespect and disobedience that caused repercussions for the offspring of the offender.

A fundamental idea related to Tongan notions of misfortune appears to be that there exists a host of hostile or indifferent components of the environment with a natural capacity to harm people who have been rendered without protection. But notions of misfortune in some cases also involve a strong emphasis on a kind of symmetry between cause and consequence. For example, the particularly painful death of a middle-aged man on Kotu in 1987 was held by many to have been caused by him killing his neighbour's pig in anger by spearing it through the stomach. This, people claimed, explained why the man should suffer from such stomach pains on his deathbed and why a man in his prime should die at all. Almost thirty years later, his death was described by one villager as having been caused by his 'bad-tempered nature' (*angaʻiteʻita*) and his tendency to become 'very angry' (*ʻita lahi*) and respond in a disproportionate manner. Likewise, birth defects in Tonga have quite often over the years been represented as the outcome of angry or greedy acts or a failed duty to submit to a higher authority or to respect higher rank. For instance, when a child was born with only two fingers on each hand, the cause was said by one informant to be that the child's mother during pregnancy had cut off and stolen some of the legs of an octopus that her father's sister was drying at the back of her compound. Likewise, a child born with a crooked leg was said to be the result of the mother's act of cutting holes in her husband's trousers during pregnancy because she was angry with him.

As a response to a question in 2012 of whether it was always the mother's transgression during pregnancy that was to blame for birth defects, 'Isikeli, who was then acting president of the Free Constitutional Church of Tonga, answered after hesitating for a few moments: 'No, since the left side of the body is the female side and the right side of the body is the male side, the cause of defects on the left side is something done by the mother while the cause of defects on the right side is something done by the father.' He looked pleased with the neatness of this explanation, and after a short pause he added: '*mālie e?*' or 'well composed, don't you think?' While the expression *maau* in Tonga is used to commend an aesthetic material constellation like a food presentation for being well 'composed' (*ngaohi*) or assembled, *mālie* is used to commend the artistic value of songs, dances, speeches and stories. Verbal performances like 'speeches' (*lea*) and 'stories' (*talanoa*) are often responded to in terms of their perceived truth value as well as their aesthetic value. Thus, audiences routinely support performers by shouting out *mo'oni!* ('So true!') as well as *mālie* ('So well composed!') The fact that he described his comment on gendered causation as *mālie* may indicate that he was more concerned about the aesthetic value than the truth value of the explanation. Since all actual cases of defects appeared to blame mothers' acts during pregnancy, I would suggest that his Biblical association of the left hand side with women and the right hand side with men may not have been widely shared. The church president's particular beliefs quite clearly find resonance in the Old Testament with the principle of 'an eye for an eye and a tooth for a tooth'.

Likewise, in the Bible, there is a widely held notion equating 'generous/compassionate deeds' (*'ofa*) with good fortune. Thus, just as unexpected misfortune tends to be discussed in terms of antisocial transgression, lucky breaks tend to be described as *tāpuaki* (a sign of 'blessing') (Churchward 1959: 457).

One central idea within Tongan Christian morality, then, appears to be that punishment and reward for sinful and virtuous deeds are not necessarily postponed until Judgement Day and neither are they only a question for the afterlife. The overwhelmingly dominant theme in church services was not punishment, however, but God's power to protect and safeguard people from *mala'ia* or 'misfortune' and the gratitude to which this entitles him. Above all, the message from the pulpit was that people should 'not trust the strength of man' (*'oua te ke falala he ivi 'o e tangata*), and that man relies on God's protective intervention to keep at bay all that may harm and destroy life. Above all, the required response from the congregation was voluble expressions of gratitude (*fakefetaʻi*) for being 'spared and granted life and well-being to this day' (*malo e tau lava/ malo e moʻui ki he ʻahoni*). And such a strong concern with the necessity to have access to God as a protective ally with the power to ward off harm and destruction and thus achieve well-being was by no means limited to church services. Thus, many everyday routines appeared to exist to reconfirm the bond with God as the ultimate source of protection and well-being.

From Chapter 5, we may recall the significance of 'nurturing spaces' (*tauhi vahaʻa*) in establishing and reproducing relations of everyday sociality. Everyday religiosity in Tonga, I would argue, may also be approached in terms of constitutive flows nurturing a space understood to be of singular importance for survival and well-being; the space between God and Tonga, which was initially opened by the Covenant of Land offering in Vavaʻu. In this space, the hierarchy of church ministers and presidents clearly has a key role in mediating or facilitating the flows that create a 'good space' (*vā lelei*) between people and their protector against destruction; the ultimate source of well-being.

Everyday protective practices routinely involve generous acts of *ʻofa* or 'love/compassion' towards church ministers and church presidents or other people in positions of high rank within the realm that was placed in God's hands through the Covenant. Thus, many informants over the years have explained that if you buy a new car, the *faifekau* or 'minister' should always be brought an 'envelope of money' (*sila*) and offered transport to the market or his garden lands to acquire yams or other food crops as a sort of spiritual insurance policy against future accidents. But also persons of rank, such as a man's sister (*tuofefine*) or father's sister (*mehekitanga*), may be brought gifts and offered transport in order to 'open up' a new car for safe use. Rather than being elaborate or highly ritualized, these strategies of 'nurturing a space', which includes God, are often quite low key and may sometimes be hard to notice.

Thus, visiting a friend who had moved from Kotu to Tongatapu in 2004, it was only after the event that it became clear that such insurance had been taken out right under my nose in the form of what is known as *hopoki* or 'a first embarking/inauguration'. This happened whilst we were sitting out, once, in front of the house. The head of the household's wife's brother and some of his children stopped by in his car. He sat down with us for a smoke and to exchange news but rose when his sister and a few other women and children of the household came out. They all went over to his car and drove off, leaving me and the head of the household to continue our conversation about the 'old days' on Kotu. After an hour, they returned with a couple of baskets of yams and sweet potatoes, which were carried into the kitchen house. Shortly after, the brother and his children took their leave and went off back home. When the wife joined us again, I asked where her brother had taken her. The household head answered on her behalf:

> He has just bought a new van and came to offer to transport his sister and her food. It was a *hopoki* ('first embarking'). It is just like the *hopoki vaka* ('the first embarking of the boat') that used to be done with new boats in order to avoid sinking. *Hopoki* is still very important, and often the sister, the *faifekau* ('minister') or both are offered transport in order to avoid future accidents.

Apparently, the higher the rank – within kindred, church or kingdom – of the position towards which generous and compassionate *'ofa* is offered, the more emphatically it reconfirms the 'binding contract' (*alea pau*) of the covenant. Also, I would argue, the more substantial the 'sacrifice', understood as work and that which is surplus channelled into this space (and that could have been channelled elsewhere), the more forcefully it nurtures the 'space' (*vaha'a/vā*) between people and their ultimate protector and source of future well-being and security from surrounding destructive forces. Thus, in June 2012, before the 'official opening' or *huufi fale* of the brand new central church building of the Free Constitutional Church of Tonga in Nuku'alofa, many resources were channelled towards the very summit of the Royal hierarchy of the Kingdom of Tonga. The high-ranking sister of King Tupou V, Princess Pilolevu, had agreed to officially open the new church. A few nights before the official opening, a delegation headed by the church president made a substantial presentation to the Princess. It consisted of a very large *puaka toho* or 'tusked pig' (with an estimated value of 1000 US$) the size of a small van, large amounts of yams and kava (agricultural produce collectively referred to as *ngoue*) as well as printed 'barkcloth' (*ngatu*) and fine mats (collectively referred to as *koloa fakatonga* or 'Tongan wealth') in addition to an 'envelope' (*sila*) containing 10,000 TOP (equalling about 5,000 US$ in 2012). According to the president, it was partly done in order to fortify Princess Pilolevu or lend her 'strength' (*ivi*) to succeed in the work of opening the new house of God and thus secure God's protection of the new church and its members and to acquire his blessing for future undertakings. He compared it to the spiritual strengthening of the one giving the *malanga* or 'sermon' achieved through the kava ceremony that always precedes the main Sunday service of Methodist congregations. Thus, he emphasized that acquiring God's protection and blessing is very taxing and exhausting work and requires sacrifices in order to be successful. Other informants confirmed that material fortification of church ministers, presidents and other high-ranking people in order to activate their capacity to create a 'good space' (*vā lelei*) between people and protector in fact constitutes a very significant part of their economic income. In many Methodist churches salaries are so low that the ministers in fact rely on the generous and compassionate *'ofa* of church members based on the ministers' key position in what might be called an economy of security and success related to an enduring entanglement of *mala* ('misfortune'), *monū* ('fortune') and morality.

Tuku Moʻui; 'Placing Life'

We have seen how everyday religiosity in Tonga, with its strong emphasis on not trusting the strength of man, is accompanied by numerous everyday strategies for gaining security and success by reaffirming the covenant, agreement or pact of protection. We have also seen how this reaffirmation takes the form of channelling a substantial flow of material resources towards positions held to be particularly significant for gaining security and success. We have seen how the rank of the recipient within kindred, church or kingdom and the magnitude of the offering make a difference with regard to how well the offering may be expected to work in gaining protection and prosperity. In the previous chapter, we saw how nurturing flows between hands that let go constituted a dynamic of everyday sociality where things understood to be strongly attached to people were also understood to be particularly potent for establishing and affirming alliances. Thus, I argued that the pervasive fostering practices that characterized local sociality on Kotu may partly be understood as sacrificial in terms of a detachment and offering of something to which one is strongly linked in order to nurture promising spaces for achieving a good life. Likewise, I would argue that everyday religiosity as an ongoing quest for security and success in Tonga relies on a similar sacrificial mechanism where frequent worship in which offering what is intimately attached to or a part of you is seen as key to achieving protection and prosperity.

In anthropological theories of sacrifice, it is common to follow the distinction the English language makes between 'sacrifice' and 'offering'. Thus, Huber and Mauss in their classical essay about the nature and function of sacrifice (Hubert and Mauss 1964) 'designate as sacrifice any oblation, even of vegetable matter, whenever the offering or part of it is destroyed' (ibid.: 12) and define sacrifice as '… a religious act which, through the consecration of a victim, modifies the condition of the moral person who accomplishes it …' (ibid.: 13). As Bourdillon has pointed out in the introduction to his anthology on *Sacrifice* (Bourdillon 1980), many of the later theories have focused on sacrifice '… in its common form of ritual slaughter' (ibid.: 1) – that is, on the consecration, killing/destruction of worthy victims and the offering of their life force in the hope of influencing life-controlling powers. Beattie in the same anthology says that what is sacrificed is '... usually and ideally, another living creature, precisely because, being living itself, it most appropriately symbolizes the life that is being offered' (ibid.: 30). Thus, Beattie perceives religious sacrifice as ' ... a dramatic, symbolic expression of man's awareness of his dependence on forces outside himself. And ... sacrificial ritual provides a means of influencing, or rather hoping to influence, these forces' (ibid.: 32).

Sacrifice in the form of offering body parts or the lives of humans for the benefit of ailing chiefs was, according to Meredith Filihia, quite common in Tonga until the turn of the nineteenth century. Thus, 'the cutting off of finger joins was prevalent in Tonga' (Filihia 1999: 6) to the extent that Captain Cook reported from his visit to Tonga in 1772 that: 'the greatest part of the people ... had lost one or both of their little fingers' (see ibid.: 6). According to Filihia, sources indicate that the cutting off of fingers as well as the strangulation of children was part of a healing strategy when high-ranking chiefs were suffering a serious illness believed to be brought about by breaking a taboo. Those offering fingers for the benefit of an ailing chief were his low- ranking relatives and, according to Mariner, who lived four years in Tonga from 1806, '... children as young as five competed to have the privilege of sacrificing their fingers' (Mariner, see ibid.: 7). Those sacrificed through strangulation were apparently the ailing chief's own children born to low-ranking wives. Both practices were abandoned very soon after the conversion to Christianity in the first decades of the nineteenth century and for contemporary Tongan Christians belong to the 'dark time' or *taimi fakapo'uli* before the coming of the 'light' or *maama* of Christianity. Contemporary religious offerings made as a part of the ongoing quest for protection and prosperity clearly do not involve sacrifices of this order. Nevertheless, I would argue that a sacrificial mechanism whereby protection and prosperity may be hoped for by offering what is strongly attached to you or part of yourself remains a significant component of contemporary Christian sociality in Tonga.

This sacrificial mechanism may be particularly well illuminated by focusing on the most important occasion of offering in the many Methodist churches of contemporary Tonga, the *Misinale* or 'Annual money collection', usually arranged on the last Sunday of October. This is the annual collection of money to support the activities of the local congregation and the central church. My findings both before and after the new Millennium clearly support Van der Grijp's findings that many resources in the form of '... much time, energy, material produce and money' (Van der Grijp 1993a: 207) were dedicated to church activities. Thus, a very significant amount of 'Tongan wealth' (*koloa fakatonga*) and cash income from and agricultural and marine produce was channelled into the church, not just in annual (*misinale*) but quarterly (*faka kuata*) and monthly (*lī pa'anga*; lit. 'throwing money') money collections as well as in relation to 'quarterly' (*kuata*) district meetings and the annual church 'conference' (*konfelenisi*). Van der Grijp reports that his informants represented their motives for contributing produce, 'wealth' (*koloa*), and money in markedly transactional terms:

> Ultimately, the people of Taoa see the *pola* [food presentation at church conference] as a gift to God and not to the church and his ministers. However, God does not eat earthly food, but the ministers do. The ministers pass the gifts on to God through prayer, in which they ask him to bless the faithful and to reward them. (ibid.: 207)

Van der Grijp therefore concludes: 'This set of religious ideas is thus a discourse of reciprocity: it is a question of giving and receiving' (ibid. 207). I would agree with Van der Grijp that giving generously and receiving fortune in return indeed was and remains an important emphasis in everyday religious discourse in Tonga. I would add, however, that so was the emphasis on foregoing inherently desirable things and putting in inherently exhausting efforts into 'doing duties' (*fai fatongia*) and 'carrying burdens' (*fua kavenga*). I would also add that a general emphasis on God's power to 'protect' (*le'ohi*), in terms of everyday ritual techniques for avoiding accidents and explanations of root causes of unexpected calamities, suggests that God's 'blessing' is quite as much a question of avoiding misfortune as that of achieving spectacular success. I have suggested that a willingness to let go or sacrifice what is inherently desirable or understood to be dear to you energizes the constitutive flows of everyday sociality. Likewise, I suggest that a willingness for such self-sacrifice lies at the heart of a religiosity aimed at everyday security and that this sacrificial theme dominates the annual *misinale* offering of money.

In the *misinale* of the Kotu congregation of the Free Wesleyan Church of Tonga in November 2014, a total of 11,500 TOP (equalling about 5,750 US$) was collected. This was quite impressive given that the congregation now numbered only a handful of households, that annual cash income to these households was generally very low, and that few of them were supported by overseas relatives. Van der Grijp has described *misinale* money offerings in Tonga as highly competitive and potentially shaming because of the role public announcements play in the collection procedure (ibid.: 205–6). Thus, in 2014 the initial sum in the 'plates' or *peleti* of the congregation's 'donating groups' (*kalasi*) was loudly announced before the plates were sent around church for the *tokoni* or 'assistance' of the congregation, accompanied by loud encouragements to '*ofa mai* ('show love/compassion'). Also the church choir was encouraged by the one in charge of sending round the plate to sing loudly to lend support and strength to give generously. Likewise, some of the elder, married and widowed women of the congregation danced with sexually suggestive and mock-aggressive body movements, much too close to respectable elders, and wearing either fierce countenances or masks. They behaved in ways that were pretty much the inversion of appropriate public conduct and that would normally be referred to as *launoa*, *laupisi* and *pauʻu*, signifying to speak 'silly/nonsense', 'rubbish' or 'naughty'. In the context of the *misinale*, however, people referred to their dances as *fakafiefia* or 'to behave joyfully/celebrate' on account of what was described as women's greater inherent capacity for 'warmth' or *mafana* and therefore through *fakafiefia* cause others to warm up sufficiently to feel *ʻofa* or 'compassionate love' and to be generous or 'let go of their grip' (*nimahomo*). Thus, from the point of view of members of the congregation, the significance of publicizing the donated sums and the competitive nature of the procedure of donation was not primarily that it produced shame or pride but that it was part of a process of offering that generated sufficient warmth and strength within people to release desirable assets. The notion that it requires *ivi* or 'strength/energy' to be generous and to release desirable assets to my mind constitutes a very significant part of the hope that *misinale* money offerings might produce protection and prosperity or security and success through God's intervention. And clearly the focus on *ivi* or 'strength/energy' was very strong in the *misinale* as a collective achievement of the congregation; not only in terms of how taxing or *fakahela* ('exhausting') the effort was implied to be for those who contributed on the day of the *misinale* itself but also in terms of all the energy spent over the year that had passed since the last *misinale* to produce the current money offering. This emphasis that the money offered in the *misinale* was really a sort of condensation of *ivi* or strength/energy was indicated by the term or expression people used to describe the *misinale* money offering in the course of the event itself. As an institution of the church year, the annual money collect appeared generally to be referred to as *misinale*. In the course of the performance, however, it was referred to as *tuku moʻui*, or 'placing/offering life'. After the *misinale* collect in 2014, the middle-aged man who had been in charge of collecting money offerings elaborated on his understanding of the *misinale* as *tuku moʻui*:

> It means to 'present/give' (*foaki*) to God or to 'place' (*tuku*) with God. It is *tuku moʻui* ('placing of life') because the money offered comes from all the work we have done to grow things in our gardens, to catch fish from the sea, to prepare and plait mats and all other kinds of work since the last *tuku moʻui*.

He was on his way to the congregation's meeting hall, where the *misinale* feast was to take place as soon as the *tuku moʻui* in church was finished.

He felt that the feast was important because it expressed the congregation's gratitude to all who had 'helped' (*tokoni*) and 'carried the burdens' (*fua kavenga*) in the work of the *misinale*, and it was also an essential means for refuelling or 'renewing strength' (*fakafo'ou 'a e ivi*) after spending so much 'energy' (*ivi*) on 'placing life' in church.

The term *tuku*, like so many Tongan terms, has a wide variety of applications, varying between 'to place/devote', 'set aside/keep', 'to desist' and 'to abandon/forsake' (Churchward 1959: 507–8). In the context of the *misinale*, the meanings 'to place', 'to leave with' and 'to entrust' (ibid.) appeared closest to people's understanding of what was done with this money. As for the value of this offering, people emphasized that what is entrusted to God is in fact 'life', indicating that not only 'another living creature' '… living itself … appropriately symbolizes the life that is being offered' (Beattie 1980: 30). People's emphasis on the energy required both to get money and release it, and the need to regain strength afterwards, implies '… man's awareness of his dependence on forces outside himself. And … sacrificial ritual provides a means of influencing, or rather hoping to influence, these forces' (ibid.: 32). I would hesitate, however, to say that money 'appropriately symbolizes the life that is offered' (ibid.: 30). Rather, I would argue that what makes money an appropriate offering is that it materializes in a very condensed form energy spent and growth achieved in a medium that is endlessly useful and therefore inherently desirable. Thus, money in the ritualized *tuku mo'ui* does not, I would argue, stand for life but is life. Letting go of a significant part of the fruits of work and growth by overcoming an urge to close the hand and by releasing it at points of particular conductivity in the 'space' (*vaha'a*) between people's everyday struggles to survive and succeed and their ultimate protector becomes a kind of self-sacrifice: the giving up of a part of the fruits of labour and growth in the hope of influencing forces, the dependence on which few find reason to doubt in Tonga. It is a dependence that people are constantly reminded about from the pulpit in being told "*Oua teke falala he ivi 'o e tangata!*" ('Do not rely on the strength of Man!')

The *faifekau pule*, or 'district minister', left little doubt in his *malanga* or 'sermon' of the *misinale* of 2014 that securing good conditions for prosperity and well-being, for vitality, growth and health, was what one might hope to achieve through the 'placing of life' in church. This was expressed in terms such as hoping for enough rain and avoiding droughts so that the crops would thrive and grow. It was also expressed in terms of a hope to avoid being hit by catastrophes in the form of destructive cyclones in the upcoming 'cyclone season' (*taimi afā*) or by destructive 'red waves' (*peau kula*) over the next year. After the money offered had been counted, it was put in a white linen bag and placed in the lap of a young maiden dressed in white and sitting on a chair under the high altar of the church. She was addressed as the *Sea 'o e tuku mo'ui* or the 'Chair of the placing of life'. During his main sermon, the minister focused on Bible verses stating that the Kingdom of God belongs to innocents and that what is done to one of God's innocents is also done to God. Thus, he emphasized that 'generous and compassionate love' or *'ofa* directed toward the 'Chair' was guaranteed to reach all the way to God. After the 'Chair' had read out the total sum of the money placed in her lap, she brought it to the district minister, the local minister and the local church steward, who all held onto the bag of money offered while the district minister consecrated the offering by praying over it. The prayer, like his initial sermon, 'gave thanks' (*fakafeta'i*) for being granted life and protection since the previous *tuku mo'ui* and the hope for continued protection, growth and prosperity over the next year.

We saw how the foundational story of Tongan Christianity was about *tuku kelekele* or 'entrusting/placing the soil' under God's protection in order to be spared from misfortune and to prosper. If so, then the annual *tuku mo'ui* or 'entrusting/placing life' in the form of placing a significant part of what emerges or 'grows' (*tupu*) out of that soil in God's hands constitutes a reconfirmation of an *'alea pau* or 'binding agreement'. We also saw how the breaking of this contract may quite easily be turned into the root cause of *mala* or 'misfortune'. Clearly this makes being the victim of misfortune potentially morally damning. We have also seen how a striking reticence with regard to broadcasting the ongoing environmental transformation through which the wild forest and weather coast of Kotu has deteriorated may partly be related to a tendency to ridicule remote places as backward/uneducated. But with the very strong emphasis in everyday religiosity on the significance of God's protective intervention for achieving security and success in an environment where worship is seen as the key to holding at bay unpredictable and potentially very destructive forces, one should probably not expect that claiming victimhood with regards to environmental change is very attractive to people.

Over the three decades that I went to Kotu, I repeatedly encountered two sayings that people identified with and would like to be recognized for. Both emphasize a willingness to combat narrow self-interest by committing to and making sacrifices for a common good. '*Ha'afeva ē, tala ki Kotu mo mālie fakamotu!*' ('Ha'afeva tell Kotu, you both did well in coming away from your island!') refers to the heroic role people from the islands of Ha'afeva and Kotu are reputed to have played when they decided to support King Taufa'āhau Tupou I during his campaign in Fiji in 1854 and is used to emphasize the moral value of 'breaking out of isolation' (*fakamotu*) in order to contribute to a greater, common cause. The other saying that people would clearly like to be associated with and that indeed has also become the name of a Facebook group consisting of people originating on Kotu is this: '*Kotu 'iloa he lotu moe poto*' ('Kotu is known by worship and (scholarly) competence'), which emphasizes people's willingness to devote themselves to 'worship' (*lotu*), to 'carrying burdens' (*fua kavenga*) and 'perform duties' (*fai fatongia*) within church to keep darkness at bay and to seek enlightenment through education. Clearly, with people seeing themselves as achieving God's protection through *lotu* and also seeing themselves as engaging the environment in a *poto* manner (i.e. with 'competence/wisdom'), being associated with environmental calamities in the form of both sudden disasters and gradual degradation may be unwelcome to people. Clearly, also, from a local perspective, the most attractive option may be to look the other way, not dwell too much on the implications and not spread the news about what is going on.

In his book *Why We Disagree about Climate Change* (Hulme 2009), Mike Hulme discusses controversy, inaction and opportunities related to climate change discourses. He concludes that we shall probably never be able to think alike or agree about the causes and consequences of climate change because what we think about it is informed by many things, including what we think about science, our social, political and moral values, our faith and our fears. The extent to which the environmental changes that have happened on Kotu over the last few decades are related to climate change is not entirely clear, neither from a scientific nor from a local perspective. But just like Hulme claims to be the case for global climate change discourses and disagreements, the drastic transformation of the surroundings that people have been engaging for countless generations on Kotu Island and *Namolahi* Lagoon appears to be understood and responded to in terms of attitudes to science, enduring social and moral values, fears and faith. Global and regional climate change debates have the potential to challenge or change the significance of faith for understanding and coping with what is going on. But for now, people's trust in the lasting efficacy of the King's 'placing of land' under God's protection in Pouono appears firm in Tonga. And on Kotu, there is no indication that people will stop identifying their island as *Kotu 'iloa e lotu* ('a place known by its worship') and thus under God's protection anytime soon.

Everyday Experience and Cultural Continuity

In exploring modes of conceptualizing and of engaging with what in Tim Ingold's terms might be called the 'weather-world' (Ingold 2011), some enduring understandings have been revealed about the world that largely 'go without saying' (Bloch 1992). An important outcome of the exploration has been that by following threads from routines of conceptualizing and coping within fields of everyday experience, a constitutive motion that relates diametrically opposed qualities or states of being has been discovered. The dynamics discovered in everyday routines of production, aesthetics and sociality also resonate with what has been identified as widespread 'culture themes' of the Austronesian world. According to Fox, interrelated notions of growth and precedence make up 'origin structures' of varying sorts (Fox 1995: 218) that play a significant part in creating, reproducing or undermining hierarchical relations in many parts of the world of Austronesian- speaking peoples: 'In many Austronesian societies, origins are conceptualized as a form of growth' (ibid.: 218–19).

In Chapter 5, we saw that Koloa used the artificial 'Tongan house' (*fale tonga*) rather than a growing thing as a metaphor for the Tongan family. But the correspondence between the careful 'building of the house' (*langa fale*) and the manner in which natural growth produces 'hard' (*fefeka*) and enduring things clearly inscribes the force of growth into the structure of the house. Thus, we saw that the hardest end of the 'inner ridgepole' (*toʻufūfū*) closest to the tree's 'base' or 'reason for existence' (*tefitoʻi*) 'leads the way' (*muʻa mai*), with parts that 'follow after' (*mui mai*) toward the 'frontal end' (*tāmuʻa*) and 'chiefly' (*ʻeiki*) position of pre-eminence. Most ways of referring to genealogical relations in Tonga do so in terms of prior and later occurrences. Genealogical tracing is referred to in a true mode of temporal precedence as *hokohoko*, meaning 'to join one after another, or to be/happen in succession one after another' (Churchward 1959). If that which produces social pre-eminence does so by a process articulating the process of growth, then the relationship between 'base/foundation' (*tefitoʻi*) and 'tail' (*hiku*) is first of all one of precedence. The crucial motion in the cultivation and growth of nurturing *ʻufi* (yam) and *niu* (coconut), strong kava and the beautifying and protective mulberry (*hiapo*) and hard/enduring ironwood (*toa*) is that some occurrences 'lead the way' (*muʻa mai*) to constitute the 'reason' (*tefitoʻi*) for occurrences that 'follow after' (*hoko mai/mui mai*). Dealing with components of the environment in an effective manner means dealing with a practical experiential realm of precedence. Indeed, dealing with this kind of precedence was probably a significant aspect of what the old Tongan calendar of yam cultivation was all about. Thus, the pre-eminent worth of the *kahokaho* yam of the 'early yam crop' (*tokamuʻa*) was that of its antecedence, making it a yam 'leading the way' (*muʻa mai*) so that the 'late yam crop' (*tokamui*) or the 'large crop' (*tokalahi*) and the 'collectivity of cultivated food' (*toʻu kai*) may 'follow after' (*mui mai*). A narrow focus on structures such as the house or peaks of ceremonial elaboration would tend to produce images of fixed hierarchical structures, but these structures are not all there is. Focusing instead on the building of houses, the ceremonial processes of transforming food into presentable 'boards of food' (*kaipola*) and the opening up of potent flows of relating at 'interfaces of enhanced conductivity' (*mata*) produces images of precedence embedded in a procreative dynamic of merging and separation as an encompassing process of growth and life. Such a focus opens up a vista on a flux that makes outstanding moments of unambiguous order beautiful, moving and important in the continual labour of re-creating a society fit to live in. Put differently, the enduring cultural significance of the phases of 'sea coming in to unite with land' (*hu'a mai ke tau 'a e tahi*) and 'sea detaching from land to become almost empty' (*mahu'i ke mamaha 'a e tahi*), 'night/darkness' (*po*) and 'day/light' (*'aho*), 'dead moon' (*mate 'a e māhina*) and 'mutual day' (*fe'ahoaki*) at full moon and other states of *noa* ('haphazard', 'indiscriminate') and *maau* ('orderly', 'well proportioned') does not lie in their fixed oppositeness. Rather, it lies in the encompassing process of merging and separation running through the environment people must engage with to achieve a good life. In Tonga, as elsewhere in Polynesia and Austronesia, people clearly remain preoccupied with etiquette, distinctions and boundaries due, perhaps, as Gell has claimed, to an enduring 'need to keep things apart' (Gell 1995: 36). This preoccupation does not, I believe, reflect a wish to live in a world of chronic 'orderliness' (*maau*) or a need to keep things constantly apart. First of all, such a wish would appear quite unrealistic to people. Secondly, it would mean existing in a frozen and barren world devoid of highly valued qualities like desire, courage and creativeness cropping up from 'within' (*'i loto*) to 'give zest to life' (Toren 1995: 76).

Picking up threads from different practical fields, I have traced enduring notions about qualities of the environment that people engaged with in everyday life, which has made it possible to produce an ethnography that may provide '… some intuition into the evocative power of [the] symbolism' (Bloch 1993: 114) by which social relatedness and orders of precedence are elaborated and constituted. In the ethnographic exploration of Kotu in the final decade of the twentieth century, I have made an effort to anchor 'conceptualizations in the material – the body, houses, wood, styles of speaking – and in practices – cooking, cultivation, eating together' and, thus, to approach symbolic expressions in the context of 'the wider processes of ecological, biological, and geographical transformation of which human society is a small part' (Bloch 1992: 144). My discoveries would seem to imply that the legitimacy of those whose pre-eminent positions are constituted by such articulation would tend to be confirmed through modes of conceptualizing and coping with the dynamics of several fields of everyday experience. Put differently, it would seem hard to uproot a leader whose pre-eminence is constituted in a mode that recapitulates practical modes of transforming 'useless wild growth' (*tupu noa 'ia pē*) into nurturing foods, strong drink and enduring and valued materials. The resonance between conceptualizations of tidal, diurnal and lunar dynamics in which many productive practices were still embedded on Kotu in the last decades of the twentieth century indicates that the calendar of yam cultivation that was centred around the Tu'i Tonga was once a powerful tool of naturalization for a centralized apparatus of government. Clearly, also, both the position of the Tu'i Tonga and the calendar of yam cultivation are institutions that have long since lost their significance in Tonga. Nevertheless, the motion of merging and separation that once was elaborated in stories about the world and its makings, and in terms of the role of Tu'i Tonga for security and well-being, did not grind to a halt with the appearance of new narratives, new faith and new important positions. In Kotu, it lingered on in many everyday engagements with dynamics and components of the environment and continued to nurture shared ideas about the importance of cultivation, of beauty, of orderliness and of sacrifice in the ongoing struggle to achieve 'good spaces' (*vā lelei*) in a world where that may never be taken for granted.

It is on the background of shared expectations that responses to environmental changes also play themselves out. It goes without saying that instability, unpredictability and vulnerability to powerful surrounding forces are to be expected. As we have seen, Tongan Christianity looms large on contemporary shared horizons of expectations and partly rests precisely on trust in God's protective intervention against overwhelming and potentially destructive surrounding forces. There is reason to doubt that neither sudden 'red waves' nor gradual sea level rise will shake this trust anytime soon. And who, after all, offers anything more reliable to trust with regard to protection against possible future scenarios of low islands in a vast ocean in an era of global warming? Few that remained on Kotu in 2016 felt certain that predictions of higher sea levels and more violent weather in the future were wrong. This did not appear to shake their trust in God's protective power, however. Thus, a laconic sentiment expressed by some was this: 'Even if Kotu should sink and red waves should keep moving in, one might perhaps hope for God's help in moving out ….'.

Notes

1. He was the biological father of my informant and the father's brother of the boy my informant had fled with. He was thus 'father' or *tamai* to both in terms of Tongan classificatory kin terminology.
2. *Lapila* is the Tongan term for a kind of tilapia fish endemic to freshwater lakes in Africa, where it is used as a measure to control mosquitoes and hence

malaria. It is farmed extensively in Asia and was probably introduced to Tongan brackish lakes in the twentieth century.

3. Pointing or beckoning by using the index finger is generally perceived as extremely rude in Tonga unless it is done by a person whose position of authority is incomparably higher than the one being beckoned. Even then, it is considered a crude gesture of self-aggrandizement. According to the Kotu interpreters of the misfortune on Fotuhaʻa, the act of *tuhuhuuʻi* is also associated with an act of 'cursing' (*talatuki*).

Appendix

Words of a World in Motion

◆●◆

States of the Tides and the Sea

Tau 'a e tahi	High tide; the sea is attached to/joined with land
Mahuʻi ke mamaha:	*Ebb tide:*
Tau mahuʻi	High tide that has turned
Takapau ʻuluaki	First dependable sign of ebb tide
Takapau ua	Second dependable sign of ebb tide
Lotoʻone ʻa e tahi	The sea is in the middle of the sand
Toukilikili ʻa e tahi	The sea is at the pebbles
Hā ʻa e pala	The appearance of the *pala* ('soggy seaweed')
Mamaha mahuʻi ʻa e tahi	Low tide that has not yet turned; the sea is almost empty but still becoming detached
Mamaha ʻa e tahi	Low tide; the sea is almost empty
Huʻa mai ʻa e tahi:	*Flow tide:*
Mamaha huʻa mai ʻa e tahi	The sea is empty and flowing here
Puli ʻa e pala	The *pala* ('soggy seaweed') has disappeared
Puli ʻa e toukilikili	The pebbles have disappeared
Lotoʻone huʻa mai ʻa e tahi	The sea flowing here is in the middle of the sand
Tau huʻa mai ʻa e tahi	The sea has arrived/connected but is still flowing here

Occasional Tidal Qualities

Tahi lahi	Big sea; spring high tide
Ngata 'i 'uta 'aupito 'a e tahi	The sea ends inland; extreme high tide
Maha 'aupito 'a e tahi	The sea is very empty; spring low tide
Pakupaku 'a e namo	The lagoon is absolutely dry; extreme low tide
Tahi si'i	Small sea; neap high tide
Ngata he loto'one 'a e tahi	The sea ends/turns in the middle of the sand; extreme neap tide high
'Oku 'ikai ke fu'u mamaha 'a e tahi	The sea is not very empty; neap tide low
Loka 'a e namo	The lagoon is on the move/astir; turbulent sea/strong current in the lagoon
Loka fakatokelau 'a e namo	The north of the lagoon is on the move; turbulent sea/strong current in the northern part of the lagoon;
Loka fakatonga 'a e namo	The south of the lagoon is on the move; turbulent sea/strong current in the southern part of the lagoon
Loka takai 'a e namo	Lagoon on the move all around; rough sea and strong current throughout the lagoon

States of Night and Day

Pō:	*Night*:
Tu'uapō	Deep night
Longo'aho:	*The feeling of day; late night*:
Mokomoko'aho	The coolness of (the coming) day
Tangi 'a Teiko	The call of the Teiko bird
'U'ua 'a e Moamu'a	First cockcrow
Kauata	(Phenomena) belonging to dawn
Lea fakamuimui 'a e Teiko	The last speech of the Teiko bird
Ata 'a fa'ahikehe	Twilight of the other side/kind
Tataki 'aho	Leading the day
Kio 'a manumu'a	First bird call

'Aho:
Hengihengi/Uhu:
'U'ua tu'o ua 'a e moa
Kiokio tu'o ua 'a e manu
Ata 'a puaka
Kio 'a e Fuleheu
'U'ua fakaholo koe 'uhi
Manu tala'aho
Kuo mafoa 'a e ata
Ata 'a tangata
Kuo ma'a 'a e 'aho

Pongipongi:
Halani 'o e la'ā
Mofisi 'a la'ā
Hopo 'a la'ā
Maluafonua
Funga'ulufonua
Fanga'ilupe

Ho'atā:
Ho'atā pongipongi
Ho'atā mālie
Ho'atā efiafi
Kuo pale efiafi
Fakalulunga
Koe fasi 'a e malu

Efiafi:
Ko e malu efiafi
Ko e hohole ke tō 'a la'ā
Ko e taitai tō 'a la'ā
Tō 'a laā

Day:
Early morning:
Second cockcrow
Second bird call
Dawn of the pig
Call of the Honeysucker bird
Cockcrows all around
Birds announcing the day
The twilight has shattered
Twilight of man
Day has become clean

Bright morning:
The road/path of the sun
The sparks of the sun
Sunrise
Hidden by the land
The surface of the head of the land
Favourite place of the pigeon

Midday:
Bright midday; midday morning
Exact midday
Midday afternoon
Decline towards afternoon
The first move west/first descent
The shadow has broken

The lighting of cooking fires; afternoon:
The shade of afternoon
The lowering of the sun to set
The sinking of the sun to set in the sea
Sunset

Efiafi poʻuli:	*Darkening afternoon:*
Tapalika	The narrow flash of light
Ataata efiafi poʻuli	The twilight of the darkening afternoon
ʻUʻuli kelekele	The darkness of the soil/ground
Feʻiloʻilongaki	Mutual recognition
Hopo ʻa e moa	The roosting of the hen
Efiafi fakapoʻuli	Dark evening
Mamalu poʻuli	The shade of night
Keiefiafi:	*Still afternoon; evening:*
Tūmaama	The lighting of the lamps
Hopo ʻa e kaveinga	Rise of the steering stars
Tamate maama	Putting out the lamp/light
Vaeua pō	The night is divided in two
Mafuli ʻa e Kaniva	The turning of the Milky Way

States of the Moon

Māhina foʻou:		*New moon; first quarter:*
Fua tuʻu ʻa e māhina	(1)	First standing of the moon (or supporting the standing of the moon)
ʻIloa ʻe he faʻahikehe		Known by the other side/kind
Pō faʻahikehe		Night of the other side/kind
Fakaua	(2)	The second
ʻIloa ʻe he toutai		Known by the fishermen/navigators
Pō toutai		Night of the navigators/fishermen
Fakatolu	(3)	The third
ʻIloa ʻe he maama		Known by the world/light
ʻIloa ʻe he tangata		Known by man
Fakafā	(4)	The fourth
Fakanima	(5)	The fifth
Fakaono	(6)	The sixth
Fakafitu	(7)	The seventh

Appendix 179

Tu'u efiafi 'a e māhina		The moon stands in the early evening; second quarter:
Fakavalu	(8)	The eighth
Tu'u efiafi 'a e māhina		The moon stands in the evening
Fakahiva	(9)	The ninth
Fakahongofulu	(10)	The tenth
Fua'aho	(11)	Carrying/supporting day
'Aho punifanga		The two sides facing one another
Fuofua vale	(12)	Incomplete/incompetent shape
Fakatauata		Exposed to the twilight of dawn/moving toward dawn
Fuofuanoa	(13)	Unimportant shape/shape of no account
Māhina kātoa		Whole/complete moon; third quarter:
Māhina kātoa	(14)	Complete moon (14)
Fē'ahoaki		Reciprocal day
Fu'u maama lahi 'a e māhina		The moon lights very much
'Uluaki māhina hopo		First moonrise
Fakamāhina hopo	(15)	Corresponding with moonrise
Fakamāhina hopo	(16)	Corresponding with moonrise
Fakamāhina hopo	(17)	Corresponding with moonrise
Kaupo'uli	(18)	The dark ones
Kaupo'uli/Matofi	(19)	The dark ones/cut, hacked off/cuttings
Kaupo'uli/Matofi tele	(20)	Peeling the cuttings
'Aho ika	(21)	Fish day
'Aho 'o e tafe	(22)	The day of running water
Vaeua mālie 'a e māhina		The moon is divided in two equal parts
Kalipa		Fourth quarter
Kalipa	(23)	V-shaped moon
Māhina vai	(24)	Weak moon
Māhina vai	(25)	
Fungaata	(26)	The surface/top of the twilight of dawn
Lekeleka		Small, low (of growing/living things)
Lekelekamate	(27)	Small, low and dying

Māhina ʻasi vaivai	(28)	A weakly appearing moon
Mate ʻa e Māhina	(29)	The moon is dead

Words of the Seasons

Lihamuʻa[1]	(1)	The first/leading child of the louse; 'The crop of the *tokamuʻa* (early planted yam crop) is small (like the child of the louse). All growing things of nature are still small' (Hafoka n.d)
Lihamui	(2)	The following child of the louse; 'The crop of the *tokamui/taʻu lahi* (late planted/large yam crop) is small (like the child of the louse)' (ibid.)
Vaimuʻa	(3)	Early water; 'Rain falling to cause the first yam crop to have tubers. The first rain of the growing crops' (ibid.)
Vaimui	(4)	Late water; 'If there has been no rain during the moon of early water the farmer would hope for rain in this month' (ibid.)
Fakaofomoʻui/ Fakahulimoʻui	(5)	The living foliage of the yam crop; 'The green leaves of the yam crop appear above ground bearing witness to the vitality of the crop' (ibid.)
Fakaafumate	(6)	The dying of the hair of the yam; 'The leaves of the yam crop dry out as a normal part of the process of growth toward maturation' (ibid.)
Hilingakelekele	(7)	Placing on a mound of earth; 'This is the time for uprooting the seed yams of the early crop to place them on a mound of earth covering the pit in which they grew. The last month of the 'harvesting season' (*utu taʻu*). This is the moon where the parts of the year called *Utu taʻu* and *Tō taʻu* collide. All growing things awaken in this month when the Seven Sisters (*Mataliki*) rise just before sunrise as the moon of *Hilingakelekele* is divided in two equal parts (*ʻi he vaeua ʻo e Hilingakelekele*[2])' (ibid.)

Hilingameʻa/ *Hilingameaʻa*	(8)	Placing the clean yam; 'This is the time to place the yam on the platform after the earth that sticks to it when it is dug out of the ground has dried and fallen off by itself so that there is no risk of ripping the skin of the yam while cleaning it' (ibid.)
ʻAoʻao	(9)	Multiplying the heads; 'This is the time to cut in several pieces the late seed yams (for planting)' (ibid.)
Fuʻufuʻunekinanga/ *Fufunekinanga*	(10)	The continual gathering and heaping; 'This is the time to collect the rubbish and waste of the garden and heap it up, as it can no longer be burned because the first yam has started to grow. It is also the time to clear away rubble in preparation for the planting of the 'late/large crop' *tokamui/taʻulahi*' (ibid.)
Uluenga	(11)	'The yellow head; 'This is the time when the top of a small portion of the early yam crop may become exposed as the rain wears down the mound of earth covering the pits in which the seed yams were planted. Exposure to the sun causes these yams to get a yellowish taint on the top' (ibid.)
Tanumanga	(12)	Buried together; 'This is the time to "house" (*fakafale*) the seed yams to delay their giving birth or sprouting until there is time to plant them' (ibid.)
ʻOaakifangongo	(13)	Making baskets for the gathering of empty shells of dried-out green coconuts; 'This is the time to collect the empty shells of green coconuts that were discarded without scraping out the meat of the coconut after drinking it. This must be done to add to the meagre diet of the final part of the planting season in times of famine. The next month is the first month of the 'Harvesting/Eating season' (*Utu/Kai Taʻu*)' (ibid.) 'This moon is the end of the year, when you have come there you must stop planting the crop' (*Ngata ai ʻa e taʻu, ʻosi haʻu ki ai ʻoua te ke toe tō taʻu*³)

Notes

1. These words and the elaborations of the phenomena to which they refer are from the section *Ko e ta'u* of the typescript *Ko e lau taimi moe kuonga* held by the Tongan Tradition Committee, Palace Office, Nuku'alofa (Hafoka, n.d.).
2. Two interpretations of the description '*i he vaeua 'o e Hilingakelekele* seem possible. Thus, it may refer either to the night described as *vaeua mālie 'a e māhina*, when the moon enters the final quarter, or to the night referred to as *Kātoa 'a e māhina*, when the moon is full and thus divides (*vaeua*) the *lunation* of *Hilingakelekele* in two. If the second interpretation is chosen, then the *Mataliki* rising 'just before sunrise' may also be described to be rising in the east just as the full moon sets in the west. The second interpretation also seems the more likely because of the stronger association between the final quarter of the moon with lack of vitality rather than the awakening and strength of plant life.
3. Description of the same moon of transition between planting and harvesting seasons made by Heamasi Koloa of Kotu Island in 1991.

Glossary

——— ◆●◆ ———

ʻaho	day
ʻAho fakamuimui	The Last Day, Judgement Day
ʻaho fakaʻosi	last day, final moment
ʻahoia	to make it through the night
ʻaho ika	fish days; term of reference for days when the Yellowstripe Goatfish form large schools of fish
ʻaho loloa	long day; quality of the day close to the December solstice
ʻaho nonou	short day; quality of the day close to the June solstice
aka	roots
akafia	abounding in roots, root penetration; Tongan illness caused by roots penetrating the bones of dead relatives
ʻā kolo	village fence; barkcloth encircling the grave at burials
ala	to collect shellfish
alea pau	dependable agreement, binding contract, covenant
ʻalofi	supreme circuit at kava ceremony
ama uku	night-diving with torch
ʻāmio	to be crooked, to twist and turn; to shirk, to try and escape one's Obligations
ʻanga	shark
anga	disposition, mode of behaving
anga fakaʻapaʻapa	matters of respect, protocol

anga fakapālangi	the Western way of life, European custom
anga fakatonga	the Tongan way of life, Tongan custom
anga ki tahi	affinity with the sea, predisposed to deal with the sea
anga 'o e la'ā	the manner of the sun
anga 'o e tupu	manner of growth, mode of growing
'Ao'ao	July; multiplying the heads (of seed yams)
aoniu	encircling coconut; row of beams running around the exterior perimeter of the lower part of the roof of a Tongan house
'aonga	suitable, useful
apai	interior; rows of beams running around the interior perimeter of the lower part of the roof of a Tongan house
'api	home/homestead
'api kolo	town allotment
'asi	to appear, to be visible
'asi vaivai	to appear weakly; quality of the moon towards the end of the fourth quarter
ata	to be slightly clear, to be dimly perceived, dawn, to dawn, twilight,
'atā	free, unencumbered, unrestricted, vacant, spacious, space between earth and sky, freedom
ataata	to grasp slightly, to barely perceive, dim light
ataata efiafi po'uli	the dimness of darkening evening; a phase of evening; phase of the evening
ata 'a fa'ahikehe	twilight of the other side/kind; phase of the early morning
ata 'a puaka	twilight of the pigs; phase of the early morning
ata 'a tangata	twilight of man; phase of the early morning
ata 'a tevolo	twilight of the spirits, devils; phase of the early morning
'atamai	mind; lit. appearing to me
'atamai 'i tangata	of human mind, of human responsiveness; third stage of a baby's cognitive development

Glossary

	when it expresses clear recognition of its mother
ʻatamai manu	of animal mind, of animal responsiveness; second stage of a baby's cognitive development
ʻatamai noa	of a confused mind, of a mind unable to discriminate, haphazard responsiveness; first stage of a baby's cognitive development
ʻā tangata	enclosure of people (standing shoulder to shoulder around a grave)
ato	roof
ʻatu	Skipjack Tuna
au	cane thatching; house-building material
ʻau	current
ʻau lahi	strong current
ava	opening, gap, passage
Ava lahi	great passage; place name referring to the widest passage in the outer reefs of the Kotu lagoon
ʻāvanga	sickness caused by a 'spirit' (faʻahikehe/tevolo)
Ava pipiko	reluctant passage: place name for passage into the Kotu lagoon
ave ʻo pusiaki	to send away for adoption
efi ʻa e afi	to light the cooking fire
efiafi	afternoon, early evening
ʻeiki fakanofo	appointed chief
ʻeiki palisiteni	noble president, church president
faʻahikehe	spirits, beings of the other side/kind
faʻahinga ika	family of fishes
faʻahi ʻo tamai	father's side
faʻē	mother and mother's sister
faʻētangata	mother's brother
faʻētangata pule	leading mother's brother; elder brother of mother
fahu	position of supreme ceremonial rank
faiʻaho	celebration of first and twenty first birthday
fai fatongia	to do one's duty, to pay tribute, fulfil obligation

faifekau	church minister
faifekau pule	leading church minister, district church minister
faifekau tokoni	assistant church minister
faihala	to do wrong, to sin
faimavae	to wean
fa'iteliha	to please oneself, to be unrestrained
fa'itoka	cemetery
faka'afu	make hot and steamy; light up the fuel of an earth oven
Fakaafumate	April; the dying of the foliage
faka'apa'apa	respectfulness, to show respect
fakafeta'i	to give thanks, gratitude
fakafiefia	to behave joyfully, to celebrate
fakafonua	pertaining to/in the manner of the homeland/island
fakahela	exhausting, taxing
fakahingoa	to name
fakahoko	to transmit, to attach, to make into one
Fakaholofononga	Day Star; star rising in the early morning
fakahuhu	to inject, to suckle, to cause to suck
fakakāinga	in the manner of kinsmen
Fakakaufue	place name for coral formation in the Kotu lagoon
fakakelekele	menstruation
fakalahi 'a e 'api	to make the household larger
fakalahi fonua	to extend/make the land larger
fakalau 'a e ata	twilight begins to come on, quality of illumination in the late night
fakalotu	in the manner of fellow Christians
fakamāhina	according to the moon, pertaining to the moon
fakamāhina hopo	corresponding with moonrise; reference to a number of moon nights of the third quarter

fakamotu	to come away from an island, break isolation, join in a task of cooperation
fakamuimui	last, final
fakanofo	to appoint
faka'ofa	moving, stirring (to pity)
Fakaofimo'ui	March; the living foliage
faka'ofo'ofa	beautiful, aesthetically moving
Fakapapanga	without projecting features, smooth; place name referring to a place of passage into the Kotu lagoon
fakapikopiko	laziness
fakapoi	sham thrust
fakapo'uli	darkness, night-time, unenlightened
fakasio	to watch or examine intensely or for a long time
fakasio 'e tahi	to examine the sea
fakataha ika	school of fish
fakatatau	to compare, to make a parallel, to make a replica, copy
fakatauata	leading to twilight; name of moon night in the third quarter
fakatele	to troll for fish
fakatōkilalo	to be humble, self-abasing
fakatolu	the third; name of moon night in the first quarter (the first night that the new moon may be seen low on the western horizon)
fakaua	the second; name of a moon night in the first quarter
faka'uluaki	the first; name of moon night in the beginning of the first quarter
fakavalu	the eighth; name of moon night in the beginning of the second quarter
fala	plaited pandanus mat
fale tonga	Tongan house
faletu'a	beams running lengthwise to which the loft beams of a Tongan house are attached

faliki	floor
falikiaki	using something to make floor mats
fāmili fakatonga	the Tongan family
Fanga lahi	great landing place; place name for a part of the waterfront of Kotu Island
fanofanoʻi	to wash the hands with someone in order to transfer special power/knowledge
fata	loft or rack supporting the roof of a Tongan house
faʻu/fatu maau	to create, build, construct order/orderliness; to compose poetry
fēʻahoʻaki	reciprocal/mutual day; name of moon nightaround full moon
fefeka	hard, enduring
feilaulau	to offer a sacrifice, to make a conciliatory offering
feʻiloʻaki	to know one another
fēʻiloʻilongaki	mutual recognition, phase of the evening
feitama	pregnancy, being pregnant
feiʻumu	the cooked food of an earth oven
fēliuliuʻaki ʻa e ʻea	changing weather, climate change
femahinoʻaki	to understand one another
fēʻofaʻaki	mutual love, mutual kindness, to act with kindness/compassion to one another
feʻofaʻofani	acts of mutual love
feohi	companionship, communion, to have fellowship
fesiofaki	to face one another, to see one another
fetokoniaki	mutual help, to help one another
fetuʻu ʻaho	the morning star
fiefia	to be happy, happiness
fie lahi	to want to appear large; to be conceited
fiepoto	to want to appear competent; conceited, pretentious
foaki	to give, to present, to donate

foʻi ava	a single passage
foʻi hakau	a single unit of coral formation
foʻi limu	a patch/field of seaweed
foʻi loto	deep spot/area, marine pool
foʻi maka	a single (coral) boulder
foha	tuber, bulb, son (of a man)
fono	monthly village meeting
fonu	turtle
fonua	homeland, island, territory, placenta
Fonuaeʻa	place name for partly exposed coral formation close to the widest passage into the Kotu lagoon
fonualoto	vault, chiefly stone grave
Fotuʻa	several Sweetlips fish
fua kavenga	carry the burdens
fua tuʻu ʻa e māhina	the moon prepares to stand; name of moon night in the beginning of the first quarter
Fufunekinanga	August; heaping the rubbish
fuke ʻa e ʻumu	to open up the earth oven
fungaata	the upper part of twilight, name of moon night towards the end of the fourth quarter
funga fonua	surface of the land
haʻa	people, race, tribe
hā ʻa e pala	the drenched seaweed has appeared; tidal phase of ebb tide
Hafukinamo	drifting before the wind to the lagoon; title of subchief (*motuʻa tauhi fonua*) of Kotu
hakau	reef
Hakau fakapapanga	smooth reef; place name for part of the outer reefs of the Kotu lagoon
hakau kahifi	brittle tabulate corals
Hakau mavahe	separated reef; place name for a part of the outer reefs of the Kotu lagoon
Hakau pupunu	filled/stopped up reef; place name for a part of the outer reefs of the Kotu lagoon
hako loa	to grow to become long and narrow of shape

halani ʻa e laʻā	the road (here) of the sun; phase of the morning just before sunrise
Halia	the graze; place name for a shallow place of passage into the Kotu lagoon
Hefau	the haul; place name for a shallow and sandy part of the Kotu lagoon
heliaki	to say one thing and mean another, to speak ironically
hengihengi	early morning before sunrise
hiapo	Paper mulberry tree
hiki hake	to uplift/raise, to praise
hiku ʻi niu	tail of the coconut, the top crown of the coconut tree
hiku ʻi puaka	lower back of the pig
Hilingakelekele	May; placing on a mound of earth
Hilingameaʻa	June; placing the clean yam
hingoa fakamatāpule	talking-chief title
hoʻatā	midday
hōʻatā mālie	noon
hokohoko	to join one after another, to be/happen in succession one after another
hoko mai	to come from, to occur before
holisi	wall
holisiaki	to make walls
hopo	to rise, to embark
hopo ʻa e fetuʻu ʻaho	rise of the day star, occurrence in the early morning
hopoʻanga laʻā	the place of the sunrise
hopoki	first embarking, inauguration
houʻeiki	chiefs
houhau laa	Red Firefish
huʻa mai ke tau ʻa e tahi	flood tide
hu mei mui	to enter by way of the back door
huo	to weed, to clear, a digging stick
huufi fale	to officially open a building

ika fakafonua	fish belonging to a place, land, island, territory
ika fuoloa	fish from the days of old
'ikai ke fu'u mamaha 'a e tahi	neap low tide
ika tupu'a 'i Kotuni	fish originating in Kotu
'ilamutu	sister's child
'iloa	known, recognizable, famous
'iloa 'e he fa'ahikehe	known by the other side/kind/spirits; moon night in the beginning of the first quarter
'iloa 'e he tangata	known by man; moon night in the first quarter
'iloa 'e he toutai	known by the fishermen/sailors; moon night in the first quarter
'ilokava	chiefly kava ceremony
'i loto mala'e	inside the place of the funeral; central area during the ceremonial process of the funeral
'inasi	share, presentation of first fruit to the Tu'i Tonga
'inasi 'ufimotu'a	tribute of first mature yams
'i tu'a mala'e	outside the place of the funeral; peripheral area during the ceremonial process of a funeral
ivi	strength, energy
kafa fonu	turtle net
kaho	reeds used in house building
kahokaho	chiefly yam, early planted yam, first crop
kahoki	rafters extending from the circumference to the summit of a Tongan house
kai efiafi	afternoon/evening meal
kai fakaafe	feast to which the participants are specifically invited
kai fakamavae	food/eating of separation; farewell meal
kai ho'atā	midday meal
kāinga ofi	close kin
kaipola	board of food, food presentation
kai pongipongi	morning meal
kai talitali	food/feast of welcome

kai ʻumu	to eat the food prepared in an earth oven
kakaha	red hot stones of the earth oven
kakapu	thick mist, fog
kakeʻi	to wrap the food to be cooked in an earth oven in leaves
kālia	large sailing canoe
kali lei	whale-tooth neckrest/headrest
kalipa	waning half moon; name of first moon night of the fourth quarter
kape	giant taro: *Alocasia macrorrhiza*
kataʻi kava	limb of kava root, section of kava from one joint to another
kātoa ʻa e māhina	the moon is full
kato ʻo Taufatōfua ki Loto ā	Taufatōfua's basket: tribute to the Royal House
kauata	belonging to the twilight; phase of the late night
Kauhakau fakatonga	southern reefs; place name for the southern part of the outer reefs of the Kotu lagoon
kau lotu	fellow worshippers, congregation
kaungāʻapi	neighbours
kau ngāue	workers, working people
kau poto	the educated/knowledgeable ones
kaupoʻuli	the dark ones; reference to several nights in the third and fourth quarters of the moon
kautā lalo	the lower curved ones; beams making up the lower curve of the curved ends of the roof of a Tongan house
kautā loto	the inner ones; beams making up the upper curve of the curved ends of the roof of a Tongan house
kautehina	group of younger brothers (relative to the *taʻokete*: oldest brother)
kautevolo	spirits, ghosts
kautuʻa	the outsiders; persons of low rank relative to the deceased at a funeral
kava	*piper methysticum*, root of the kava plant, kava powder mixed with water

Glossary

Kava tokoua	twin kava; place name for pools by the sandstone barrier in the Kotu lagoon
kavenga	duty, obligation, burden
kei mui	still young/later
kei si'i	still small/young
kei talavou	still young and handsome
kei vale	still incompetent, ignorant, unknowing
kele	mud, dirt, clay
kelekele	land, soil, dirt, earth, ground
kili ma'a	clean light bark, inner bark
kili 'uli	dark/dirty bark, outer bark
kio 'a e manumu'a	first bird call; sequenced occurrence in the early morning
kio 'a fuleheu	call of the Honeysucker bird; sequenced occurrence in the early morning
kio fakaholo	bird calls all around; sequenced occurrence in the early morning
kio fe'ilo	bird calls of mutual recognition; sequenced occurrence in the early morning
kiokio tu'u ua 'a e manu	second bird calls, sequenced occurrence in the early morning
koango	Emperor fish (probably Thumbprint and Grass Emperor)
kofukofu he ngatu vala	to wrap in a piece of barkcloth for burial
kole	solicitation, to request, to beg
koloa fakatonga	Tongan goods, wealth
kolo tangata	village of people; persons encircling the grave at burials
konfelenisi 'o siasi	annual church conference
kongaloto	middle part
kongamu'a	foremost part/top
kongamui	anterior part/bottom
konga po'uli	partly night/dark
kuata	quarterly church district meeting
kuitangata	grandfather

kumala	sweet potato
kumete	wooden bowl, container
kuo maʻa ʻa e ʻaho	day has become clean, phase of the morning
kuo mafoa ʻa e ata	twilight has shattered; phase of the early morning
kuonga	period of time
kupenga	net, fishing net
laʻā	the sun
lalava	rope latching, latchwork
lalo	down, below; part of Kotu village
langa	to build
langi	sky, burial place of persons of royal descent
Langi tuʻu lilo	the hidden burial mound; place name for chiefly grave on Kotu Island
lanu	colour
laulalo	lower layer, underside of bark cloth
lau māhina fakatonga	the reckoning of the moons in the Tongan way
launoa	nonsense, silly, idle talk
lauʻolunga	upper layer, surface of barkcloth
laupisi	(to talk) rubbish, twaddle
lau pō	the reckoning of moon nights
lausiʻi foʻou	new moon sicle
lausiʻi motuʻa	old moon sickle
lau taimi	reckoning of the passage of time
lea fakamuimui	last cry of the bird spreading the day; sequenced occurrence in the
ʻa e manu tataki ʻaho	late night
leʻo	to keep watch, to guard
leʻohi	to shelter, to protect
lepoʻi	to cover the earth oven with leaves
liʻaki	to abandon, to neglect, to sacrifice, to devote
lī paʻanga	monthly collect of money
lohu loa	the long harvesting stick; mode of defining relatedness and relative rank by tracing genealogies far back in time

loka	on the move, astir
loka ʻa e namo	the lagoon is on the move; strong currents in the lagoon
loka fakatokelau	the north is on the move; strong currents in the northern part of the lagoon
loka fakatonga	the south is on the move; strong currents in the southern part of the lagoon
loka takai	the lagoon is on the move all around; strong currents in all of the lagoon
lolo tonga	Tongan scented coconut oil
longo	silence, a vague feeling that something is about to happen
longoʻaho	late night, a feeling that day is coming; phase of the early morning
longolongo	a feeling that something is about to happen
longolongoʻuha	it feels like rain
loto	inside, personal disposition, wish, desire, heart
loto fale	inside the house
loto lahi	confidence, courage, to be brave
loto māfana	warm inside, commitment
loto mamahi	to hurt inside, to suffer
lotonamo	sea inside the lagoon
lotoʻone ʻa e tahi	sea in the middle of the sand; tidal phase
lotoʻone huʻa mai	flood tide on the middle of the beach; phase of flood tide
lotoʻone mahuʻi	ebb tide on the middle of the beach; phase of ebb tide
loto siʻi	timid disposition
lotu	worship, prayer, to pray
lotu kākā	deceitful praying
lotu loi	false praying
lotu mālohi	powerful/forceful praying
Luapunga	place name of permanently submerged reef formation of the Kotu lagoon
Lula lalo	lower ruler; place name for the deep end of a field of seaweed in the Kotu lagoon

Lula ʻuta	higher ruler; place name for the shallow end of a field of seaweed in the Kotu lagoon
Luo	the hole; place name for deep area/pool in the Kotu lagoon
luo fonua	pit, earth grave
mā	shame, shamefulness
maʻa	clean, clear, free of dirt and impurity
maama	light, lamp
maau	well ordered, properly arranged, tidy, poem, poetry
Maau lahi	the large tidy; place name for coral formation in the Kotu lagoon
Maau siʻi	the small tidy; place name for coral formation in the Kotu lagoon
mafoa	to shatter, to be shattered
mafoa ʻa e ata	twilight has shattered, phase of the early morning
maha ʻaupito ʻa e tahi	the sea is completely empty; spring low tide
mahaki fakafefine	the sickness of women; menstruation
mahaki fakamāhina	the moon sickness; menstruation
mahaki fakatonga	Tongan illness
mahakiʻia ʻa e huhu	breast inflammation
māhina	the moon
māhina foʻou	new moon; first quarter of the moon
māhina kātoa	full moon; name of moon night
māhina lekeleka	tiny moon; name of moon night towards the end of the fourth quarter
māhina motuʻa	old moon
māhina tuʻu efiafi	moon standing in the evening; waxing half moon
māhina vai	weak moon; quality of the moon towards the end of the fourth quarter
mahino	to understand, to know, to recognize, to deduct, understandable, recognizable
māhoaʻa	arrowroot

mahu'i	to tear from, to separate forcefully, to wean away from
mahu'i ke mamaha 'a e tahi	The sea is separating/detaching to become almost empty; ebb tide
mahu'inga	important, importance
makafale	tabulate corals
maka feke	catching octopus with lure, octopus lure
maka feo	staghorn coral
Maka he afe	Boulder of the bend; place name in the Kotu lagoon
Maka ngatala	coral cod rock; place name for coral boulder within the Kotu lagoon
maka papa	stone barrier
Maka tangafa	giant maori wrasse rock; place name for coral boulder within the Kotu lagoon
mala	misfortune
mala'ei 'a e la'ā	the sun moves a little to one side; phase of the late part of midday
mala'ia	unlucky, unfortunate, cursed
malanga	public speech, sermon
malili	Yellowfin Goatfish
malimali	smiling face, responsive looks
mālohi	strong, power, powerful, force, forceful, strength
malu efiafi	shady afternoon; phase of the late afternoon
mamaha	almost empty
mamaha 'a e tahi	low tide
mamaha hu'a mai	low tide that has turned; tidal phase
mamaha kaha'u	next low tide
mamalu 'a e po'uli	shade of the night; phase of the evening
mamalu efiafi	evening of deep shades; phase of the evening
mana	miracle, wonder, sign
manu tala'aho	birds announcing day; sequenced occurrence in the early morning
mā'olunga	high

mata	face, eye, interface, top, front, edge, projection, point
matāfonua	coast/front of the land from the perspective of the sea
matahakau	front of the reef from the perspective of the deep sea
mata hele	knife edge
mataʻihuhu	teat, nipple
mataʻiniu	sprouting point of a coconut
mataʻitalo	top of the taro tuber used for planting
mataʻitofua	suckers/slips used for pandanus planting
mata lavea/mata ʻi lavea	wound
Mataliki	the seven sisters; the Pleiades star constellation
mata moʻui	lively face/eyes
Matangi taulau	favourable wind (from SE towards NW); talking chief title on Kotu
mata nifo	the biting edge of the teeth
mata ʻo e fingota	the eye/opening of the clam
matapā ʻi muʻa	frontal doorway
matapā ʻi mui	posterior doorway; back door
matapā ki hala	door leading to the road; front door
matāpule	talking chief
matātahi	beach, waterfront
mata tao	spearpoint
matapā	door, doorway
matatau	battlefront, vanguard
mate	to die, dead, death, to be unconscious, to be extinguished
mate ʻa e māhina	the moon is dead; name of moon night at the end of the fourth quarter
matengataʻa	hard to kill, not dying easily
matengofua	vulnerable, easy to kill, dying easily
matofi ʻa e māhina	the moon is chopped up; name of moon night towards the end of the third quarter
maʻu	to have, to take

māʻulalo	low
māʻuli	midwife
maumau ʻa e ʻatamai	to destroy the mind
mavae	farewell, to be separated, to be weaned, weaning
mavahe mei	divided off, separated from
mavaheua	divided into two
mavahevahe	to place separately
meʻa	thing, matter, affair, substance
meʻa fakaʻeiki	corpse at a funeral
meʻa fakafafangu	wake-up call, warning
meʻakai	starchy food
meʻakiki	non-starchy food
meʻa ʻofa	thing of love; gift
meʻa pau	dependable thing
mehekitanga	father's sister
misinale	annual money collection in church
moana	deep sea
mohenga ʻo e kafa fonu	site for placing a turtle net
mokomoko ʻaho	coolness of the (approaching) day; phase of late night
mokopuna	grandchild
monū	success, luck
monūʻia	lucky, abounding with fortune, blessed
motuʻa	old, mature
motuʻa tauhi fonua	old man taking care of the land; subchief
motumotu	worn and torn; large and coarse woven matting covering most of the body; appropriate attire for persons of low relative rank at a funeral
Moʻunga ʻe ua	twin peaks; talking-chief title on Kotu
Moʻunga Tōfua	the mountain of Tōfua; place name for deep area in the Kotu lagoon
muʻa	front, anterior, before, preceding
muʻa mai	to lead the way here, to precede, to occur before
muʻa ʻo e pola	the anterior/preceding end of a food presentation

mui	posterior, after, following
mui mai	to follow after, to occur later
muimui mai	following someone here
muimui mai ʻa e ʻaho	day following in the wake
mui ʻo e pola	the posterior/following end of a food presentation
muiʻulu ʻi puaka	upper back of the pig
namo	lagoon
Namolahi	large lagoon; term of reference to the Kotu lagoon
namu lelei	nice smell
namu palakū	putrid smell, bad smell
nenefu	haze
ʻofa	love, compassion
ohi	to adopt, an adopted child, banana plant or fruit resulting from transplantation
omi ke pusiakiʻi	to bring a child to be adopted
ngakau	intestines
ngaohi	to build, to construct, to create, to compose, to assemble
ngaohi fanau	to build/put together children, to raise, educate, form children
ngaohi lea	to assemble words, compose a speech
ngaohi mata lelei	to build, compose a good face
ngaohi pola	to build a board of food; to compose a food presentation
ngaohi ʻumu	to make an earth oven
ngata	to end, to last, to reach full extension
Ngataʻanga	end, turning point
Ngataʻanga ʻo e pō	the end of night
Ngataʻanga ʻo e tahi	the turning point of the tide
Ngataʻanga ʻo e taʻu	the end/turning point of the year crop
ngata he lotoʻone	
ngata ʻi ʻuta ʻa e tahi	spring high tide

ngatala	term of reference for numerous rock cod, coral trout, groupers
ngata 'o e tahi	the turning of the tide
ngatu	painted barkcloth
ngoto'umu	volcanic crater, earth oven (synonymous with *'umu*)
nimahomo	hand from which things slip; open handedness, generosity
niu	coconut palm tree, coconut, coconut cream
noa	of no account, of no consequence, haphazard, dumb, futile
noa'ia pē	whimsical, aimless, without consideration, unimportant, worthless
nofo'anga ika	haunt, dwelling place of fish
'Oaakifangongo	October/November; making baskets to collect empty shells of used green coconuts
'ofa	to love, to be fond of, to have compassion, to be kind to
'ofa mo'oni	sincere love, true compassion
'oho	sudden appearance
'ohovale	startled by a sudden occurrence
ongo vai	*the pair of pools*
'Otua	God
pakupaku 'a e namo	the lagoon is completely dry; spring low tide
pala	soggy, drenched, rotting
pale 'a e la'ā	the sun beginning to decline; phase of the early afternoon
pale efiafi	beginning of the sun's decline
Papa	term of reference to rock barrier along the weather coast of Kotu
papaka	to flinch
pau	certain, dependable, predictable
pau'u	naughty, naughtiness
pō	night
pō 'a e maama	night of the world/light; name of moon night in the first quarter

pō faʻahikehe	night of the other side/kind/spirits; name of moon night in the beginning of the first quarter quarter
pola	'table'/board of food
pongipongi	morning from immediately before sunrise
pongipongi mamaha	low tide in the morning
pō ʻo e tuʻu ʻa e māhina	night of the standing moon; name of moon night in the first quarter
popongi	dazzling brightness
popotu	small crab
poto	competent, competence, knowledge
pō toutai	the night of fishermen/sailors; name of moon night in the first
pou	posts supporting the *toka ʻo e fale* or foundation of a Tongan house
poʻuli	night, darkness, to be night, to be dark
pule ngāue	work leader
puke nima	miserliness greed, greedy, lit. to grasp, hold
pule toutai	fishing leader
puli	disappear, vanish
puli ʻa e pala	the drenched seaweed has disappeared; phase of flood tide
puli ʻa e toukilikili	the pebbles have disappeared; phase of flood tide
puluʻi he ngatu	to encase in a sheet of bark cloth for burial
punga	brain coral, head coral
Punifanga	filling out to get two sides; name of moon night in the second quarter (also *Fuaʻaho*)
pupunu	to fill up, to plug, to stop up
pusiaki	adopted child, to adopt, to give up in adoption
setuata	church steward
sīlī	casting net
sino lelei	full-bodied, well-built, well-proportioned, healthy
sino ʻo e putu	the substance/body of the funeral; persons of high rank relative to the deceased

siu	birds flying to catch fish, men going out in boats to catch sharks, chiefs going out in boats to catch fish
ta'eako	uneducated
ta'efaka'apa'apa	lack of respect, without respect
ta'e feohi	uncompanionable, without companionship
ta'elata	homesick, dissatisfied
ta'engaohi	badly composed/raised, lack of manners
ta'e'ofa	without love, without compassion, unkind
ta'eole	no fun, boring
ta'epau	unpredictable, uncertain, not to be depended on
tafa'aki 'o e ngatu	the two sides of a piece of barkcloth
tafa puaka fakakioa	carving up the pig along the throat
tafe	flow of running liquid, stream
tahi	sea as opposed to land (*'uta*)
tahi lahi	spring high tide
tahi si'i	neap high tide
taimi fakapo'uli	pre-Christian era, time of darkness, night-time
taimi mafana	warm season
taimi momoko	cool season
taimi 'uha	rainy season
takapau	green palm leaf mattings, young coconut leaves used for making floor mats
taka pau ua	second dependable sign; phase of ebb tide
taka pau 'uluaki	first reliable sign; phase of ebb tide
talangata'a	insubordinate
talangofua	obedient
tali 'a e kole	to respond (positively) to solicitation
talinga	waiting place, place of welcome
Talinga vete	Goatfish waiting place; place name for a part of Kotu Island affording a good view of the lagoon and a part of the beach of Kotu
talo	taro

tamahā	eldest daughter of Tu'i Tonga's eldest sister; the position of supreme rank in former system of Tongan ranking
tamai	father and father's brothers
tamate maama	to put out the lamp/light
tāmu'a	anterior curved end of a Tongan house
tāmui	posterior curved end of a Tongan house
tangi 'a Teiko	the cry of the Teiko bird, sequenced occurrence in the early morning
Tanumanga	October; buried together in one place
tanutanu	term of reference for some Emperor fishes (probably Pink-eared or Orange-striped Emperor)
ta'o	to place the food in the earth oven to be cooked
tā 'ofa	to strike/punish out of love/compassion
ta'okete	eldest brother (of a man)
ta'olunga	Tongan dance performance, to perform a Tongan dance
ta'ovala	woven matting worn around the waist
tapalangi	the edge of the sky, the sky side
tapalika	the slim edge (of the disk of the sun); final moment of sunset
tapu	restriction, forbidden, constrained, sacred
tataki	to spread
ta'u	year, yam crop
ta'u lahi	big yam crop; late yam crop
tau	layer of leaves covering the food in the earth oven
tau	to be joined with, to copulate, to come all the way to, to reach
tau 'a e tahi	high tide
tau 'a e tahi mo e 'uta	sea and land unite
taufa	rainstorm, squall
tauhi	to maintain, to nurture, to care for, to look after, to foster, fostered/adopted child
tauhi vaha'a	to nurture/feed the space/gap (between people)

tau huʻa/tau huʻa mai	high tide that has not yet turned
tau kahaʻu	next high tide
Taulanga lahi	big anchorage; place name in the Kotu lagoon
Taulanga siʻi	small anchorage; place name in the Kotu lagoon
tau mahuʻi	high tide that has turned
taumataʻu	to fish with hook and angle
tefitoʻi	essential, fundamental, cardinal, principle, cause/reason of existence
tefitoʻi fāmili	family head in the extended sense of the term *fāmili* (synonymous with *ʻulumotuʻa*)
tefitoʻi niu	base of the coconut tree
tehina	a younger brother (relative to the *taʻokete*: eldest brother)
teungahina	white clothes; appropriate attire for persons of high rank relative to the deceased at a funeral
teungaʻuli	black clothes; appropriate attire for persons of low rank relative to the deceased at a funeral
teuteu	decoration, to decorate, to prepare
tō	sugar cane, to plant, to set, to fall
toa	species of hardwood tree
tō ʻa e laʻā	sunset
tōʻanga laʻā	the place of the sunset
tofi ke tō	cut up seed yam to plant
Tofuke	place name for coral formation in the Kotu lagoon
tō he taʻu	to plant with the crop/year/season
Tohi tapu	the Bible, the Holy Book
toka ʻo e fale	the foundation of the house; beams resting on the posts of the Tongan house to support the roof
tokamuʻa	early yam crop (*kahokaho*-yam crop)
tokamui	late yam crop; a variety of yams planted later than the early crop of *kahokaho*-yams and maturing more slowly

Tōkilangi	dedicated to the chiefly burial mound; place name for freshwater pool on Kotu Island
tokonaki	bring together, collect food, Saturday
tokoni	to help, food
tokotuʻu	standing studs; smaller posts to which the walls of the Tongan house are attached
tokoua	same-sex siblings
tongo	mangrove
tongo lei	a variety of mangrove
toʻotoʻonga ʻo e puaka	entrails of the pig
tō taʻu	to plant the yam crop, planting season
toʻu	generation
tou-	prefix often denoting a prolonged, productive or procreative union between constituent parts
touʻa	group of kava-makers, kava girl
touʻaki	to feed, nurture so as to build up the strength gradually
toʻufūfū	inner ridge beam running along the interior of the apex of a Tongan house
touʻia	to be with foal, animal pregnancy
toʻu kai	generation of food, crop
toʻu kai mo hono lohu	the crop and its harvesting stick; idiom; each generation has its own leaders
toukilikili ʻa e tahi	the sea is at the pebbles; phase of ebb tide
tou-mohomoho	limp and softened leaf covering (*tau*) over the cooked food in an earth oven
toutai	fishing, marine activity
toutama	to suckle a child
tuʻa fonua	the other side of an island from where one is facing (*matāfonua*)
tuʻa ʻi puaka	mid-back of the pig
tuʻa namo	sea outside the lagoon
tuʻa ʻo e putu	the outsiders of the funeral; persons of low rank relative to the deceased
tufa he kakai	to distribute food and wealth to the participants at a funeral

tuhutuhuʻi	threaten; lit. shake the index finger
tuku	to place, to set aside, to hand over, to entrust, to devote, to abandon, to neglect, to desist
tuku kelekele	to place/hand over/devote/entrust land/soil
tuku moʻui	to place/hand over/devote/entrust life
Tukulalo	low-lying land near the coast; term of reference to Kotu Island
tukuʻuta	interior
tumaama	to light the lamp; evening after dark
tumuʻaki	summit, outer ridge beam running along the exterior summit of a Tongan house
tuofefine	sister (to a man)
tuongaʻane	brother (to a woman)
tupu	grow, grow up, to originate, to rise, to swell
tupu ki loto	to grow, spring from the middle part
tupu ki muʻa	to grow, spring from the foremost part
tupu ki mui	to grow, spring from the posterior part
tupu noa ʻia pē	to crop up all around, wild growth
tutu	to burn, to put something on a fire
tuʻuapō	deep night
tuʻu efiafi ʻa e māhina	the moon stands in the evening; name of moon night in the beginning of the second quarter
tuʻu lilo	hidden, secret, isolated
tuʻunga	pedestal, perch, standing place
Tuʻunga kupenga	place of net fishing; place name for passage into the Kotu lagoon
Tuʻungatala	the perch of the *Tala* bird; place name for rock on the outer reefs of the Kotu lagoon
Tuʻu peau ala	standing in the waves collecting shellfish; place name in the Kotu lagoon
tuʻu tonu ʻa e laʻā	the sun stands straight up; quality of illumination/heat at midday
tuʻu tonu ʻa e māhina	the moon at its zenith
tuʻutuʻuni ʻo e putu	leader of the funeral
tuʻutuʻuni ʻo e ʻumu	master of the earth oven

ʻufi	yam
ʻūfia	to cover, to be covered, to veil, to be veiled
ʻufi ʻeiki	chiefly yam
ʻufi motuʻa	mature yam, seed yam
ʻuha	rain
uike lotu	week of devotion; reference to first week of January
ʻuliʻi	to make dirty, to soil, to work in the garden (of chiefs)
ʻuliʻuli	black, dirty
ʻulu	head
ʻuluaki hopo ʻa e māhina	first moonrise after full moon on the eastern horizon; name of a moon night in the third quarter
ʻUluenga	September; the yellow head (of the yam)
ʻulu ʻi puaka	head and neck of the pig
ʻulumotuʻa	family head, ancestor
ʻuta	garden land as opposed to village (*kolo*) or uncultivated bush (*vao*)
ʻuta	dry land as opposed to sea (*tahi*)
ʻUta	place name for one side of Kotu village as opposed to the *Lalo* side of the village
utu taʻu	to harvest the yam crop, harvesting season
ʻuʻua ʻa e moamuʻa	first cockcrow; sequenced occurrence in the early morning
ʻuʻua fakaholo	crowing all around, sequenced occurrence in the early morningʻ
uʻua tuʻo ua ʻa e moa	second cockcrow, sequenced occurrence in the early morning
ʻuʻuli	soiling, darkening
ʻuʻuli kelekele	the darkness of the ground, phase of the evening
ʻuʻulu	booming sound, rumbling, outer reefs
ʻumu	earth oven, stone oven
ʻUtu popotu	small crab rockface; place name for a part of the outer reefs of the Kotu lagoon

vā	space
vaeua mālie 'a e māhina	the moon is divided in two; half moon
vaeua mālie 'a e matātahi	the beach divided in two equal parts; tidal phase
vaha'a	gap, space between
vahe 'o e māhina	part/quarter of the moon
Vai fefine	women's water; place name for pool on Kotu
vai māhanga	twin waters/pools
vai melie	fresh sweet water
Vaimu'a	January; 'first water'
Vaimui	February; 'late water'
vaiola	water of life
vai tahi	sea/salt water
Vai tangata	men's water; place name for pool on Kotu
vai tonga	Tongan medical water
vaitupu	well/spring of water
vaivai	weak
vale	incompetent, ignorant
vā lelei	a good space/harmonious relations
valevale	unable to think for oneself, baby (synonymous with *pepe*)
Vāsia	food made from taro leaves, coconut cream and arrowroot; term of reference to pool by the sandstone barrier along the weather coast of Kotu Island
Veifua	first food to be eaten by a woman who has married or given birth; men who have been out shark fishing; place name for pool on Kotu Island
vete	Yellowstripe Goatfish

References

Aoyagi, Machiko. 1966. 'Kinship Organization and Behaviour in a Contemporary Tongan Village', *Journal of the Polynesian Society* 75(2): 141–76.
Barnes, Robert. 1977. '*Mata* in Austronesia', *Oceania* 47(4): 300–19.
Barth, Fredrik. 1987. *Cosmologies in the Making: A Generative Approach to Cultural Variation in Inner New Guinea*. Cambridge: Cambridge University Press.
_____. 1989. 'The Analysis of Culture in Complex Societies', *Ethnos* 54(3–4): 120–42.
_____. 1993. *Balinese Worlds*. Chicago and London: The University of Chicago Press.
Bataille-Benguigui, Marie-Claire. 1986. 'Les Polynesiens des Iles Tonga et leur representation du milieu marin', unpublished doctoral thesis, Universite de Paris X (Microfiche No. 87.50.3287.86 Universite de Lille III).
_____. 1988. 'The Fish of Tonga: Prey or Social Partners?', *Journal of the Polynesian Society* 97(2): 185–98.
Beaglehole, Ernest and Pearl. 1944. *Pangai, a Village in Tonga*. Wellington: Polynesian Society Memoir 18.
Beaglehole, John C. 1967. *The Journals of Captain James Cook on His Voyages of Discovery: The Voyage of the Resolution and Discovery 1776–1780*. Cambridge: Hakluyt Society.
Beckwick, Martha W. 1932 'Kepelino's Traditions of Hawaii', *Bulletin 95*. Honolulu: Bernice P. Bishop Museum.
Bennardo, Giovanni. 2009. *Language, Space and Social Relationships: A Foundational Cultural Model in Polynesia*. Cambridge: Cambridge University Press.
Beattie, John H.M. 1980. 'On Understanding Sacrifice', in M.F.C. Bourdillon (ed.), *Sacrifice*. London: Academic Press, pp. 29–44.
Besnier, Nico. 2004. 'The Social Production of Abjection: Desire and Silencing amongst Transgender Tongans', *Social Analysis* 12(3): 301–23.
_____. 2011. *On the Edge of the Global: Modern Anxieties in a Pacific Island Nation*. Stanford: Stanford University Press.
Bible. 1976. *Good News Bible*. The Bible Societies: Collins/Fontana.

Biersack, Aletta. 1991. 'Kava'onau and the Tongan Chiefs', *Journal of the Polynesian Society* 100(3): 231–68.
———. 1994. Book Reviews. *Tongan History Association Newsletter* 5(2): 2–3.
Bloch, Maurice. 1992. 'What Goes Without Saying: The Conceptualization of Zafimaniry Society', in Adam Kuper (ed.), *Conceptualizing Society: Models of Society, the Individual, and Nature*. New York: Routledge, pp. 127–46.
———. 1993. 'Domain-Specificity, Living Kinds and Symbolism', in P. Boyer (ed.), *Cognitive Aspects of Religious Symbolism*. Cambridge: Cambridge University Press, pp. 111–20.
Bott, Elisabeth. 1958. *Discussions of Tongan Customs with Her Majesty Queen Salote Tupou and the Hon. Ve'ehala*. Nuku'alofa: Typescript in Palace Records Office.
———. 1972a. 'Psychoanalysis and Ceremony', in J. La Fontaine (ed.), *The Interpretation of Ritual*. London: Tavistock Publications, pp. 205–37.
———. 1972b. 'The Significance of Kava in Tongan Myth and Ritual', in J. La Fontaine (ed.), *The Interpretation of Ritual*. London: Tavistock Publications, pp. 205–82.
———. 1981. 'Power and Rank in the Kingdom of Tonga', *Journal of the Polynesian Society* 90(1): 7–81.
———. 1982. *Tongan Society at the Time of Captain Cook's Visits*. Wellington: The Polynesian Society.
Bourdieu, Pierre. 1963. 'The Attitude of the Algerian Peasant Toward Time', in J. Pitt-Rivers (ed.), *Mediterranean Countrymen*. Paris: Mouton & Co, pp. 55–72.
Bourdillon, Michael F.C. 1980. *Sacrifice*. London: Academic Press.
Campbell, Ian. 1992. *Island Kingdom: Tonga Ancient and Modern*. Christchurch: Canterbury University Press.
Carroll, Vern. 1970. 'Adoption in Nukuoro', in V. Carroll (ed.), *Adoption in Eastern Oceania*. Honolulu: University of Hawaii Press.
Churchward, Clerk M. 1953. *Tongan Grammar*. London and New York: Oxford University Press.
———. 1959. *Tongan Dictionary*. Tonga: Government Printing Press.
Collocott, Ernest E.V. 1919. 'A Tongan Theogony', *Folklore* 30(3): 234–38.
———. 1921. 'Legends from Tonga: The Maui', *Folklore* 32(1): 45–58.
———. 1928. 'Tales and Poems of Tonga', Bulletin 46. Honolulu: Bernice P. Bishop Museum.
Cowling, Wendy. 1990a. 'Motivations for Contemporary Migration in Tonga', in Phyllis Herda et al. (eds), *Tongan Culture and History*. Canberra: Department of Pacific and Southeast Asian History, ANU, pp. 187–206.
———. 1990b. 'Eclectic Elements in Tongan Folk Belief and Healing Practice', in Phyllis Herda et al. (eds), *Tongan Culture and History*. Canberra: Department of Pacific and Southeast Asian History, ANU, pp. 72–93.
Decktor Korn, Shulamit R. 1974. 'Tongan Kin Groups: The Noble and the Common View', *Journal of the Polynesian Society* 83(1): 5–13.

———. 1975. 'Household Composition in the Tonga Islands: A Question of Options and Alternatives, *Journal of Anthropological Research* 31(3): 235–59.

———. 1976. 'Demographic Aspects of Ethnography: Data from the Tonga Islands', *Ethnos* 41(1–4): 133–45.

———. 1978. 'After the Missionaries Came: Denominational Diversity in the Tonga Islands', in James Boutilier et al (eds), *Mission, Church, and Sect in Oceania*. Lanham: University of America, pp. 395–422.

Decktor Korn, Frederic and Shulamit R. 1983. 'Where People Don't Promise', *Ethics* 93(3): 445–51.

Donner, Simon D. 2007. 'Domain of the Gods: An Editorial Essay', *Climatic Change* 85(3–4): 231–36.

Douglas, Mary. 1966. *Purity and Danger: An Analysis of the Concepts of Pollution and Taboo*. London: Routledge.

Dye, Tom S. 1983. 'Fish and Fishing on Niuatoputapu', *Oceania* 53(3): 242–71.

Eliade, Mircea. 1958. *Patterns in Comparative Religion*. London: Sheed and Ward Stagebooks.

Encyclopedia Britannica Online, 1999: *Myth*. http://www.eb.co.uk [https://www.britannica.com/].

Fall, Patricia. 2010. 'Pollen Evidence for Plant Introductions in a Polynesian Tropical Island Ecosystem, Kingdom of Tonga', in Simon G. Haberle (ed.), *Altered Ecologies: Fire, Climate and Human Influence on Terrestrial Landscapes*. Canberra: ANU Press, Terra Australis 32, pp. 253–73.

Fanua, Tupou P. 1986. *Tapa Cloth in Tonga*. Nukuʻalofa: Secondary Teacher Education Program.

Filihia, Meredith. 1999. 'Rituals of Sacrifice in Early Post-European Contact Tonga and Tahiti', *The Journal of Pacific History* 34(1): 5–22.

Firth, Raymond. 1936. *We, the Tikopia*. London: George Allen and Unwin.

———. 1992. 'Art and Anthropology', in. J. Coote and A. Shelton (eds), *Anthropology Art and Aesthetics*. Oxford: Clarendon Press, pp. 15–40.

Fox, James J. 1995. 'Austronesian Societies and their Transformations', in Peter Bellow et al. (eds), *The Austronesians: History and Comparative Perspectives*. Canberra: Research School of Pacific Studies, ANU, pp. 214–29.

———. 2008. 'Installing the "Outsider" Inside: The Exploration of an Epistemic Austronesian Cultural Theme and its Social Significance', *Indonesia and the Malay World* 36(105): 201–18.

Freeman, Derek. 1983. *Margaret Mead and Samoa: The Making and the Unmaking of an Anthropological Myth*. Cambridge: Harvard University Press.

Gailey, Christine W. 1987. 'State, Class and Conversion in Commodity Production: Gender and Changing Value in the Tongan Islands', Journal *of the Polynesian Society* 96(1): 67–80.

———. 1990. *From Kinship to Kingship*. Austin: University of Texas Press.

Gell, Alfred. 1992. *The Anthropology of Time: Cultural Constructions of Temporal Maps*. Oxford: Berg Publishers.

———. 1995. 'Closure and Multiplication: An Essay on Polynesian Cosmology and Ritual', in D. de Coppet and A. Iteanu (eds), *Cosmos and Society in Oceania*. Oxford: Berg Publishers, pp. 21–57.

———. 1998. *Art and Agency: An Anthropological Theory*. Oxford: Clarendon Press, pp. 155–220.

Gifford, Edward W. 1924a. 'Euro-American Acculturation in Tonga', *Journal of the Polynesian Society* 33(4): 281–92.

———. 1924b. 'Tongan Myths and Tales', *Bulletin 8*. Honolulu: Bernice. P. Bishop Museum.

———. 1929. 'Tongan Society', *Bulletin 61*. Honolulu: Bernice P. Bishop Museum.

Gordon, Tamar. 1996. 'They Loved Her Too Much: Interpreting Spirit Possession in Tonga', in J.M. Mageo and A. Howard (eds), *Spirits in Culture, History and Mind*. New York and London: Routledge, pp. 55–74.

Grijp, Paul van der. 1993a. *Islanders of the South: Production, Kinship and Ideology in the Polynesian Kingdom of Tonga*. Leiden: KITLV Press.

———. 1993b. 'The Making of a Modern Chiefdom State: The Case of Tonga', *Bijdragen Tot de Taal-, Land-, en Volkenkunde* 149(4): 661–73.

Gunson, Neil P. 1990. 'Tongan Historiography: Shamanic Views of Time and History', in P. Herda et al. (eds), *Tongan Culture and History*. Canberra: Department of Pacific and Southeast Asian History, ANU, pp. 12–21.

Hafoka, Havili. n.d. 'Tohi 'a Havili Hafoka and Queen Salote on Tongan Traditions', Nuku'alofa: Tongan Traditions Committee at Palace Office, *Miscellaneous manuscripts*.

Halapua, Sitiveni. 1982. *Fishermen of Tonga: Their Means of Survival*. Suva: Institute of Pacific Studies, University of the South Pacific.

Hau'ofa, 'Epeli. 1994. 'Our Sea of Islands', *The Contemporary Pacific* 6(1): 148–61.

Herda, Phyllis. 1987. 'Gender, Rank and Power in 18th Century Tonga', *Journal of Pacific History* 22(4): 195–208.

———. 1990. 'Genealogy in the Tongan Construction of the Past', in P. Herda et al. (eds), *Tongan Culture and History*. Canberra: Department of Pacific and Southeast Asian History, ANU, pp. 21–30.

Hirsch, Eric. 1995. 'Introduction. Landscape: Between Place and Space', in E. Hirsch and M. O'Hanlon (eds), *The Anthropology of Landscape, Perspectives on Place and Space*. Oxford: Clarendon Press.

Howard, Alan, and Robert Borofsky. 1989. *Developments in Polynesian Ethnology*. Honolulu: University of Hawaii Press.

Hubert, Henri, and Marcell Mauss. 1964. *Sacrifice: Its Nature and Function*. London: Cohen & West.

Hulme, Mike. 2009. *Why We Disagree about Climate Change: Understanding Controversy, Inaction and Opportunity*. Cambridge: Cambridge University Press.

Hviding, Edvard. 1996. *Guardians of Marovo Lagoon: Practice, Place and Politics in Maritime Melanesia*. Honolulu: University of Hawaii Press.

Ingold, Tim. 1992. 'Culture and the Perception of the Environment', in E. Croll and D. Parkin (eds), *Bush Base: Forest Farm. Culture, Environment and Development*. London: Routledge, pp. 39–56.

———. 2000. *The Perception of the Environment: Essays in Livelihood, Dwelling and Skill*. London and New York: Routledge.

———. 2011. *Being Alive: Essays on Movement, Knowledge and Description*. London and New York: Routledge.

James, Kerry E. 1983. 'Gender Relations in Tonga 1780 to 1984', *Journal of the Polynesian Society* 92(2): 233–43.

———. 1990. 'Gender Relations in Tonga: A Paradigm Shift', in P. Herda et al. (eds), *Tongan Culture and History*. Canberra: Department of Pacific and Southeast Asian History, ANU, pp. 93–101.

———. 1991. 'Migration and Remittances: A Tongan Village Perspective', *Pacific Viewpoint* 32(1): 1–23.

Kaeppler, Adrienne L. 1983. 'Dance in Tonga: The Communication of Social Values through an Artistic Medium', *Journal of Anthropological Studies of Human Movements* 2(3): 122–28.

———. 1985. 'Structured Movement Systems in Tonga', in Paul Spencer (ed.), *Society and Dance*. Cambridge: Cambridge University Press, pp. 92–115.

———. 1990. 'Art, Aesthetics and Social Structure', in P. Herda et al. (eds), *Tongan Culture and History*. Canberra: Department of Pacific and Southeast Asian History, ANU, pp. 59–72.

———. 1993. 'Poetics and Politics of Tongan Laments and Eulogies', *American Ethnologist* 20(3): 474–501.

Kaʻili, Tevita O. 2005. 'Tauhi Vā: Nurturing Tongan Socio-spatial Ties in Maui and Beyond', *The Contemporary Pacific* 17(1): 86–105.

Keesing, Felix M. 1947. 'Acculturation in Polynesia', in K. Luomala et al. (eds), *Specialized Studies in Polynesian Anthropology, Bulletin 193*. Honolulu: Bernard P. Bishop Museum, pp. 32–47.

Kingdom of Tonga. 1976. *Population Census*. Nukuʻalofa: Government of Tonga, Statistics Department.

———. 1986. *Population Census*. Nukuʻalofa: Government of Tonga, Statistics Department.

Kitekeiʻaho, Fuka. 2012. 'PASAP/ Lifuka Project', Pacific Community, Geoscience division. Retrieved 26 August 2021 from http://gsd.spc.int/marinecoastalsciencesurvey/geohazardmapping.

Koch, Gerd. 1955. *Sudsee- Gestern und Heute: Der Kulturswandel bei den Tongarnen und der Versuch einer Deutung dieser Entwicklung*. Braunschweig: A. Limbach Verlag.

Leach, Edmund. 1972. 'The Structure of Symbolism', in J. La Fontaine (ed.), *The Interpretation of Ritual*. London: Tavistock Publications, pp. 239–76.

Lebot, Vincent. 1995. 'The Origin and Distribution of Kava', *Canberra Anthropology* 18(1–2): 20–33.

Lebot, Vincent, Mark Merlin and Lamont Lindstrom. 1992. *Kava: The Pacific Drug*. New Haven: Yale University Press.

Leivestad, Karen. 1995. 'Fra en Ring av Steiner: En Etnografisk Studie av Matpraksis og Mening i Marovo (New Georgia, Solomon Islands)', unpublished MA thesis. Bergen: Institute of Social Anthropology University of Bergen.

Leslie, Heather E.Y. 2007. '… Like A Mat Being Woven', *Pacific Arts NS 3*: 115–27.

Levy, Robert I. 1973. *Tahitians: Mind and Experience in the Society Islands*. Chicago: Chicago University Press.

Luomala, Katharine. 1949. 'Maui-of-a-Thousand-Tricks: His Oceanic and European Biographers', *Bulletin 198*. Honolulu: Bernice P. Bishop Museum.

Māhina, 'Okusi. 1990. 'Myths and History: Some Aspects of History in the Tu'i Tonga Myths', in P. Herda et al. (eds), *Tongan Culture and History*. Canberra: Department of Pacific and Southeast Asian History, ANU, pp. 30–46.

Manderson, Lenore. 1986. 'Food Classification and Restriction in Peninsular Malaysia: Nature, Culture, Hot, Cold?', in L. Manderson (ed.), *Shared Wealth and Symbol: Food, Culture and Society in Oceania and Southeast Asia*. Cambridge: Cambridge University Press, pp. 127–43.

Marcus, George E. 1980. *The Nobility and the Chiefly Tradition in the Modern Kingdom of Tonga*. Wellington: The Polynesian Society [Memoir 42].

Martin, John. 1991. *Tonga Islands: William Mariner's Account*. Tonga: Vava'u Press.

MORDI. 2016. 'Nuku'alofa: Tonga'. Retrieved 26 August 2021 from http://www.morditonga.to/.

Morton, Helen. 1996. *Becoming Tongan: An Ethnography of Childhood*. Honolulu: University of Hawaii Press.

Morton, Keith L. 1972. 'Kinship, Economics and Exchange in a Tongan Village', unpublished Ph.D. thesis. Portland: University of Oregon.

———. 1976. 'Tongan Adoption', in I. Brady (ed.), *Transactions in Kinship*. Honolulu: University of Hawaii Press, ASAO Monograph 4: 64–81.

———. 1980. 'The Atomization of Tongan Society', *Pacific Studies* 10(2): 47–73.

Müller, Max. 1856. *Comparative Mythology: An Essay*. London: Routledge and Sons.

Naylor, Paz B. 1986. 'On the Semantics of Reduplication', in Paul Geraghty et al. (eds), *Focal I: Papers from the Fourth International Conference on Austronesian Linguistics*. Canberra: Department of Linguistics, Research School of Pacific Studies, ANU, pp. 175–85.

Perminow, Arne A. 1993a. *The Long Way Home: Dilemmas of Everyday Life in a Tongan Village*. Oslo: Scandinavian University Press.

———. 1993b. 'Between the Forest and the Big Lagoon: The Microeconomy of Kotu Island in the Kingdom of Tonga', *Pacific Viewpoint* 34(2): 179–93.

———. 1995. '"Recreational" Drinking in Tonga: *Kava* and the Constitution of Social Relationships', *Canberra Anthropology* 18(1–2): 119–36.

———. 2001. 'Captain Cook and the Roots of Precedence in Tonga', *History and Anthropology* 12(3): 289–314.

———. 2003. '"The Other Kind": Representing Otherness and Living with it on Kotu Island in Tonga', in I. Hoëm and S. Roalkvam (eds), *Oceanic Socialities and Cultural Forms: Ethnographies of Experience*. New York and Oxford: Berghahn, pp. 157–76.

———. 2011. '"It is a Tree that Fights": Engaging Notions of Qualitative Difference in Tonga', in I. Hoëm and R. Solsvik (eds), *Identity Matters: Movement and Place*. Oslo: Kon Tiki Museum, Occasional Papers, Volume 12, pp. 111–23.

———. 2015. 'Food Presentations Moving Overseas: Ritual Aesthetics and Everyday Sociality in Tonga and among Tongan Migrants', in Ø. Fuglerud and L. Wainwright (eds), *Objects and Imaginations: Perspectives on Materialization and Meaning*. New York and Oxford: Berghahn, pp. 111–32.

———. 2018. 'Moving Moorings, Nurturing Flows: Scales of Tongan Mobilities', in K. Larsen and J. Simonsen (eds), *Movement and Connectivity: Configurations of Belonging*. Oxford: Peter Lang, pp. 131–59.

Pollock, Nancy. 1992. *These Roots Remain: Food Habits in Islands of the Central and Eastern Pacific since Western Contact*. Laie: The Institute for Polynesian Studies.

———. 1995. 'Introduction: The Power of Kava', *Canberra Anthropology* 18(2–3): 1–19.

Poltorak, Mike. 2007. 'Nemesis, Speaking, and Tauhi Vahaʻa: Interdisciplinarity and the Truth of "Mental Illness" in Vavaʻu Tonga', *Contemporary Pacific* 19(1): 1–36.

Randall, John E., Gerald R. Allen and Roger C. Steene. 1990. *Fishes of the Great Barrier Reef and Coral Sea*. Honolulu: University of Hawaii Press.

Redfield, Robert. 1956. *Peasant Society and Culture: An Ethnographical Approach to Civilization*. Chicago: University of Chicago Press.

Rogers, Garth. 1968. 'Politics and Social Dynamics in Niuafoʻou: An Outlier in the Kingdom of Tonga', MA thesis. Auckland: University of Auckland.

———. 1975. 'Kai and Kava in Niuatoputapu: Social Relations, Ideologies and Contexts in a Rural Tongan Community', Ph.D. thesis. Auckland: University of Auckland.

———. 1977. 'The Father's Sister is Black', *Journal of the Polynesian Society* 86(2): 157–82.

Rosaldo, Renato. 1993. *Culture and Truth: The Remaking of Social Analysis*. Boston: Beacon Press.

Sahlins, Marshall. 1995. *How "Natives" Think: About Captain Cook, for Example*. Chicago: The University of Chicago Press.

Shore, Bradd. 1982. *Salaʻilua: A Samoan Mystery*. New York: Columbia University Press.

_____. 1989. 'Mana and Tapu', in A. Howard and R. Borofsky (eds), *Developments in Polynesian Ethnology*. Honolulu: University of Hawaii Press, pp. 137-75.
_____. 1996. *Culture in Mind: Cognition, Culture and the Problem of Meaning*. Oxford: Oxford University Press.
Taumoefolau, Melenaite. 1990. 'Is the Father's Sister Really "Black"?' *Journal of the Polynesian Society* 100(1): 91-99.
Thaman, Konai Helu. 2008. 'Nurturing Relationships and Honouring Responsibilities: A Pacific Perspective', *International Review of Education* 54: 459-473.
Thomas, John. 1825-67. *Journals (1825-59)*. Mitchell Library Microfilms FM 4/1439 (MMS 48). Sydney: Library of New South Wales.
Tohi Tabu. 1990. *Koe Tohi Tabu Katoa*. Suva: The Bible Society.
Topouniua, Penisimani. 1986. *A Polynesian Village: The Process of Change*. Suva: South Pacific Social Science Association.
Toren, Christina. 1990. *Making Sense of Hierarchy: Cognition as Social Process in Fiji*. LSE Monograph on Social Anthropology No. 61. London: The Athlone Press.
_____. 1995. 'Cosmogonic Aspects of Desire and Compassion in Fiji', in D. de Coppet and A. Iteanu (eds), *Cosmos and Society in Oceania*. Oxford: Berg, pp. 57-83.
Turner, Victor. 1969. *The Ritual Process: Structure and Anti-structure*. New York: Cornell University Press.
Urbanowicz, Charles F. 1973. 'Tongan Adoption Before the Constitution of 1875', *Ethnohistory* 20(1): 109-24.
Valeri, Valerio. 1989. 'Death in Heaven: Myths and Rites of Kinship in Tongan Kingship', *History and Anthropology* 4(1): 209-47.
Webster's dictionary. 1979. *Webster's New Collegiate Dictionary*. Springfield, MA: G. & C. Merriam Co.
Weiner, Anette B. 1992. *Inalienable Possessions: The Paradox of Keeping-While-Giving*. Berkeley: University of California Press.
Weiner, James F. 1991. *The Empty Place*. Indianapolis: Indiana University Press.
Wendt, Albert. 1986. *The Birth and Death of the Miracle Man and Other Stories*. Auckland: Penguin Books.
_____. 1987. *Poʻuliʻuli*. Auckland: Penguin Books.
Whistler, Arthur. W. 1992. *Tongan Herbal Medicine*. Honolulu: University of Hawaii Press.
Witoszek, Nina. 1998. *Norske Naturmytologier: Fra Edda til Økosofi*. Oslo: Pax Forlag A/S.

Index

adopting children, 135–39
ad option (by choice), 135–39
akafia (Tongan illness caused by root penetration), 86
allegories, 70, 72. *See also* myths; tales
alliances, 164
anga fakatonga (Tongan way), 55
Annual money collection (*Misinale*), 165, 166, 167
The Anthropology of Landscape (Hirsch), 12
attraction, 67, 70–73

background realities, 12
Bali, 151
Balinese Worlds (Barth), 151
Barth, Frederik, 151
beaches, 115–18. *See also* sea
Beaglehole, Ernest, 14
Beaglehole, Pearl, 14
beautification, 84–86, 93, 94
beauty/beautiful (*faka'ofo'ofa*), 91, 93
Bennardo, Giovanni, 104, 105
Besnier, Nico, 13
Bible, 161. *See also* Christianity
bird calls, 38, 39, 40
birth defects, 160
births, 137. *See also* children
blood-relatedness, 101. *See also* relationships
board of food (*kaipola*), 78, 97, 100, 101, 103, 124, 172

body parts, sacrifices of, 165
bones, taboo and, 85
Book of Havili Hafoka and Queen Sālote on Tongan Traditions (Hafoka), 36
borderlands, 115–18
Bourdillon, M.F.C., 164
building/assembling of the board of food (*ngaohi pola*), 100–105
building by naming/teaching, 133–35, 139
burial traditions, 54, 55, 87

calamities, attitudes toward, 151, 152
catastrophic environmental events, 10
cemeteries, 87
ceremonial processes, 82–84, 93, 94
ceremonial slippage, 81
Chair of the placing of life (*Sea 'o e tuku mo'ui*), 169
changing environments, coping with, 149–53. *See also* environmental changes
childcare, 119, 131
children, 120–24; adopting, 135–39; building by naming/teaching, 133–35; communication, 130; composing, 132–33, 145; coping with one another, 144–46; growth of, 132–33; mutual sacrifice of adopting, 139–44; parenting, 129, 130; relocation of, 135

Christianity, 33, 50, 151, 152, 153; burial traditions and, 55; pre-Christian myths of creation, 46, 156; pre-Christian Polynesian cosmology, 45; Tonga and, 72, 158, 165, 169

churches: Free Chiefly Church of Tonga (*Siasi Tauatahina 'o Tonga Hou'eiki*), 157; Free Constitutional Church of Tonga (*Siasi Tauatahina Konisitutone 'o Tonga*), 157, 161, 163; Free Wesleyan Church of Tonga, 1, 77, 166; life in, 168; Methodist, 156, 157, 164; in Tonga, 156, 157. *See also* Christianity

climate change, 170

Collocott, Ernest E.V., 67, 68. *See also* myths

communication: flows, 131; Kotu Island, 93; parents and children, 130

Comparative Mythology (Müller), 71

compassionate love (*'ofa*), 144

composing/assembling/building (*ngaohi*), 132

compromise culture, 16

connectedness, 114

constitutive flows, 125–26, 131

constitutive motions, 45–46

constraints, ceremonies and, 93, 95

Cook, James, 8, 13, 26, 102, 165

cool season (*taimi momoko*), 98

coping with one another, 144–46

coral formations, 116

cosmic order, state of, 46–51

cosmology, 49*f*; pre-Christian Polynesian, 45

Covenant of Land, 162

crops, 102. *See also* food

culinary tableaus, 100, 105. *See also* food; tableaus

cultivation of kava, 62, 63

cultural continuity, 35, 170–73; Tonga and, 12–17

cultural traditions, 14, 15

cures, 86

cycles of night and day, 36–39; constitutive motions, 45–46; feeling that day is coming, 39–41; motions of merging, 43–45; united phrases of, 41–42

Cyclone Ian (2014), 4

Cyclone Isaac (1982), 122

cyclones, deaths and, 4

Cyclone Winston (2016), 4, 151

daily activities: in *Namolahi* Lagoon, 22–23; synchronization of, 20

darkness (*fakapo'uli*), 43, 45, 46. *See also* day; night

dawn, descriptions of, 38

day: concept of, 66; constitutive motions, 45–46; cycles of, 36–39; feeling that day is coming, 39–41; motions of merging, 43–45; state of cosmic order, 46–51; states of, 176–78; transformations (night to day), 51–52; united phrases of, 41–42. *See also* cycles of night and day

dead, body of, 85, 86

death, 160; food and, 98, 99; Tonga and, 85

deaths: cyclones and, 4

Deep night (*Tu'uapō*), 46

diets, 97, 99

differentiation, 50

diurnal cycle, 36, 41, 50, 56, 70, 107; concepts of, 66; constitutive motions, 45–46; diurnal dynamics, 47*f*, 48*f*; oscillations, 65; state of cosmic order, 46–51; tidal dynamics, 48*f*; transformations (night to day), 51–52. *See also* cycles of night and day; day; lunar motions; night

doorway (*matapā*), 113–14, 123*f*; borderlands and, 115–18; definitions of, 114–15; homes, 120–24; to nurture/care for the space between

(*tauhi vā* or *tauhi vaha'a*), 118–20; relationships and, 125
Douglas, Mary, 44
duty, to pay tribute, fulfil obligation (*fai fatongia*), 78, 81, 92, 113, 150
dying *vao* (forest), 5, 6f, 149, 153–56

Early morning (*hengihengi*), 37
earth oven, stone oven (*'umu*), 79, 100, 101, 102, 106
earthquakes, 1, 2, 3, 10
eating. *See* meals
education, 13, 152
electricity, 73
emergency warnings, 1, 2, 4
environmental changes, 17, 155; adopting children, 135–39; borderlands, 115–18; composing children, 132–33; coping with one another, 144–46; doorway (*matapā*), 113–14; from face to interface, 114–15; flows of everyday living, 127–30; holding onto possessions, 130–31; interest in (or lack of), 9; mutual sacrifice of adopting children, 139–44; *Namolahi* Lagoon, 21–22; responses to, 112; *tauhi vā* or *tauhi vaha'a*, 118–20
environmental consequences, 10–11
environments: daily engagements with, 66; engaging, 31–33
European houses, 122. *See also* homes; Tongan house (*fale tonga*)
everyday living, 127–30, 170–73
everyday meals, 97–99, 106
examine, inspect (*fakasio*), 26–29, 30
experience, concepts of, 97

fa'ahikehe (spirits, beings of the other side/kind), 38, 40, 45, 57, 70, 87
Facebook, 170
fahu (position of supreme ceremonial rank), 84, 85, 89

fai fatongia (duty, to pay tribute, fulfil obligation), 78, 81, 92, 113, 150
faka'apa'apa (respectfulness, to show respect), 3, 79, 103, 126, 158
faka'ofo'ofa (beauty/beautiful), 91, 93
fakapo'uli (darkness), 43, 45, 46. *See also* day; night
fakasio (examine, inspect), 26–29, 30
fakasio e tahi (inspect the sea), 19. *See also* marine environments
fale tonga (Tongan house), 120–24, 123f, 124–25
fāmili fakatonga (Tongan family), 121
farewells, 112–13
father's sister (*mehekitanga*), 119, 126, 132, 138, 162
female things (*me'a fakafefine*), 129
fertility, 60, 66
fetokoniaki (help, to help one another), 100, 101, 113, 114, 127, 128, 140
Fiji, 169
Filihia, Meredith, 165
fingers, cutting off, 165
firewood, 154. *See also* forest (*vao*), dying
fishermen, Kotu Island, 30
fishing: lunar motions and, 58; night, 98
flood tides, 41. *See also* tidal motions
flows: communication, 131; constitutive, 125–26, 131; of everyday living, 127–30; of interchanges, 139
food: bringing together of, 106; death and, 98, 99; everyday meals, 97–99; *kaipola* presentations, 78, 97, 100, 101, 103, 124, 172; *ngaohi pola* (building/assembling of the board of food), 100–105; ranking of, 106. *See also* meals
foreground notions, 12
forest (*vao*), dying, 5, 6f, 149, 153–56
formal education, 152. *See also* education
Free Chiefly Church of Tonga (*Siasi Tauatahina 'o Tonga Hou'eiki*), 157

Free Constitutional Church of Tonga (*Siasi Tauatahina Konisitutone 'o Tonga*), 157, 161, 163
Free Wesleyan Church of Tonga, 1, 77, 166
fruits, 102

garden, fertility, 66
Gell, Alfred, 19, 20, 157
generosity, 91, 92, 130, 131
ghost stories, 86
Gifford, Edward W., 68, 69. *See also* myths
giving, act of, 91
global climate dynamics, 155
God: power of, 151, 158, 160 (*see also* Christianity); protection of, 168, 169
Government Primary School (Kotu Island), 153
greed, 95
greetings, Kotu Island, 45
growth, 144, 168; of children, 132–33; lunar motions and, 54, 56–60 (*see also* lunar motions); optimal time of, 63; origin and, 123; process of, 105; relationships and, 126; wild and cultivated, 93–95
Gunson, Neil P., 48, 49, 49*f*

Ha'afeva island, 2, 13
Ha'apai group, earthquakes, 1, 2
habits, personal, 128
Hafoka, Havili, 37, 38, 40, 41, 42, 43
Hala siulolovao, 5
Hawaiian nights of the moon, 63–64
headaches, 86. *See also* pain
help, to help one another (*fetokoniaki*), 100, 101, 113, 114, 127, 128, 140
hengihengi (Early morning), 37
the hidden burial mound (*Langi tu'u lilo*), 8, 10
Hina, mythical cycle of Sinilau and, 66–70, 72, 73

Hirsch, Eric, 12
homes, 120–24; composing children, 132–33; Cyclone Isaac (1982), 122; doorway (*matapā*), 123*f* (*see also* doorway [*matapā*]); entering, 113–14; from face to interface, 114–15; flows of everyday living, 127–30; holding onto possessions, 130–31 (*see also* possessions); social relations and, 124–25
horizons of expectations, 152
Hulme, Mike, 11, 170
human nature, truths about, 95–97
Hviding, Edvard, 21, 22

illnesses, 85, 86, 159, 160
'*ilokava* ceremony, 80
importance, occasions of, 93. *See also* ceremonial processes
'*inasi* (share, presentation of first fruit), 102
Ingold, Tim, 4, 12, 13, 105
inspect the sea (*fakasio e tahi*), 19. *See also* marine environments
International Date Line, 2
Islanders of the South (van der Grijp), 15, 16
isolation, 91, 169

Japan, 1, 2, 3. *See also* earthquakes
just staying (*nofo pē*), 153, 155

kahokaho (yam), 62, 102, 171
kai fakaafe (eat by invitation), 100
Kai manna, 159
kaipola (board of food), 78, 97, 100, 101, 103, 124, 172
kau poto (the knowledgeable ones), 150, 159
kava, 97, 103; ceremonial processes, 82–84, 93, 94; ceremony, 80–82 (*See* Mata'aho [Queen]); cultivation of, 62, 63; drinking, 98

Keauokalani, Kepelino, 63, 64
Kepelino's Traditions of Hawaii (Beckwick), 63
kerosene lamps, 35
kin: expectations of, 101; limiting freedom, 125–26. *See also* relationships
King's Church (Free Wesleyan Church of Tonga), 77
kinship, 113; adopting children and, 140 (*see also* children)
knowledge, distribution of, 15, 104
the knowledgeable ones (*kau poto*), 150, 151, 159
koloa fakatonga (Tongan goods, wealth), 77, 129, 131, 163
Koloa, Heamasi, 24, 25, 29, 30, 31, 38, 39, 41, 42, 43, 45, 55, 56, 57, 59, 60, 61, 62, 64, 77, 78, 79, 80, 82, 88, 95, 102, 103, 104, 113, 116, 120, 122, 123*f*, 124, 125, 127, 128, 159
Korn, Decktor, 16
Kotu Island, 3; burial traditions on, 54; changes on, 35; communication, 93; Cook, James, 8, 26; coping with changing environments, 149–53; cycles of night and day, 36–39; death and, 85, 86, 87; doorway (*matapā*), 113–14; dying *vao* (forest), 6*f*; earthquakes, 1, 2; electricity on, 73; emergency warnings and, 4; engaging environments, 31–33; fishermen, 30; Government Primary School, 153; greetings, 45; homes, 120–24; importance of the moon, 54–55; inspection of marine environments, 26–29; kava ceremonies, 94 (*see also* kava); *loka* (on the move/astir), 29, 30; loses land (*mole e fonua*), 5–10; lunar motions, 54; mosquitoes and, 9; *Namolahi* Lagoon, 21–22, 33 (*see also Namolahi* Lagoon);

over-exploitation of resources, 154; phone booths, 101; royal visits, 77–80; rules for reading the sea, 29–30; social events in, 12; solar panels, 35, 36; telecommunications and, 13, 14; time conceptions, 20; *Vai fefine/Tōkilangi* pool, 7*f*, 8; *Vai tangata/Veifua* pool, 7*f*; weather coast (*liku*), 5, 6

lagoons: borderlands and, 116; on the move, 30, 31
land and sea, borderlands, 115
Langi tuʻu lilo (the hidden burial mound), 8, 10
lapila fish, 155
Last Day, 55
late night/early morning (*longoʻaho*), 39. *See also* day; night
Lātū, ʻAhokava, 84
Laukau, Amini, 84
lausiʻi foʻou (new moon sickle), 65
lausiʻi motuʻa (old moon sickle), 65
Lifuka Island, 10
light (*maama*), 43
light, transformations to, 51–52. *See also* cycles of night and day
liku (weather coast), 5, 6, 7*f*, 149, 153–56
linguistics, 104, 105
local sociality, 112, 113
Lohu Loa harvesting stick, 88–90
loka (on the move/astir), 29, 30, 31
longoʻaho (late night/early morning), 39. *See also* day; night
loses land (*mole e fonua*), 5–10
lotu mālohi (powerful/forceful praying), 151
love/compassion (*ʻofa*), 162, 163
lunar cycles, 60, 107; Hawaiian nights of the moon, 63–64; merging and separation in the sky, 64–66; sun-moon relationships, 70

lunar motions, 54, 70; concepts of, 66; fishing and, 58; growth and, 56–60; importance of the moon, 54–55; mythical cycle of Hina and Sinilau, 66–70; planting season (*tō ta'u*), 57; rise of the moon, 60–63; tales of attraction, 70–73
lunation, description of, 59

maama (light), 43
maau (well ordered, properly arranged, tidy, poem, poetry), 84, 88, 90, 93, 95, 157
mala'ia (unlucky, unfortunate, cursed), 161
male things (*me'a fakatangata*), 129
Marcus, George, 13
marine environments: engaging, 31–33; inspection of, 19–21, 26–29; rules for reading the sea, 29–31; terminology of tidal motions, 27–28
Mata'aho (Queen), 97; ceremonial processes, 82–84; kava ceremony, 80–82; visit to Kotu Island, 77–80
matapā (doorway), 113–14, 123f; borderlands and, 115–18; definitions of, 114–15; homes, 120–24; to nurture/care for the space between (*tauhi vā* or *tauhi vaha'a*), 118–20; relationships and, 125
matāpule (talking chief), 81
me'a fakafafangu (wake-up calls), 158, 159
me'a fakafefine (female things), 129
me'a fakatangata (male things), 129
meals: death and, 99; everyday, 97–99, 106; *kaipola* presentations, 103; *ngaohi pola* (building/assembling of the board of food), 100–105
meats, 103
mehekitanga (father's sister), 119, 126, 132, 138, 162

merging, 35–36, 145, 156; borderlands, 117; constitutive motions, 45–46; cycles of night and day, 36–39; definition of, 44; feeling that day is coming, 39–41; motions of, 43–45; and separation in the sky, 64–66; state of cosmic order, 46–51; tableaus, creating, 106–7; transformations (night to day), 50, 51–52; united phrases of night and day, 41–42
Methodist churches, 156, 157, 164
ministers, 168
misfortunes, 160
Misinale (Annual money collection), 165, 166, 167
missionaries, 100
modernity, Tonga and, 14
modernization, 73
mole e fonua (loses land), 5–10
moon: activities and, 57; changing states of, 56; Hawaiian nights of the, 63–64; importance of the, 54–55; myths and, 67; new moon sickle (*lausi'i fo'ou*), 65; night fishing and, 98; old moon sickle (*lausi'i motu'a*), 65; rise of the, 60–63; sickness and birth, 55, 56, 59; states of, 178–80; waxing moons, 59, 61; weak moon, 70. *See also* lunar motions
morality, 112, 161
MORDI (Mainstreaming of Rural Development Innovation), 149, 150
Mormons, 158. *See also* Christianity
morning, 46. *See also* cycles of night and day
Morton, K., 16
mosquitoes, Kotu Island and, 9
mounds, 8, 10
Müller, Max, 71
mutual sacrifice of adopting children, 139–44
mutual support (*fetokoni'aki*), 127, 128

myths: aesthetics and, 73, 74; ghost stories, 87; mythical cycle of Hina and Sinilau, 66–70, 72, 73; study of, 71

naming, 139; building by, 133–35
Namolahi Lagoon, 21–22; daily activities in, 22–23; places of, 23–26; tidal dynamics of, 48*f*; transformation of, 98
Namolahi Lagoon (Kotu Island), 33; changes on, 35
narratives, 67, 71. *See also* myths
natural disasters: cyclones, 4; earthquakes, 1, 2
networks, 127. *See also* relationships
new moon, 56, 60, 66. *See also* moon
new moon sickle (*lausiʻi foʻou*), 65
New Zealand, 1
ngaohi (composing/assembling/building), 132
ngaohi pola (building/assembling of the board of food), 100–105
ngataʻanga (turning point), 26
ngatu (painted barkcloth), 78, 84, 85, 86, 87, 88, 93, 108, 129, 163
night: concept of, 66; constitutive motions, 45–46; cycles of, 36–39; motions of merging, 43–45; state of cosmic order, 46–51; states of, 176–78; transformations (night to day), 51–52; united phrases of, 41–42. *See also* day
night fishing, 98
nipples, 116, 117
Niuatoputapu Island, 2
noaʻia (of no account, of no consequence, haphazard, dumb, futile), 107
nofo pē (just staying), 153, 155
nongovernmental organizations (NGOs), 149, 150
Norwegian Mythology of Nature (Witoszek), 71

Nukuʻalofa (Tonga), 5, 149, 150
to nurture/care for the space between (*tauhi vā* or *tauhi vahaʻa*), 118–20
nurture spaces (*tauhi vahaʻa*), 129, 162

ʻofa (love/compassion), 144, 162, 163
offerings, 16, 164, 166, 167
old moon sickle (*lausiʻi motuʻa*), 65
Old Testament (Bible), 161. *See also* Christianity
On the Edge of the Global (Besnier), 13
on the move/asti (*loka*), 29, 30, 31
orderliness, 50
origin, growth and, 123
over-exploitation of resources, 154

Pacific Adaptation Strategy Assistance Program (PASAP), 9, 10
Pacific Ring of Fire, 2, 4, 10
pain, roots of, 86–88
painted barkcloth (*ngatu*), 78, 84, 85, 86, 87, 88, 93, 108, 129, 163
parenting, 119, 129, 130; adopting children, 135–39; communication, 130; coping with one another, 144–46; mutual sacrifice of adopting children, 139–44; rights and duties, 135
Patolo, Soane, 150
peau kula (red wave), 149
personal beautification, 93, 94
personal habits, 128
personhood, concepts of, 95
phone booths, Kotu Island, 101
pigs, 103, 163
Pilolevu (Princess), 163
pilot projects, 10
planting: fertility, 66; moons for, 63, 64
planting season (*tō taʻu*), 57
plants, cultivation of, 116
poetry (*maau*), 84, 88, 90, 93, 95, 157
politics, 13
Poltorak, Mike, 159

Polynesia, 12
Polynesian cosmology, 49f
pork, 103
position of supreme ceremonial rank (*fahu*), 84, 85, 89
possessions, 128, 129; holding onto, 130–31
powerful/forceful praying (*lotu mālohi*), 151
precedence, 123
pre-Christian myths of creation, 46, 156, 157
pre-Christian Polynesian cosmology, 45
pregnancy, 137; moon and, 60 (*see also* moon)
private experiences, concepts of, 97
processions, 81
protective practices, 162
Pterois volitans (Red Firefish), 160
public arena, participation in, 91
pusiaki (adopted child, to adopt, to give up in adoption), 135–39, 139–44

qualitative nuances, 20
Queen Mataʻaho. *See* Mataʻaho (Queen)

radio, emergency warnings, 1, 2
Radio Tonga, 2
raising children, 119
Red Firefish (*Pterois volitans*), 160
red wave (*peau kula*), 149
red waves, 2, 3. *See also* natural disasters
regeneration, lunar motions and, 54. *See also* lunar motions
relationships, 104; adopting children, 135–39; building by naming/teaching, 133–35, 139; composing children, 132–33; coping with one another, 144–46; doorway (*matapā*), 125; expectations of kin, 101; farewells, 112–13; flows of everyday living, 127–30; generosity, 131 (*see also* generosity); harmonious, 129, 130; limiting freedom, 125–26; mutual sacrifice of adopting children, 139–44; to nurture/care for the space between (*tauhi vā* or *tauhi vahaʻa*), 118–20; socialization (*see* socialization); sun-moon, 70 (*see also* moon; sun); *tauhi vā* or *tauhi vahaʻa*, 118–20; Tongan house (*fale tonga*), 124–25
religion, 13
religious offerings, 16, 165, 166, 167
repulsion, 67
resonance, quality of, 72
resources, over-exploitation of, 154
respectfulness, to show respect (*fakaʻapaʻapa*), 3, 79, 103, 126, 158
rise of the moon, 60–63
rituals, 35
root crops, 102, 105. *See also* food
root penetration, 88
routines, 22, 23. *See also* daily activities
royal visits, 77–80, 97; beautification and, 84–86. *See also* Mataʻaho (Queen)
rules for reading the sea, 29–31

Sacrifice (Bourdillon), 164
sacrifices, 164–70
safety, seeking after earthquakes, 3
Sālote (Queen), 15, 36
Samoa, 2, 67, 68, 96
scents, masks of, 93
sea, states of, 175–76
seabirds, 40. *See also* bird calls
sea levels, 150; changes in, 8
Sea ʻo e tuku moʻui (Chair of the placing of life), 169
seas: borderlands, 115–18; tidal motions (*see* tidal motions)
seasons, states of, 180–81
sea temperatures, 30
sea walls, 150
security, gaining, 164
self-sacrifice, 168

self-sufficiency, 91, 92, 95
separations, 35–36, 145, 156; borderlands, 117; constitutive motions, 45–46; cycles of night and day, 36–39; feeling that day is coming, 39–41; and merging in the sky, 64–66; motions of merging, 43–45; state of cosmic order, 46–51; tableaus, creating, 106–7; transformations (night to day), 50, 51–52; united phrases of night and day, 41–42
sermons, 168
sexual aggression, 95
shaman, 46
share, presentation of first fruit ('inasi), 102
sharp points, 115–18
Shore, Bradd, 91
Siasi Tauatahina Konisitutone 'o Tonga (Free Constitutional Church of Tonga), 157, 161, 163
Siasi Tauatahina 'o Tonga Hou'eiki (Free Chiefly Church of Tonga), 157
signal events, 38, 39
sinfulness, 152. See also Christianity
Sinilau (chief), 68, 69, 70
Sinilau, mythical cycle of Hina and, 66–70, 72, 73
social isolation, 91
sociality, Tongan Christianity, 153, 157. See also Christianity
socialization, 92, 113–14, 126
social media, 170
social relations, Tongan house (fale tonga), 124–25
solar motions, 59. See also lunar motions
solar panels, 35, 36
solar technology, 14
South Pacific, 19. See also marine environments
spears, 116
speeches, 161
spirits, beings of the other side/kind (fa'ahikehe), 38, 40, 45, 57, 70, 87

stars, descriptions of, 39
state of cosmic order, 46–51
stereotypes, 152
sun, 59; myths and, 67
sun-moon relationships, 70. See also moon
systems of exchange, 113

tableaus, creating, 76–77; beautification and, 84–86; building/assembling of the board of food (ngaohi pola), 100–105; ceremonial processes, 82–84; concepts of beauty, 88–90; everyday meals, 97–99; merging and separation, 106–7; Queen Mata'aho's kava, 80–82; roots of pain, 86–88; royal visits, 77–80; truths about human nature, 95–97; warmth inside, 91–92; wild and cultivated growth, 93–95
taboo, 85
taimi fakapo'uli (times of darkness), 55
taimi momoko (cool season), 98
tales, 67; aesthetics and, 73, 74; of attraction, 70–73; ghost stories, 87. See also myths
talking chief (matāpule), 81
tapu (restriction, forbidden, constrained, sacred), 8, 93, 94, 107, 117
Taufa'āhau Tupou (King), 158
tauhi vaha'a (nurture spaces), 129, 162
tauhi vā or tauhi vaha'a (to nurture/care for the space between), 118–20
teaching, building by, 133–35
telecommunications, Kotu Island and, 13, 14
threats: adopting children, 135–39; borderlands, 115–18; composing children, 132–33; coping with one another, 144–46; doorway (matapā), 113–14; from face to interface, 114–15; flows of everyday living, 127–30; holding onto possessions, 130–31; mutual sacrifice of adopting

children, 139–44; responses to, 112; *tauhi vā* or *tauhi vahaʻa*, 118–20
tidal motions, 31, 37, 41, 46, 50, 70, 107; concepts of, 66; *loka* (on the move/astir), 29, 30, 31; rules for reading the sea, 29–31; terminology of, 27–28; tidal dynamics, 48*f*
tides, states of, 175–76
time conceptions, 19, 20; synchronization of daily activities, 20
times of darkness (*taimi fakapoʻuli*), 55
timing of everyday meals, 97–99
Tōfua island, 62, 63
tokamuʻa (early yam crop [*kahokaho*-yam crop]), 57, 88, 102, 104, 171. See also yam
Tonga: anxiety and, 13; burial traditions, 54; Christianity and, 72, 151, 153, 158, 165, 169; churches in, 156, 157 (*see also* Christianity); compromise culture, 16; constitutive motions, 45–46; cultivation of kava, 62, 63; cultural continuity, 12–17, 35; cultural traditions, 14, 15; cycles of night and day, 36–39; electricity and, 73; environmental changes, 17; environmental consequences to, 10–11; fishing techniques, 21; Haʻafeva island, 13 (*see also* Haʻafeva island); homes, 120–24; importance of the moon, 54–55; Kotu Island (*see* Kotu Island); Lifuka Island (*see also* Lifuka Island); lunar cycles, 60; modernity and, 14; modernization, 73; Mormons, 158; myths, 67 (*see also* myths); Nukuʻalofa, 5; public decoration in, 84 (*see also* beautification); qualities of cultural aesthetics, 31; solar technology, 14; state of cosmic order and, 46–51; stereotypes, 152; Tōfua island, 62, 63 (*see also* Tōfua island)
Tongan Christianity, 50. See also Christianity

Tongan family (*fāmili fakatonga*), 121
Tongan goods, wealth (*koloa fakatonga*), 77, 129, 131, 163
Tongan house (*fale tonga*), 120–24, 123*f*; social relations and, 124–25
Tongan illness caused by root penetration (*akafia*), 86
Tongan Ministry of the Environment and Climate Change, 10
Tongan Tradition Committee, 36, 63
Tongan way (*anga fakatonga*), 55
Tonga Trench, 2
tō taʻu (planting season), 57
traditions, 153
transactions: adopting children, 135–39 (*see also* children); wealth and, 166
transformations (night to day), 43, 50, 51–52. See also day; night
transitions (night to day), 44, 45. See also day; night
tropical cyclones. See cyclones
tsunamis, earthquakes and, 1, 2
Tuʻi Haʻatakalaua (King), 68
tuku, definitions of, 168
tuku moʻui (to place/offer life), 164–170
Tupou V, (King), 163
turning point (*ngataʻanga*), 26
tusked pigs, 163
Tuʻuapō (Deep night), 46
twilight, descriptions of, 38, 40. See also day; night

ʻumu (earth oven, stone oven), 79, 100, 101, 102, 106

Vai fefine/Tōkilangi pool, 7*f*, 8
Vai tangata/Veifua pool, 7*f*
Vaitokelau (chief), 67, 68, 69
vai tonga (waters of healing), 6
Van der Grijp, Paul, 15, 16, 85, 165, 166
vao (forest), dying, 5, 6*f*, 149, 153–56
villages, entering, 113–14
violence, 95

wake-up calls (*me'a fakafafangu*), 158, 159
warmth inside, 91–92
warnings, 159
waters of healing (*vai tonga*), 6
waxing moons, 59, 61
weak moon, 70
weather, attitudes toward, 4

weather coast (*liku*), 5, 7f, 149, 153–56
Why We Disagree about Climate Change (Hulme), 11, 170
Witoszek, Nina, 71
women: pregnancy, 60 (*see also* moon); sickness and birth, 59

yam (*kahokaho*), 62, 102, 171

www.ingramcontent.com/pod-product-compliance
Lightning Source LLC
Chambersburg PA
CBHW051538020426
42333CB00016B/1982